بِسْمِ اللهِ الرَّحْمَنِ الرَّحِيمِ

İSTANBUL - 1434 / 2013

ERKAM PUBLICATIONS————————————

Organize Sanayi Bölgesi Turgut Özal Cad. No: 117 / 4   İkitelli / İSTANBUL
Tel: (0212) 671 07 00 (Pbx) Faks: (0212) 671 07 17
Ankara Cad. No: 60/5 Cağaloğlu / İSTANBUL   Tel: (0212) 513 35 80

ISLAM
SPIRIT AND FORM

By
Osman Nuri Topbaş

ERKAM PUBLICATIONS

Published by:
Erkam Publications
Ikitelli Organize Sanayi Bölgesi
Turgut Özal Cd. No: 117/2
Ikitelli, Istanbul, Turkey
Tel: (90-212) 671-0700 pbx
Fax: (90-212) 671-0717
E-mail: erkam@altinoluk.com
Web site: http://www.altinoluk.com

ISBN: 975-6736-62-3

Cover photo	: Blue Mosque Istanbul
Cover design	: Altinoluk Graphics
Typeset by	: Altinoluk Graphics
Printed by	: Erkam Printhouse

TABLE OF CONTENTS

ZAKAT AND INFAQ
(POOR-DUE AND SPENDING FOR OTHERS) / 185

PILGRIMAGE TO MECCA / 231

THE HOLY MONTH OF RAMADAN
AND FASTING / 263

PREFACE

$\mathcal{D}$ear Readers!

Praise be to Allah the Almighty, who has granted us the serenity of belief in Islam, and peace be upon Prophet Muhammad who has guided mankind from darkness to light.

Every sound human being can understand that this world has been created for a purpose. In order to fulfill this purpose Allah the Almighty has sent prophets with religions to guide mankind. All these religions have been the same in essence and they have been called Islam. Islam is Allah's greatest gift to man since through Islam people of faith may preserve the purity of their divine-given nature and may change their world into a rose garden. At our core is a deep longing to return to the Creator and the state of tawhid in Islam makes this possible. It enables us to spiritually return to our Lord and this is life's greatest pleasure.

Those who want to be sincere servants of Allah should cultivate an understanding of the inner aspects of Islam and should fulfill its commandments. Those who realize a high level of religious practice both in form and spirit will attain to the love and reward of Allah. On the other hand, those who do not heed Allah's invitation to return to Him, will be doomed and will be losers in the Hereafter. The blue skies have never shed tears over sinners, and it is the same skies that have destroyed the enemies of Allah through fierce thunder and torrential rain. Our sun is the same sun that once illuminated the castles and palaces of Pharaoh, Nimrod and other unfortunate people. Today it illuminates the ruins of their kingdoms. Hence none of them could attain eternal life as they had wished. Only those who have served Allah sincerely have attained this felicity and its concomitant rewards.

The essence of Islamic faith is to declare that there is no God but Allah and Prophet Muhammad is his messenger. After declaring this fact one becomes a believer, but Islam is not only a religion of dogma. One needs to complement his faith with good deeds. The holy Quran always mentions having faith in Allah and doing good deeds together. Faith is perfected through both the worship of Allah the Almighty and good deeds. Historically, those believers who have perfected their faith have found neither life's difficulties nor the threats of the non-believers to be problematic. When the tyrant Pharaoh severely punished the magicians for their faith in Moses (a.s.) they did not abandon their faith but rather said: **"Our Lord: Pour out upon us patience and cause us to die in submission"** (Araf, 7:126) Likewise, the early Christians who were thrown to wild animals because of their faith did not renounce faith in the unity of God but chose instead to taste the spiritual pleasure of martyrdom. Hadrat Sumayya, who had feared even a needle prick in her past, did not fear the hot irons as they branded her body due to her strong faith in Islam. Her husband followed suit as he refused to turn back from the path of Islam even though he was savagely killed. The lives of the companions of the Prophet (pbuh) and the lives of some of the followers of other holy religions before the advent of Islam repeatedly testify to the ability of faith to conquer disbelief.

History bears witness that so long as Muslims have practiced Islam as dictated by Allah the Almighty, their civilization has embodied in all aspects of life a culture known for great refinement. They have been in the forefront of science, politics, economics and other fields of life. However, when they have abandoned the practice of Islam or they have only practiced it in form and not in spirit they have correspondingly lost their strength and unity. They have ceased to be world leaders in politics, economics and other fields of cultural inquiry. Hence, once more we deeply need to return to our faith with sincerity and to practice it not only in form but also in spirit.

It is with this need in mind that I have analyzed the spiritual dimension of Islam. Initially, the foundation of our faith has been explored and to the best of my ability the wisdom behind it has been unveiled. Following the principles of faith, I have delved into the spiritual aspects of Islamic worship. Although Islam as a faith may be noted for the degree to which it is practiced, unfortunately usually in our times this practice has lacked the spirit of Islam. The rituals are mechanically performed as if only a kind of social custom while the spirit of Islam has been almost totally lost. This book aims to illuminate the spiritual radiance of Islamic worship and to clothe it in stories of the lives of the prophets and their companions and also in the lives of exemplary Sufis. In particular many references to the poetry of Rumi, Yunus Emre and other Sufis aim to bond the passion of our practice with its ritual form.

The chapters on paying charity and poor-due have been emphasized. The deep analysis they afford of the economic philosophy integral in Islam, abundantly demonstrates their inherent value in our grossly material world. Islam strives not only to render spiritual but also material guidance. Hence I have emphasized the economic commandments of Islam in order to assist us in our battle against material want.

In the course of writing this book, I would like to render special thanks to Mr. Muhammad Eshmeli for both his ongoing support and too in the editing of the book. I also pray for the other brothers who have taken part in the printing process and pray that this book will be a source of spiritual blessing and a continuous source of charity for all of them in the Hereafter.

I would also like to extend my very special thanks to Dr. Suleyman

Derin and to Dr. Ali Köse for their assistance in the translation of this book and also to the editors who have struggled to make it as articulate as possible. May Allah accept their well-intentioned efforts and reward them generously.

May Allah make those who are touched by this book benefit from it as they grow to more deeply understand Islam both in form and spirit, and may Allah bless us with a due portion of light flowing from the meaning of the following verse when we meet our Lord in the Hereafter:

"Verily among those who followed his Way was Abraham, Behold! he came unto his Lord with a sound heart" (Saffat, 37:84)

Amen

Osman Nuri Topbaş

01-16-2003

Uskudar

ISLAM AND ITS SUBLIME NATURE

"To Him (Allah) belong the Most Beautiful Names" (Tâ-Hâ, 20:8)

*T*hroughout the history of mankind all religions, the first of which was revealed to Adam, have in essence been the same. The only religious changes that have occurred have been in regard to social laws since the communities of man have been in a continual process of development. Nevertheless, these changes have not pertained to the essence of these faiths. Thus, all religions which have been revealed from Adam (a.s), who was the first human being and the first prophet, up to the last Prophet Muhammad (ﷺ) are in fact at the core level essentially the same as Islam.

Therefore the Prophet (ﷺ) said:

Narrated by Abu Huraira:

"I heard Allah's Apostle saying, 'I am the nearest of all people to the son of Mary, and all the prophets are paternal brothers, and there has been no prophet between me and him (i.e. Jesus)'." (Bukhari, Volume 4, Book 55, Number 651)

Therefore it is a wrong supposition to think that Islam is restricted solely to the Qur'an, since it contains all the previous religions that have been revealed by Allah. Of course, here the word religion signifies their original forms prior to their distortion by human beings. The Qur'an confirms this in the following verse:

3

"The Religion before Allah is Islam (submission to His Will): Nor did the People of the Book dissent therefrom except through envy of each other, after knowledge had come to them. But if any deny the Signs of Allah, Allah is swift in calling to account."(Al-i Imrân, 3:19)

This verse also demonstrates that Islam is the sole solution for the problems of humanity. Here we are referring to the Qur'anic declaration that it is salvation both in this world and in the Hereafter. The following verse clarifies this fact even more clearly:

"If anyone desires a religion other than Islam (submission to Allah), never will it be accepted of him; and in the Hereafter He will be in the ranks of those who have lost (All spiritual good)." (Al-i Imrân, 3:85)

Hence, Islam is a religion that has been continually revealed from Adam through to the last Prophet Muhammad (ﷺ), and has been perfected through the stages of human history, finding its most perfect form in the Qur'an.

The description of Islam can be summarized in two principles:

1. Faith (Iman): To believe in the five principles of Islam sincerely.

2. Good deeds ('amal al-sâlih): To do good deeds that are demanded by Allah with sincere faith.

Islam practiced under these two principles organizes our life, thought, and behavior in a balanced way. Islam is a path that leads the believer to Allah by connecting logic, ear, eyes, tongue and heart to divine light. If the beauties of Islam were to fall on a piece of rock, it would turn the rock into soft fertile soil. On the other hand, the hearts of those far from Islam are turned into hard rocks. Only Islam has the ability to soften and cure them.

Islam perfects the intellectual and practical life of human beings and takes them from darkness into light. Those who embrace Islam are elevated from the lowest of states to the highest peak. It has the capacity to transform an ordinary human being into a perfect man. Islam achieves this spiritual transformation by returning man to his original form.

Islam is a robe of guidance extended from Allah to all of humanity. Those who submit to it, will rise above their mortality and will attain the elixir of immortality. Allah has summoned all prophets, who are beings at the peak of servanthood to Allah, to one condition: "When Allah said unto them: Surrender! Each of them said: I have surrendered to the Lord of the Worlds."

In the personality of the great prophet Abraham (a.s) this reality is declared in the Qur'an:

"When his Lord said unto him: Surrender! he said: I have surrendered to the Lord of the Worlds." (Baqara, 2:131)

This submission is realized in experiencing the closeness of Allah through mentioning His names. In fact, the aim of all forms of worship is to attain proximity to Allah, to attain to the knowledge and love of Allah.

One preacher was speaking in a mosque about death and its aftermath. He was explaining those questions that we will be asked after burial such as: "How did you spend your life, where did you spend your wealth and health, did you practice what you learned, were you following the commandments of Islam and did you refrain from what was forbidden? He was speaking about details and was not addressing the essence. Among the listeners, the great Sufi Master Shibli was present, and in order to remind the preacher of the essence of the matter he said:

"O preacher! You have forgotten the most important question that Allah will ask His slaves in the Hereafter. When we meet Allah in the Hereafter, He will ask: O my servant! I was with you at all times, whose company were you in?"

Based on this form and level of respect, Islam is to lead a life where we feel the presence of Allah at all times:

"And He is with you wheresoever ye may be." (Hadîd, 57:4)

The well being of the earth and the sky is dependent upon our obedience to Allah. In the absence of this obedience, the wrath of Allah will descend upon us.

"Corruption has appeared in the land and the sea (the order of the

universe has broken, natural calamities appeared) on account of what the hands of men have wrought, that He may make them taste a part of that which they have done, so that they may return (from the wrong path that they follow)." (Rûm, 30:41)

What this verse means is that abandoning Islam causes corruption of the harmony and order of nature. Here natural disasters are perceived as warnings to return to Islam.

People of insight can perceive the difference between the Creator and His products. Such an individual looks at the outer form while he perceives its inner form. He understands the reality of this world as he remembers the Hereafter. He gazes at the boundless heavens as he leads a life constantly remembering the divine majesty behind them. He knows his weakness as a servant and never ceases behaving like a servant. On his travel to the eternal world, Allah bestows upon him many of His divine secrets. Thus, the servant falls into prostration in yearning for his Lord. In this way, the purpose of creation is fulfilled and the servant gains eternal bliss as stated in the following verse of the Qur'an:

"And whomsoever it is Allah's will to guide, He expandeth his bosom unto the Surrender," (An'âm, 6:125)

However, the verse proceeds to go on and state that some of creation runs away from His divine mercy.

"And whomsoever it is His Will to send astray, He maketh his bosom close and narrow as if he were engaged in sheer ascent. Thus Allah layeth ignominy upon those who believe not." (An'âm, 6:125)

In short, salvation for mankind is only possible in Islam as the Prophet (ﷺ) states:

"Whoever accepts Allah as his Lord, Islam as his religion, Muhammad as prophet and is pleased with them Allah rewards him with Paradise." (Abu Dawud, Salât, 36; Tirmidhi, Salât, 42)

Islam comes from the root of silm and salam, meaning peace, submission, purity and sincerity. The first chapter of the Qur'an, Fatihah, summarizes the essence of Islam. According to this chapter, Islam aims to take mankind to Allah's bounties and to the right path without attracting His wrath:

"In the name of Allah, Most Gracious, Most Merciful.

Praise be to Allah, the Cherisher and Sustainer of the worlds;

Most Gracious, Most Merciful;

Master of the Day of Judgement.

Thee do we worship, and Thine aid we seek.

Show us the straight way,

The way of those on whom Thou hast bestowed Thy Grace, those whose (portion) is not wrath, and who go not astray." (Fatiha, 1:1-7)

Hence, Islam equally fulfills the needs of faith and reason. It protects man from that which harms his life and his possessions as well as the health of younger generations. The benefits of Islam can be summarized as follows:

- *The finest religion of faith:* Islam provides the best mode of faith while protecting the honor of man from heretical beliefs such as the worship of idols.

- *Islam nurtures the soul of man through acts of worship:* The kinds of worship in Islam address both the soul and the body since their performance involves both body and soul. Those fulfilling the obligations of Islam live paradisiacally in this very world.

- *Islam is a religion of mercy:* Islam strives to carry man to felicity and the mercy of Allah although most of his acts more nearly deserve destruction and punishment. Allah, the Almighty states that His mercy exceeds His wrath.

Narrated Abu Huraira:

The Prophet (ﷺ) said, "When Allah created the Creation, He wrote in His Book -and He wrote (that) about Himself, and it is placed with Him on the Throne- 'Verily My Mercy overcomes My Anger'." (Bukhari, Volume 9, Book 93, Number 501)

The *basmalah* which is mentioned in the beginning of the every chapter involves the names of Allah which enlighten His attribute of mercy: In the name of Allah, Most **Gracious**, Most **Merciful**. These two attributes are also mentioned in the first chapter of the Qur'an in its second verse:

All praise is due to Allah, the Lord of the Worlds. Most Gracious, Most Merciful; *al-Rahmân*, meaning compassionate, merciful. The first two verses of this chapter inform us that due to His mercy Allah taught us the Qur'an:

"The Beneficent Allah, It is He Who has taught the Qur'an."

(Rahman, 55:1-2)

These verses signify in addition that the content of the Qur'an is also a mercy for humanity. In the chapter Isra this reality is clearly stated:

"We send down (stage by stage) in the Qur'an that which is a healing and a mercy to those who believe: to the unjust it causes nothing but loss after loss." (Isrâ, 17:82)

Not only is the Qur'an a mercy for humanity, but this is also true for the Prophet of Islam who transmitted the Qur'an:

"We sent thee not, but as a Mercy for all creatures." (Anbiyâ, 21:107)

As a matter of fact this reality has been proven in the life of the Prophet (ﷺ) since he never cursed those who harmed him. In the town Tâif he was stoned and left bleeding due to injuries. Angels such as Gabriel came to him and told him that he could destroy the inhabitants of this town due to their mistreatment of him. The Prophet (ﷺ) did not accept this offer and answered: "No I do not want such a thing. I am a prophet of mercy."

He even prayed to Allah for their guidance and well-being. We can conclude that the first fruit of Islam is mercy. The friends of Allah who followed this golden rule summarized servanthood to Allah in two principles:

1. *Ta'zîm li amrillah:* To fulfill the commandments of Allah with full reverence.

2. *Shafkat li halkillah:* To show mercy to the creation of Allah.

- *Islam is a religion of rationality:* Although Islam is not a product of human intelligence and reason, since both religion and logic are gifts of the Creator there is no reason they should be mutually exclusive. Islam guides the human mind to the most useful and productive states, hence enabling man to lead a balanced life without falling into extremes.

In other words, human rationality can find its full expression in belief in the unity of Allah and He implores us to use our logic and rational faculties at many points in the Qur'an: *"Afala ta'qilun?"* (Do you not contemplate?).

The Prophet (ﷺ) also invites us to use our mind and contemplate upon the purpose of life. Comparing the reward of worship and contemplation he says: "An hour of contemplation is more valuable than sixty years of worship."

The human mind has been created as a vehicle to take man to Allah and guidance. It is the interpreter of the divine realities.

- *Islam is a religion of love:* Mere rationality is not enough in guiding man to divine realities. At times rationality is incapable of guiding man to Allah. Instead it takes him into a pit of doubts. Hence it is necessary for rationality to be under the rule of love and to enlighten it with love. Rumi says:

"He that is blessed and familiar (with spiritual mysteries) knows that intelligence is of Iblis, while love is of Adam." (Masnawî III, 1402)

"Love is as a ship for the elect: seldom is calamity (the result): for the most part it is deliverance." (Masnawî III, 1406)

Those individuals, like philosophers, who rely on intelligence as their guide become slaves of their external senses. They serve what their eyes see and what their ears hear without normally reminding themselves of the hidden. Reason may know Allah through love, whereas it alone is only an instrument whereby love may reach to the Creator.

Love engenders sacrifice. A believer who loves his Lord may even give up his life in the path of Allah. The companions of the Prophet (ﷺ) sacrificed everything in the path of Allah and His Prophet and thus reached the highest station in the history of mankind. Whenever the Prophet (ﷺ) requested something from them they replied: "My father and mother have been sacrificed for you."

Hence, Islam is a religion of the heart rather than merely a religion of reason. It aims first to reach the heart of man. It is also a religion of equilibrium: The most fundamental aspect of Islam is that it involves balance between the two worlds. As Allah has created the universe in complete harmony and order similarly Islam has provided a road to equilibrium in the life of man. Islam has brought balance between this world and the Hereafter, between body and soul, between men and women, poor and rich, the ruled and the ruler, and too between matter and spirit. These seeming opposites have been transformed into complements through Islam. Islam does not sacrifice or ignore the other-world for this world, or the body for the spirit. Islam removes the conflict between them and in its place establishes harmony. Through these wings man can fly to higher worlds.

- *Islam is a religion of knowledge and wisdom:* Islam is not a religion fit for the ignorant. On the contrary, Islam is the last and perfect religion that has been sent to fight ignorance. Therefore, the Qur'an states that knowledge is the most important condition of being a pious and worthy believer.

"Those truly fear Allah, among His Servants, who have knowledge: for Allah is Exalted in Might, Oft-Forgiving." (Fâtir, 35:28)

Prophet Muhammad (ﷺ) says: "The superiority of a scholar over a worshipper is like my superiority over the one who occupies the lowest rank among you." (Abû Dâwud, Ilm, 1)

Nevertheless, Islam joins knowledge and wisdom. Knowledge without wisdom harms mankind more than it benefits. As an example, knowledge of medicine without wisdom can be used to kill rather than cure. Therefore the Prophet (ﷺ) warns: "Whoever increases his knowledge without increasing his asceticism and fear of Allah distances himself from Allah." (Kanz al-Irfân, 62)

- *Islam is a religion of high morality:* Man is envisaged as the peak of creation. He is the vicegerent of Allah on earth. Although he was created out of earth, Allah blew his spirit into his body. The holy Qur'an draws our attention to this fact and warns us not to let our souls be contaminated by our base desires. It advises man to purify his soul from vices and to reach Allah with a pure heart. Prophet Muhammad (ﷺ) is the best example of one who has achieved this great purpose and has attained to the summit of morality. He has even stated that one of the main purposes of his prophethood was to exhibit the finest example of morality:

"Indeed, I was sent to complete the perfection of morality." (Muwatta, al-Hulk, 7)

The Qur'an bears witnesses to this fact and praises him with the following verse:

"And thou (standest) on an exalted standard of character." (Qalam, 68:4)

The companions of the Prophet (ﷺ) were living witnesses of his bashfulness. He was even more bashful than a veiled young girl. In order to clarify the significance of bashfulness (i.e. from Allah), he said: "Bashfulness and faith go hand in hand. If one leaves (man) the other follows (suit)." (Suyûtî, Jâmiu's-Saghîr, I, 53)

The following words of Jalaluddin Rumi illuminate the importance of hayâ (i.e. feeling bashful when a sin is committed) in relation to faith:

"I asked my mind, what is faith? My mind answered my heart: Faith is nothing but good conduct (adab), therefore those who have no adab will be further away from the mercy of Allah."

- *Islam is a religion of kindness and good behavior:* According to the Prophet (ﷺ), kindness which is not given adequate significance by the majority of people, will be taken very seriously on the Day of Judgment. The Prophet (ﷺ), whose example is the best in all aspects of life, also has left us with the best example of kindness. When he noticed any of his companions performing a wrongdoing, he would correct it without insulting the responsible one. Instead of directly addressing the wrongdoer, he would address the public: "What has occurred is that I have seen some people doing this or that", and by introducing the topic in this fashion he would veil the responsible one.

- *Islam is a religion of justice:* One of the fundamental concepts that Islam emphasizes on all occasions is the concept of justice and law. According to Islam, the most unforgivable sin beyond associating partners with Allah is to violate the rights of other. The Prophet (ﷺ) during his worst period of illness, leading up to his death, emphasized the significance of respecting the rights of others by personally going to the mosque and asking to settle any unfulfilled rights by saying: "O my companions! If I have taken the possessions of any of you by mistake, these are my possessions, let him take it. If I have hit the back of any of you by mistake, this is my back. Let him hit me and take his revenge." (Asım Köksal, Islam Tarihi, v.II, p. 38)

The Islamic concept of justice, which was established on such a strong foundation, has reached to the peak of perfection and fills any scholar who studies it with admiration. After examining all systems of law, the French philosopher Lafayet, who had a significant role in forming the ideological background of the French Revolution, expressed as follows: "O Muhammad! No one reached to your level in bringing justice among people."

The history of Islam is full of anecdotes proving the place of justice in Islamic societies. One day a man bought a horse from the market. Although the horse was young and strong it died three days after the purchase. The buyer was suspicious that the seller had poisoned the horse since he may have wanted to hurt him due to a personal conflict they had had between them. He went to the court for three days but the judge was away. Consequently, the man took the dead horse to a veterinarian. The veterinarian's findings proved that the man was justified in his suspicions. When the judge returned from his trip the buyer of the horse went to the judge again. The judge told him: "Why did you not come to me in the first place so as to enable us to see the signs of the horse?" The complainer replied: "Sir I have come to you for three days running but you were absent." The judge answered: "You are right. My mother had passed away and I traveled to my hometown in order to be present for her funeral." After contemplating a moment, the judge turned to the secretary and pronounced his verdict. The matter was solved in the following way: Absence of the judge from the court resulted in a loss for the plaintiff. Hence, the damages suffered by the plaintiff will be reimbursed by the judge.

In short, Islam is a religion of justice both materially and spiritually.

Therefore, in the past, our ancestors termed people Muslims without religion if they were non-converts who respected justice and behaved righteously. On the other hand, those Muslims who did not behave justly were referred to as disbelieving Muslims. Islam when it is practiced sincerely is capable of purifying the human soul of all sorts of imperfection. Only Islam can transform individuals who have fallen prey to their base desires, from the lowliest of the low stations to the greatest of statures.

The Prophet (ﷺ) states: "If a servant of Allah accepts Islam and practices it, all his past good deeds are valued and all his past sins are deleted. From then on, all his good deeds are rewarded from ten to seven hundred fold. However, his sin is only written one time (in the account book of the slave) unless Allah forgives it completely."

From the very early days of the religion there have always been those who have been unwilling to accept its guidance and instead have preferred to follow their base desires as the slaves of Satan. There are many examples of this in the history of Islam. Although the Meccans admitted the trustworthiness of the Prophet Muhammad (ﷺ) many of them refused to accept his life-giving message. They understood the reality of Islam through their consciousness but unfortunately were dominated by their base desires. Thus they fell into the pit of disbelief. Also, the Jews and the Christians for centuries had been foretelling the coming of Prophet Muhammad (ﷺ), but since he ultimately came from a different nation and they were dominated by their nationalism and racist bigotry, they refused to accept him. In particular, the Jews surpassed others in their rejection of Islam since they had a long history of rejecting prophets and killing them. The following incident demonstrates this fact with great clarity. Once the Prophet (ﷺ) read the Jews the following verses from the Qur'an:

"But if they dispute with you, say: I have submitted myself entirely to Allah and (so) every one who follows me; and say to those who have been given the Book and the unlearned people: Do you submit yourselves? So if they submit then indeed they follow the right way; and if they turn back, then upon you is only the delivery of the message and Allah sees the servants." (Âl-i Imrân, 3:20)

After he recited this verse to them he asked:

"Do you accept Islam?"

The Jews said:

"Yes we accept."

Upon this the Prophet (ﷺ) asked the following question:

"Do you also accept that Jesus (a.s) is Allah's word, his slave and his messenger?"

They answered:

"No, may Allah protect us from such a mistake."

Hence, by rejecting Jesus (a.s) as a prophet of Allah, they became among the unfortunate infidels.

He asked the Christians:

"Do you bear witness that Jesus (a.s) is Allah's word and His messenger."

The Christians said:

"How is it possible that Jesus (a.s) is a creature of Allah, He is the son of Allah."

On another occasion, the Prophet (ﷺ), went to a school of Jewish scholars and invited them to Islam. Nuaim b. Harith and Zaid asked him:

"What is your religion?"

The Prophet (ﷺ) answered: "I am of the religion of Abraham."

Upon hearing this answer, they claimed: "Abraham was a Jew."

The Prophet (ﷺ) said: "In that case shall we accept the Torah as our arbitrator."

They Jews hesitated and did no accept this offer. They had a famous scholar whose name was Abdullah b. Salâm. They always praised him for his knowledge. However, when he accepted Islam they forgot about their praise for him and started cursing him. They altered the chapters that foretold the advent of Prophet Muhammad (ﷺ). The Qur'an in addressing this issue states:

"Woe, then, to those who write the book with their hands and then say: This is from Allah, so that they may take for it a small price; therefore woe to them for what their hands have written and woe to them for what they earn. (Baqara, 2:79) **Of the Jews there are those who displace words from their (right) places,"** (Nisa, 5:46; Maidah, 4:13)

These activities demonstrate that the Jews and the Christians altered their religions according to their desires, thus destroying the authentic nature of their teachings. Today, the oldest copy of the Torah dates back to the 9th century before Christ. Consequently, there is a great deal of time separating Moses from the period when the Torah was compiled. Those who call for reforms in Islam, unfortunately have the same purpose. As before, they conceal their hidden aims with nice words.

The human mind cannot wholly understand either the wisdom or the hidden purposes behind the universe because it has been created by the omnipotence and omniscience of Allah. Allah knows best the nature of man since He created him. Hence His commandments and restrictions concerning the life of man are in accordance with his nature. A mind that has not been molded by divine revelation is incapable of comprehending these realities. A healthy mind will ultimately never deny the fact that the Creator knows best his creation and is thus capable of leading him to the way of life best fit for him. We can say that Islam is the only religion ideally molded to his nature.

Allah the Almighty through His boundless mercy has sent humanity Islam as a universal religion. In Islam He has designed an ideal and comprehensive system for living. As a religion Islam is capable of answer any question concerning life that may appear in the mind of man. As an example, dreams transcend the reality of our physical lives since they reside in our minds. Even so, Islam evaluates dreams and grants verdicts as to their meanings. Any value system upon which laws are based that has ignored any feature in the fundamental nature of man will be rejected by human nature and will be ultimately ignored by him. As an example, Catholics ignore the need to have a family and forbid monks and nuns from marrying. Such a law conflicts with human nature and in the end leads man towards disobedience.

Human nature contains changeable and unchangeable features. Religious systems ignoring the unchanging characteristics of human nature cannot indefinitely retain their validity. Human nature exceeds any external boundaries imposed upon it. As an example, Western Europe suffered from the pangs of an adulterated Christianity, but in the end they basically eliminated it from their lives and elected to restrict Christianity to inside the boundaries of the church. Unfortunately, many Christians have left religion in entirety due to the unnatural tendencies of the Christian faith. Furthermore, since believing in a divine being is a natural tendency some "Christians" have even started believing in Satan.

Islam, on the other hand, takes into consideration the divine nature of man and thus will not be outdated with the passage of time. To give an example, women are more emotional than men and as a consequence they cannot function legally in certain circumstances as witnesses, otherwise justice might not be fulfilled.

The commandments of Allah prevent the negative characteristics of man from developing and taking control of him. Beyond this, they assist us in developing positive character traits. Nevertheless, Islam grants us the freedom to organize our lives according to new circumstances in that realm of life subject to change and transformation. This freedom is granted for his own good. There are no definitive rulings as to the changeable aspects of life. Hence, Islam is a religion of realism that addresses the reality of human nature. It is also useful to note that human nature naturally tends towards what is positive rather than negative when it is free of contextual pressure to conform. In order to emphasize this point the Prophet (☙) states that every newborn baby is born with an Islamic nature. (Bukhari, Janaiz, 92)

Narrated Abu Huraira:

The Prophet said, "Every child is born with a true faith of Islam (i.e. to worship none but Allah Alone) and his parents convert him to Judaism or Christianity or Magianism, as an animal delivers a perfect baby animal. Do you find it mutilated?" (Bukhari, *Volume 2, Book 23, Number 467*)

As a result of Allah's all-encompassing mercy exceeding His wrath, in general there is peace and tranquility in the Universe. In a forest, we may observe that small and weak animals live side by side with those that are strong and wild. The same circumstance is true for a human being who is the essence of the universe. Although he may possess both positive and negative qualities, so long as the positive attributes exceed the negative, a condition arises where the negative features are unable to freely manifest themselves outwardly. However, this positive nature is always corrupted by the contextual social influences as discussed in the above hadith of the Prophet (ﷺ). Islam, through the way of life it points us toward, works to preserve this untarnished human nature thereby allowing the spiritual purity that was bestowed to man by Allah the Almighty to shine through. It is understood in Islam that human nature's negative features may not be entirely erased. As an example, instead of permitting the complete freedom of our sexual desires as in the case of some modern psychological systems, Islam organizes our sexual experience within the boundaries of marriage and family in order to preserve human continuity. Islam facilitates the expression of natural desires with the condition of marriage and is thus able to direct our sexual drive towards divine purposes as exemplified in the fostering of good offspring.

In relation to the possession of wealth, Islam teaches that everything in reality belongs to Allah. Believers are guided to spend what they have for the benefit of others rather than surrendering themselves to the aim of collecting wealth solely for personal use. Islam directs us to cultivate appreciation and cooperation with others rather than harboring jealousy.

In the same way, Islam organizes the intellectual faculties of man. It roots human mental inquiry on a foundation of revelation for without this support mental reflection is capable of carrying man to ridiculous consequences. It is for this reason that philosophers have always denied each other's realities. Furthermore, in ancient Athens stealing was an appreciable act if the thief did not get caught. The thieves were tolerated and not punished since their theft was a product of high intelligence. Although stealing is a self-evident wrong, this was not intellectually perceived without the help of divine revelation. If the human mind fails to perceive the self-evident, then how can it hope to perceive what is true in even more complex issues. When reason is accepted as the sole judge then there will be times when both sides will seem right and justice will not prevail. The following is a good example:

In ancient Athens, a student of law had a contract with his professor to be trained as a lawyer. The student would give half of the tuition after his training ended and the other half after he won his first case in court. Nevertheless, the student after having completed his training with the professor told him that the first installment he had paid was enough for his services and that he would not pay the second installment even after winning a court case.

The professor of law took his student to court for his breach of the agreement. On the day their case was presented to the judge, the professor told the judge: "I will get my payment in either case whether I lose this case or win it." The judge asked" "How?" The professor explained: "If I win the case the student will pay my tuition fee as an obligation to fulfill your judgment. If he does not pay, then he will be refusing your verdict, which is impossible. If I lose the case, then my student will be winning it and according to our agreement I am supposed to take my tuition fee when my student wins his first court case." The student who had been trained well said: "On the contrary, I will not pay the tuition fee whether I win the case or lose it." The judge asked him as well to explain his reasoning. He answered: "If I win the case I should not pay him, otherwise it will be against the verdict of this court and this is not acceptable. If I lose this case then according to the agreement I should not pay anything according to the agreement between us."

As can be seen in the above example, the human mind is capable of reaching absolutely contradictory conclusions with equally acceptable proofs. This is an inevitable consequence if revelation is disregarded. Islam by emphasizing the significance of respecting the rights of others above all else brings a different dimension to the relationship between adversaries. Islam teaches man to think about the needs of others more than his own. The hadith where it is stated that those who sleep well when their neighbors are hungry are not from us clearly testifies to this fact.

In this way Islam made its followers into sharing, caring, and loving brothers and sisters. Before Islam, Arabs were famous for their hatred, enmity, and plundering of other tribes' wealth through bloody wars. They were even so heartless that they used to bury their daughters alive, since they considered girls to be dishonorable. They had never ending blood feuds. The strong would crush the weak and the law always favored the strong. Describing this horrible social circumstance Mehmed Akif, the most famous Turkish poet said:

"If a human being had no teeth, his brothers might eat him."

However, with the advent of Islam, they rose to be among the most virtuous and noblest people in the world. Those who had earlier been eager to drink each other's blood, with the coming of Islam reached to a status that inspired them to consider the good of the other before their own even at the onset of death. The following incident narrated by Hadrat Hudaiyfa shows the level of kindness and generosity that the members of the early community attained. Hudaiyfa was searching the battlefield for survivors at the battle of Yarmuk. He narrates:

"I saw my cousin Harith in a pool of blood. I rushed to him to give him water, but when he was taking the water he heard the voice of Ikrimah:

'Water, a drop of water for the sake of Allah!'

Harith pointed his eyes to Ikrimah and withdrew his hand from the water, signifying that I should take the water to him. When I reached him this time we heard the voice of Iyâsh: 'Water, please water!'

Ikrimah like Harith did not accept the water and instead pointed me towards Iyâsh. I rushed to Iyâsh but he did not have time to drink the water before he gave up his life. Then I rushed back to take the water to Ikrimah but he was also dead by that time. In amazement I ran back to Harith, but unfortunately he had also passed away.

Three warriors, who were about to become martyrs, preferred to give up water offered for drink in favor of sacrificing their chance so that another person could drink first. As a result, not one of them was reached before he took his last breath and each became a martyr without drinking a drop of water."

This exemplifies the high standards of Islamic morality that became embodied in the lives of its early followers. These same people were more than happy to kill one another for the most simple of reasons during the time of ignorance. Through Islam their hearts were enveloped by a divine mercy and grace to such an extent that their time was later referred to by Muslims as the time of felicity (asr al-saadah)

Allah the Almighty reminds us this great favor in the following verse:

"And remember the favor of Allah on you when you were enemies, then He united your hearts so by His favor you became brethren; and you were on the brink of a pit of fire, then He saved you from it, thus does Allah make clear to you His communications that you may follow the right way." (Âl-i Imrân, 3:103)

This verse addresses all humanity in the person of the companions of the Prophet (ﷺ).

The same story is true in the case of the Turkish people. Before Islam, their name was not good in the annals of history. Atilla left only bloodshed and tears throughout his 7000 kilometers of campaigns. However, after they were honored with Islam this nation became one of the noblest nations and full of love and mercy for humanity. Out of this mercy they have addressed their enemies as follows:

"You are so cruel o mercy! You make my enemy lovable to us."

THE FIVE PILLARS OF ISLAM

As we have stated before Islam consists of faith and good deeds.

According to Islam man has two kinds of obligations towards Allah, one is to have faith and the other is in terms of practice. The obligations of faith are considered before the practical ones. Therefore the Prophet (ﷺ) has said:

"The thing I fear most for my Ummah is associating partners to Allah." (Musnad, IV, 124,126)

Human beings will be divided into two nations before Allah as believers and non-believers. Faith is rootel in an indivisible unith. In other words, if anyone refuses to believe in any of the principles of faith it is the same as refusing all of them. All the principles possess the same weight since man has no right to call something wrong which is termed right by Allah. In his state of total weakness, can man reject the omnipotent and omniscient Creator? Without faith good deeds are of no benefit. In Islam, faith occupies the highest place among necessities.

However, faith cannot stand alone without good deeds. Through good deeds it is protected from harm. Islam is like a fruit tree. Faith through the heart is its roots. Declaring faith by tongue is the trunk and good deeds are as the flowers and fruits of the tree. As fruit are the purpose behind the tree, similarly good deeds are the necessary consequence of faith. Marifah to Allah can be gained through good deeds. In other words, Islam is not only a matter of belief but also a matter of good practice. It is a dangerous path to expect salvation through faith only without having good practice. As a result, four out of five pillars of Islam are practical principles of good deeds. Only the first pillar of Islam is related to faith alone. It is the profession of faith. The following hadith clearly numerates the five pillars of Islam:

Narrated Ibn 'Umar:

Allah's Apostle said:

"Islam is based on (the following) five (principles):

1. To testify that none has the right to be worshipped but Allah and Muhammad is Allah's Apostle.

2. To offer the (compulsory congregational) prayers dutifully and perfectly.

3. To pay Zakat (i.e. obligatory charity) .

4. To perform Hajj. (i.e. Pilgrimage to Mecca)

5. To observe fast during the month of Ramadan."

(Bukhari,*Volume 1, Book 2, Number 7*)

However, these five principles are not the whole of Islam. They are the main pillars that support the building but there are also other principles. Islam organizes man's life from the cradle to the grave, both his spiritual and material life as well as his personal and public life. Even a cursory study of the Qur'an and the sayings of the Prophet (ﷺ) will show that they cover all aspects of life. The above hadith however, provides Muslims with the primary directives that they need to construct their life. Without a building's main pillars, no structure can stand firmly on its foundation. The other principles however support these main ones thus widening the strength of the whole structure. In keeping with this many other hadiths elucidate additional principles. As an example the following hadith states:

"Islam is made out of eight shares. The first share is believing in Islam, performing salat is one share, paying the poors' due is a share, fasting is a share, performing pilgrimage is a share, commanding goodness is a share, refraining from evil is a share, striving in the path of Allah is a share..."

The commandments of Islam function as the arms of a compass. One point is fixed and other is moving and mobile. This means that obligatory commandments are incumbent (fixed) upon all believers whereas the superogatary acts of worship are like the moving arm. One can freely do these acts as much as he can according to his capacity. Those who have a capacity similar to that of Abu Bakr should do more, it is not correct for them to behave like a weak Muslim. On the other hand, those who do not possess a high capacity like that of Abu Bakr cannot practice Islam as he did. The important principle here is that after having fulfilled the obligatory acts of worship in as perfect of a manner as possible one should then do the superogatary acts to the degree possible so as to reach Allah through renunciation of the world. Through doing this we may grow to deserve the role of being Allah's vicegerent on earth.

As it is important to understand Islam's apparent rules, so too is it important to understand Islam's hidden spiritual aspects. Allah the Almighty repeatedly informed us of these principles through His Messenger (ﷺ). In this way Allah has empowered us to teach Islam in a correct way and has also extended to us the opportunity to practice it to perfection. The following hadith, which is best known as the hadith of Gabriel, emphasizes this point:

As narrated by Umar (may Allah be happy with him)

"Umar ibn al-Khattab, told: 'One day we were sitting in the company of Allah's Apostle (ﷺ) when there appeared before us a man dressed in pure white clothes, his hair extraordinarily black. There were no signs of travel on him. None amongst us recognized him. At last he sat with the Apostle (ﷺ)

He knelt before him placed his palms on his thighs and said:

- Muhammad, inform me about al-Islam.

The Messenger of Allah (ﷺ) said:

- Al-Islam implies that you testify that there is no God but Allah and that Muhammad is the messenger of Allah, and you establish prayer, pay Zakat, observe the fast of Ramadan, and perform pilgrimage to the (House) if you are solvent enough (to bear the expense of) the journey.

He (the inquirer) said:

- You have told the truth.

He (Umar ibn al-Khattab) said: "It amazed us that he would put the question and then he would himself verify the truth."

He (the inquirer) said:

- Inform me about Iman (faith).

He (the Holy Prophet) replied:

- That you affirm your faith in Allah, in His angels, in His Books, in His Apostles, in the Day of Judgment, and you affirm your faith in the Divine Decree about good and evil.

He (the inquirer) said:

- You have told the truth.

He (the inquirer) again said: Inform me about al-Ihsan (performance of good deeds).

He (the Holy Prophet) said:

- That you worship Allah as if you are seeing Him, for though you don't see Him, He, verily, sees you.

He (the enquirer) again said:

- Inform me about the hour (of the Doom).

He (the Holy Prophet) remarked:

- One who is asked knows no more than the one who is inquiring (about it).

He (the inquirer) said:

- Tell me some of its indications.

- He (the Holy Prophet) said:

- That the slave-girl will give birth to her mistress and master, that you will find barefooted, destitute goat-herds vying with one another in the construction of magnificent buildings.

He (the narrator, Umar ibn al-Khattab) said: 'Then he (the inquirer) went on his way but I stayed with him (the Holy Prophet) for a long while. He then, said to me: "Umar, do you know who this inquirer was?" I replied: "Allah and His Apostle knows best." He (the Holy Prophet) remarked: "He was Gabriel (the angel). He came to you in order to instruct you in matters of religion." (Muslim, Iman, 1)

In short, Islam is a religion of worshipping the one Allah. Allah the Almighty states in the Qur'an:

"I created the jinn and humankind only that they might worship Me." (Zâriyat, 51:56)

Allah the Almighty commands his Prophet (ﷺ) to inform humanity about this fact:

"Say (O Muhammad): Lo! I am commanded to worship Allah, making religion pure for Him (only).

And I am commanded to be the first of those who are Muslims (surrender unto Him).

Say: Lo! if I should disobey my Lord, I fear the doom of a tremendous Day.

Say: Allah I worship, making my religion pure for Him (only)." (Zumar, 39:11-14)

Faith in Allah is not a blind, robotic imitation of religious law. It is to worship the creator of the universe, the owner of life and death, to be happy with His verdict, and to do good deeds in accordance with His will.

Establishing religion is a privilege only given to prophets. Among all of the world's religions, the sources of Islam have been best preserved. Allah has made the miracle of the Qur'an valid forever.

Islam demolished all myths, all superstitions and removed any vestige of darkness. In the place of ignorance, Islam established justice, high morality and brought forth felicity and peace to the world.

Islam helps one to discover his true identity and to teach him the secret of the verse:

"I breathed him from my own soul"

Islam polishes the mirror of the heart, prepares it to reach to Allah, adorns it with high morality, and is such a powerful elixir that it transforms the night of death into an object of desire as in the case of a young man anxiously awaiting his wedding night.

Mehmet Akif looking at the sad situation of Muslims in his time due to their weakness in submitting to Islam said:

"If Muslims do not want to be crushed by the passage of days
They should return to the bosom of Islam."

THE EXPRESSION OF FAITH
AND ITS PILLARS

"Lâ ilâha illallah, Muhammad Rasulullah"-
There is no God but Allah and Muhammad is His messenger.

*E*xpressing the profession of faith is the first step in entering the Islamic religion. It is a sentence bearing witness to the oneness and unity of Allah and to the acceptance of Prophet Muhammad (ﷺ) as Allah's last messenger. It is the root of religion. It possesses all secrets for the salvation of humanity. It also has many names that demonstrate its significance to Muslims:

Kalimah al-tayyibah; the most beautiful words,

Kalimah al-taqwa; the enunciation of Allah's awareness,

Kavl al-thâbit; the right words,

Maqâlid al-thamavât wa al-ard; the key to the heavens and the earth,

Kalimah al-ihlâs, the expression of sincerity,

And Samanu'l-Jannah; the price of paradise.

The profession of faith is the essence of Islam and is the essence of all the religion's other teachings. All details of Islam are dependent on this essence. Hence, it is the best kind of worship to utter these holy words. It is superior to all other kinds of worship. Even the best mode of worship, salât is incumbent at certain times of the day whereas the declaration of faith is incumbent at all times upon believers. Faith should always be protected from all sorts of harmful thought such as heedlessness. Fasting, salat and other kinds of worship can be postponed if there is an obstacle, however, faith can never be postponed regardless of the circumstance.

The profession of faith is:

أَشْهَدُ اَنْ لاَ اِلَهَ اِلاَّ اللهُ وَ أَ شْهَدُ اَنَّ مُحَمَّدًا عَبْدُهُ وَ رَ سُولُهُ

"Ashadu anlâ ilâha illallah wa ashhadu anna muhammadan abduhu warasuluhu"

This means that:

In order to enter Islam, one should utter these words with his tongue and accept it in his heart. The profession of faith contains all Qur'anic wisdom and all realities. In other words, the entirety of the Qur'an is the articulation of these words. The essence of the Qur'an consists of belief in one Allah, tawhîd. The following verse clearly expresses this reality:

"This is a clear message for mankind in order that they may be warned thereby, and that they may know that He is only One Allah, and that men of understanding may take heed." (Ibrahim, 14:52)

All praiseworthy acts of the servant of Allah are the consequence and fruit of these beautiful words. The more these words are established in the heart, the more a servant takes pleasure in worship. On the other hand, all acts that attract Allah's wrath are the products of disbelief in these holy words. Allah the Almighty states in the Qur'an:

"Seest thou not how Allah sets forth a parable? - A goodly word like a goodly tree, whose root is firmly fixed, and its branches (reach) to the heavens - of its Lord. So Allah sets forth parables for men, in order that they may receive admonition. It brings forth its fruit at all times, by the leave of its Lord. So Allah sets forth parables for men, in order that they may receive admonition. And the parable of an evil Word is that of an evil tree: It is torn up by the root from the surface of the earth: it has no stability." (Ibrahim, 14:24-26)

The phrase in the verse, "It brings forth its fruit at all times", is explained by the Prophet (ﷺ) as the continuous remembrance and mentioning of the names of Allah *(Fazâil al-A'mâl)*.

Explaining this verse Ibn Abbas (may Allah be happy with him) states: "This verse points to the word of profession, its roots are in the heart of the believer and its branches are in the heavens. The good deeds of the believer reach to the heavens. The filthy words are the ones that contain disbelief, and those that associate partners with Allah. No good action is accepted in the absence of faith."

Therefore Allah has informed us in the Qur'an:

"He indeed shall be successful who purifies himself," ('Alâ, 87:14)

The Prophet (ﷺ) explains the concept of purification in this verse as uttering the words of profession (لَا اِلٰهَ اِلَّا اللهُ مُحَمَّدٌ رَسُوْلُ اللهِ) with sincerity, and abandoning the worship of idols both internally and externally. (Fazail A'mâl, 466)

The friends of Allah whose duty is to purify souls from all sorts of vice, act in accordance with the guidance of the above hadith. The idols are not always apparent, sometimes human souls nurture hidden idols such as his animal desires. In the following verse, Allah the most High condemns such attitudes:

"Hast thou seen him who maketh his desire his god," (Jathiyah, 45:23)

One of the duties of the Prophet (ﷺ), as revealed in the Qur'an, is to purify the hearts of human beings from spiritual diseases and to unveil for them the deep dimensions of belief in the unity of Allah. Faith is like a mirror, and if a person is heedless of Allah this mirror is blurred. A blurred mirror prevents us from receiving and reflecting divine lights. Divine lights only manifest in a believer's heart if the heart is made tender through the mentioning and remembrance of the names of Allah (zikrullah). Zikr is the opposite of forgetfulness. The tarnished nature of the heart is removed through turning to Allah with all sincerity and devotion.

The prophets and the friends of Allah invite people to accept the profession of faith which will open the door of heaven and earth for man. The prophets have shared these sweet words with humanity in the best manner through love and mercy. Many blessed people have responded to this call and have tasted the real faith which is sweeter even than *kawthar* (Fountain in Jannah). They have pioneered carrying the torch of faith. In this vein, let us examine the following verses of Aziz Mahmut Hudai:

Obey the commandments of Allah
Come to the unity, to the unity
Refresh your faith
Come to the unity, to the unity

Do not look too far into the distance
Do not throw your heart into the fire
Do not incline to everything you see
Come to the unity, to the unity

Close your eyes to everything other than Allah
Expect from Allah whatever you want
Throw your concerns from your heart
Come to the unity, to the unity

What do you think
You who are deceived by the transient
One day you will awaken
Come to the unity, to the unity

Leave blind imitation
Profess the unity of Allah with sincerity
Find all your dreams
Come to the unity, to the unity

So do not worship the forms
Look at the meanings
Try to be close to the Real
Come to the unity, to the unity

Do not believe your carnal soul
Do not think that you know
Do not throw yourself into the fire of shirk
Come to the unity, to the unity

Leave transient loves
Do you ever mention the dead
The traveler continues his travel do not be late
Come to the unity, to the unity

The profession of faith possesses limitless wisdom. Therefore, the earth, the heavens and everything in them confirm the message of these holy words. Even Allah the most High bears witness to His Unity:

"Allah bears witness that there is no god but He, and (so do) the angels and those possessed of knowledge, maintaining His creation with justice; there is no god but He, the Mighty, the Wise." (Âl-i Imrân, 3:19)

The profession of faith possesses four meanings in short:

1. Declaring the existence of Allah,

2. Declaring the attributes of Allah,

3. Declaring the acts of Allah,

4. Declaring the trustworthiness of the messenger of Allah.

The profession of faith is the seal of the Islamic faith and is called *Âmantu*. The six pillars of faith are a summary of the entire Islamic belief system.

The translation of the Âmentu is as follows:

I believe in Allah the Most High, in His angels, in His books, in His Prophets, in the Day of Judgement, in divine predestination and in the fact that both good and evil occur through the will of Allah, the Supreme Being and that there will be life after death. I testify that Muhammad (ﷺ) is His servant and messenger.

When one accepts the five pillars of Islam he/she becomes a Muslim and when he/she accepts the six pillars of faith he/she becomes a believer. However, only uttering these words by tongue without accepting it in the heart is not enough to be a believer.

In addition to believing in the existence of Allah and the prophethood of Muhammad(ﷺ), one also needs to cultivate understanding and practice straightness in life. In other words, our faith should be strong and perfect so that it can carry us to salvation. When we speak about a strong faith it also includes accepting all the attributes of Allah.

I. FAITH IN ALLAH

The human mind cannot fully comprehend the nature of Allah, who has created the sky, the earth, and all things in between them. For this reason, contemplating the essence of Allah generates strange ideas in the imagination of man and damages correct faith. The Prophet (ﷺ) has forbidden this kind of contemplation:

"Contemplate upon the favors (His creation, power and greatness) of Allah and do not contemplate upon Him. (since no one can afford to do that)." (Kitâb al-Arbaîn)

In order to emphasize the limited nature of our mind, the leading Sufis state:

"O my Lord! You are as You are, You are above our perception and our information about You."

Perceiving the nature of Allah is beyond the range of our power. However, it is possible for the human mind to deduce from cause to the causer, from art to the artist, from results to the causes. If the human mind, with a clean perception and a good will, looks at the attributes and acts of Allah it is unthinkable that it will reject belief in Allah. Rejection of faith is the consequence of a sick mind and mentality. If the purity of mind and heart can be preserved it will guard man from the rejection of faith. Even those who have been born in disbelieving societies can discover true faith, as may be seen in the example of prophet Abraham (a.s), so long as they have purity of heart. Although Abraham (a.s) was born in a society that believed in idols, through his intellect and heart he was led to the true faith and entered belief in the unity of Allah.

Believing is easier than disbelief. Affirming that there is no Creator will not resolve the issues surrounding the origin of the world, of life and of death. The condition of disbelief resembles a person who is hungry and does not feel the pain of his hunger due to a nervous breakdown, or a person who is drugged and does not feel the pain of the cutting knife. The Qur'an terms such people as deaf and dumb.

Allah the Almighty created man's nature and bestowed in it the need for belief in Allah and the search for truth. There is no exception to this divine planning. If this does not happen it is due to spiritual blindness and dumbness. Our subconscious faith is blocked by the weight of material life as in our inability to remember our dreams.

Both in heavenly religions and in man made religions there is a conception of belief in Allah. However, the concept of Allah in man made religions has significantly deviated from the correct faith where Allah is the only creator of the universe, where He transcends all weaknesses and human attributes and instead possesses the most perfect of attributes. These attributes have been revealed to us through the Prophet (ﷺ) and are beyond alteration. According to the common division adhered to by scholars, the list of Allah's most important attributes are as follows:

ALLAH'S EXISTENCE: There exists Allah and His existence depends on nothing. Thus, He is self-existent. There is no probability of Him being non-existent. And all things, apart from Him, are His creatures and their existence is a potentiality. Their existence is not necessary. It is declared in the Qur'an:

اَللّٰهُ لاَ اِلَهَ اِلاَّ هُوَ الْحَيُّ الْقَيُّومُ لاَ تَأْخُذُهُ سِنَةٌ وَلاَ نَوْمٌ
لَهُ مَا فِى السَّمَاوَاتِ وَمَا فِى الْأَرْضِ

"There is no god But He, the Living, the Self-subsisting, Eternal. No slumber can seize Him nor sleep. His are all things in the Heavens and on earth..." (Baqara, 2:155).

It is an obvious fact that there exists an impeccable order and coherence in this immense universe. This coherent order has been running in a well-balanced and delicate way since the universe came into being. It is a known fact that if the earth had not had a 23,5 degree angle of pitch, seasons would not have come about. In that case, one part of the earth would have been in winter, and the other part in summer. Likewise, should the distance between the earth and the sun had been just a little bit longer, the earth as a whole would have turned into a frozen region; or should the distance between the two had been a little bit of shorter, the earth would have been turned into ashes. These and suchlike states of affairs demonstrate the fact that all celestial bodies are so wisely tuned into a program so that life becomes possible.

Such a mechanism of perfection and delicacy presents a sign for the existence and Oneness, Magnificence and Omnipotence of the Creator of the universe. It is declared in the Qur'an:

"**And the Firmament has He raised high, and He has set up the balance (of Justice).**" (Rahman, 55:7).

"**He who created the seven heavens one above another: no want of proportion will you see in the Creation of (Allah) most Gracious. So turn your vision again: saw you any flaw? Again turn your vision a second time: (your) vision will come back to you dull and discomforted, in a state worn out.**" (Mulk, 3-4).

If a farmer saw that the plants in his farm were irregularly chopped down he would attribute what happened to his farm to the acts of the storm or another natural disaster. However, if he noticed that the plants were chopped down regularly, for example one in three or five plants, he would not attribute what happened to his farm to a natural disaster. He would realize that this action was taken by a conscious and potent being. He would think that this action might have been taken by one of his enemies. In that case, he is supposed to ask how the perfect and delicate mechanism of the universe can take place by chance while he does not accept that such a tiny action as chopping the plants down can happen by chance. Nadjib Fadl, the famous Turkish poet, calls to those who lapse into such unawareness:

> *I see that I am wrapped all round,*
> *Does not a wrapped one require a wrapper?*
> *Who is this craftsman drawing this human face;*
> *Does not anyone ask looking at the mirror?*

Jalal al-Din al-Rûmî calls for the awakening of the eyes and the hearts by opening out the doors of wisdom and meditation:

"As you see the movement of the millstone, you had better make more effort to see the water of the river that makes it move!"

"You see the dust in the air, you had better give a look at the storm that takes it up!"

"You see the pot boiling, you also look at the fire with foresight!"

"Tell me, O foolish one! Which is logical? Do those palaces and dwellings have a builder, or do they not have a builder?

"Tell me, O my son! Which is logical? Do those writings on the walls and the pages have a writer, or do they not have a writer?

"O son of Adam! Could you ever point to a single thing that came into being on its own? See what happens when you root out a plant from its soil. Do you think it vegetates by itself?"

The poet puts this point into words so elegantly:

Should this place have come into being by itself,
This caravan would arise by itself as well!..

The chimneys on the roofs tell you,
That there is no fire, no smoke.

Should there exist no power,
Would the universe turn round by itself?

Should once the gardener leave the vineyard on its own,
Would the wheat be resolvable from the straw on its own?

When the soil is thirsty for water, the cloud in the sky tells the eye,
Is there a river flowing on its own?..

Whoever says that he had not seen behind the curtain,
His lie will turn into a snake on its own!

Satan would be ready to pour tar over the light;
And he would say to the conscience "believe only on your own!.."

*The tongue asked **Mehmedî** to appreciate his own heart;*
Without it the tongue does not run on its own!

Any naturally disposed will and heart consciously realizes that there exists a chain of causes and all these depend on the **Great Producer** of all secondary causes, the Allah, and hence believe in Allah.

However, Satan lays many traps at every corner in order to lead astray the humans in their thoughts. Jalal al-Din al-Rûmî warns humans not to be deceived by the tricks of Satan:

"Do not be deceived by Satan in this matter of belief. Satan is so wise a thief that he keeps a good look-out for dark nights to come to you and when he seizes the opportunity he knocks at your door. Then you want to answer the door to see who it is with the cresset in your hand. And every time you try to light the cresset Satan puts out the spunk by seizing it. Hence you cannot see who it is and you judge that the spunk has become moist. Thus you stay unaware of the thief who puts out the lighter. So, Satan, in this way, interferes with your belief cresset in the darkness of oversight. Therefore, Satan walks away with the virtues of your heart and makes you bankrupt of the after-life. In this manner, you stay unaware of both the creation and the Creator."

As declared in the Qur'an in the words ."..**those truly fear Allah, among His servants, who have knowledge...**" (Fatir, 35: 28), the cognizance of the Grandeur and the Magnificence of Allah adequately is, above all, a matter of knowledge (science). The following account of Einstein illustrates this reality:

"The creator of the universe does not play dice. His creation is not random and uncounted. We observe, as much as we can, the balance and harmony of this world with admiration... I may say that anybody who explores nature enjoys a religious respect as s/he discovers the Grandeur of Allah. Accordingly, I cannot think of a true scientist who does not have a profound faith. This fact may be articulated as follows: It is impossible to have faith in science having no religion. So, **a religion with no knowledge (science) is blind, and knowledge (science) with no religion is lame.**"

Thus, many non-Muslim scientists embraced Islam and many, though not embracing Islam, perceived that they had to concede to the Greatness of Allah. This is a miracle of the Qur'an. Allah says:

"**And those to whom knowledge has come see that the (Revelation) sent down to you from your Lord-that is the truth, and that it guides to the path of the Exalted (in Might) Worthy of all praise.**" (Saba, 34: 6).

"Soon will We show them Our Signs in the (furthest) regions (of the earth), and in their own souls, until it becomes manifest to them that this is the Truth. Is it not enough that your Lord does witness all things?" (Fussilat, 41: 53).

Anybody who looks at the universe taking it as a lesson beholds the countless signs mentioned in this verse.

If there only existed humans and animals in the world they would use up all the oxygen by turning it into carbon dioxide, and in a short time they would be poisoned and perish by the increasing amount of carbon dioxide. However, the Might that called the universe into being also created the plants endowing them with the ability to use carbon dioxide turning it into oxygen so that the universe could keep running in equilibrium.

On the other hand, the Creator filled three fourths of the earth with water. And He created the great majority of the remaining one fourth in the form of infertile deserts and rocks. The earthy part of the world is only a small part. However, the Most High Allah transforms this earthy part from one form to another so that it could be a source to feed all living beings.

Let us examine a species of an animal. If all the past, the present and the future members of this species had been sent down to earth at once, the space and the sustenance of the world would not have been sufficient for even this single species. However, Allah creates them in an order of time and space sequence. The same point is valid for all living-creatures. So, the world, with the mystery of time and space, may sustain a trillion times more loading. Namely, the existence of the creatures in the universe is subject to an equilibrium and limitation. For example, it is a known fact that a plane-tree breeds millions of seeds and these seeds are sent away through the wind as if they all have a parachute made of feathers. Should the seeds of even a single plane-tree have the opportunity to be a new plant, all fertile parts of the world would soon be infested with plane-trees. Namely, the world would become not spacious enough for even a single tree. This example may be extended to all creatures. This fact points out to the existence of an impenetrable harmony and balance in the universe.

Besides, the Most Supreme Being endowed all living creatures with such features that even those who live on the same sort of foods produce different products and these complement one another in order to make life entirely possible. For example, a cow or a sheep eats the leaf of a mulberry, and it produces milk and wool; but a silkworm produces silk, and a musk-deer breeds musk from the same leaf. The bee produces honey from pollens, but the human being, who is considered to be the most perfect creature, has no ability to produce honey as the bee does. The colors, odors, and the lively leaves that various flowers draw out from the nutrients of the soil are the qualities that no chemist is able to exactly produce. While an animal is able to transform the grass into meat and milk, the human being is not able to produce just a piece of meat or milk from tons of grass in chemical laboratories.

Any sensible human is supposed to see the existence and magnificence of Allah wherever s/he turns in the universe. The qualities such as sending prophets and perfecting humans with their knowledge and morality are the works of Divine grace. In addition, when the human being takes a look at himself/herself and the universe intellectually, s/he immediately understands how ridiculous and laughable that it becomes to disbelieve in the face of its grandeur and magnificence. The poet puts this point into words so nicely:

Many meanings distill through the endless systems,
The signs of Allah will always be in the heart of Adam.

What a transcendent fact; the earth and the sky have no pillars,
There is no particle with no scale!..

With the endless space above, and the black ground beneath;
O you servant, what behooves you is to prostrate on the prayer rug!..

Surely, this infinite universe is a sign for the Existence and the Grandeur of Allah. It is a gleam of faith.

The sky has black and white holes. This is a new finding of the positive sciences. Yet we find Allah swear to these holes in the Holy Qur'an.

"Furthermore I call to witness the setting of the stars; and that is indeed a mighty adjuration if you but knew." (Waqia, 56: 75-76).

This reality that contemporary science has just now discovered illustrates the magnificence facing us. The spot where stars are born is called a white hole; and the spot where they die is called a black hole. A small object comes through the white hole and instantly gets expanded a trillion times bigger than its actual size to bring forth a giant constellation. And many stars that are much more bigger than our world die in due course by drawing into the black holes. Accordingly, the sun that lightens our sky will, one day, be exposed to the fact of **"When the sun (with its spacious light) is folded up"** (Takwir, 81: 1).

That day the sun will come to an end as well. No wonder that day is the doomsday. It is the end of everything!.. And there is no way except turning to Allah by prostration.

In short, those who are vigilant perceive that this world, in the face of the Divine Grandeur, is only a dust among trillions of dust particles in space. Among them are the mountains, plains, oceans, and humans. With this impotence, man is nothing but for his servitude.

This example of the human's position, of being only a drop from the oceans, requires the logical perception of a Allah who is **All-Powerful**, **Almighty**, **Self-existent**, and **Provider** of the needs of men and beasts. However, in order to be able to perceive this reality one needs to have his/her heart open. It is stated in the Qur'an:

"Do they not travel through the land, so that their hearts (and minds) may thus learn wisdom and their ears may thus learn to hear? Truly it is not their eyes that are blind, but their hearts which are in their breasts." (Hajj, 22: 46).

Ibrahim Haqqi of Erzurum puts this point into words so wisely:

Those who are aware can see,
But those who are blind cannot.

Yunus Emre says:

The true path takes you to the right place,
The real eye leads you to perceive Allah...

Allah is watching everywhere,
But it requires an eye to see...

The earth and the sky bear many clear evidences to the existence of Allah and this reality needs no explanation. Men of Allah taste this reality with all qualities of their hearts. Their souls sense the divine secrets as they throw over the earthlings. Those who can manage the act of self-denial in accordance with the hadith, "die before your death!", are to rise in the springtime of reality. They wriggle themselves out of metaphoric beings and live in the spirit of the Prophet (ﷺ). They never ever have a doubt about truth and reality. This example clearly illustrates this fact:

Junaid al-Bagdadî, one of the Great Saints, asked the people around who were running somewhere with a rush:

"– Where are you going? Why is this hurry?"

They replied:

"– We were told that there came a scholar from somewhere! He has the ability to explain the existence of Allah with a thousand and one evidence! We are going to benefit from his explanations. You may come, if you like!"

Upon hearing this, Junaid al-Bagdadî told them with a sour smile:

"– There are countless signs and evidences in the universe for the eyes to see, and the hearts to feel. There are innumerable testimonies indicating the existence of Allah. O people! Despite all the evidence, let those of you who still have doubts go! My heart has no scrap of doubt."

Thus, those people with spiritual knowledge explain this point as follows:

"Allah is never a hidden being. However, it may be said that "Allah is hidden from our vision because human beings cannot bear the power of the sight of Him."

Namely, if a room had a bulb of five thousand volts, human eyes would not be able to see anything under so powerful a voltage. Just as in this example, the vision of Allah's is so powerful, and for this the vision of

Allah remains hidden to human beings. Namely, human beings have no ability to see Allah with their biological eyes. That is why Allah told the Prophet Musa "**By no means can you see Me (direct)!**" (Araf, 7:143).

*

ETERNAL EXISTENCE IN THE PAST: It is a logical prerequisite that all creatures came into being from a priori cause on a reason-and-result basis. This a priori cause (being) needs not be created; yet, on the contrary, it should be able to create. So, this a priori cause is Allah Almighty. This is the Being whom human beings call Allah. There is no beginning to His High Being. It is He, who is the beginning of everything. He had eternal existence in the past. It is stated in the Qur'an:

"**He is the First and the Last, the Evident and the Immanent...**" (Hadid, 57: 3).

"In the beginning there existed Allah, nothing existed before Him..." (Bukhari).

The Prophet (ﷺ) used to say in his prayers "O, my Lord! You are the beginning, and nothing existed before You..." (Muslim, 61) and he advised Muslims to pray with these words.

*

ETERNITY: Allah has no ending, He is Eternal. The Qur'an states that:

"**And call not, besides Allah, on another god. There is no god but He. Everything (that exists) will perish except His own Face. To Him belongs to command, and to him will you (all) be brought back.**" (Qasas 28:88).

"**All that is on earth will perish: but will abide (for ever) the Face of your Lord – full of Majesty, Bounty and Honor.**" (Rahman, 55:26, 27)

Nothing in this world has the attribution of eternity. That is why, everything in this world lives a life on a time-sharing basis, because Allah assigned this attribution (eternity) only to Himself and made all creation transitory.

The epitaph of "**It is only He, Who is eternal**" written on Muslims' tombstones signifies this fact. Yunus Emre reminds us of the fact that everything except for Allah is transitory:

Show me a construction,
That has no ruinous end...
Gather all your belongings,
That all you leave behind...

Therefore, men of Allah do not care about this world and long for reaching the state of annihilation in Allah. These wise men/women do not fall for the transitory delights and involvements of this world and they, being in the secret of the principle of "die before your death", set forth on a journey to the season of eternity.

Believing that "it is the flesh that perishes, not the soul", they throw off the bodily enslavement, and go on a journey of the heart. Finally, they reach Allah and say:

I have found the most beloved one,
Let my life be sacrificed.

*

THE UNITY OF ALLAH: The fact that the universe keeps running in a great harmony and order since it was created is enough to indicate that everything is only the work of a single force. If this force had partners, harmony and the order of the universe would be damaged due to the differences among them, and the chaotic atmosphere would make the life impossible. It is stated in the Qur'an:

"Allah has said: Take not (for worship) two gods: for He is just One Allah: then fear Me (and Me alone)." (Nahl, 26:51).

"Say: If there had been (other) gods with Him, as they say, behold, they would certainly have sought out a way to the Lord of the Throne!" (Isra, 17:42).

"If there were, in the heavens and the earth, other gods besides Allah, there would have been confusion in both! But glory to Allah, the Lord of the Throne: (High is He) above what they attribute to Him!" (Anbiya, 21:22).

".. Nor is there any god along with Him: (if there were many gods), behold, each Allah would have taken a way what he had cre-

ated, and some would have lorded it over others! Glory to Allah! (He is free) from the (sort of) things they attribute to Him!" (Muminun, 23: 91).

If the Qur'an is examined in depth it will be seen that the most important ability that Allah enjoins on His servants is the belief in His attributes. Among these attributes, the belief in the unity of Allah is the most sensitive one. So much so, that attributing a partner to Allah is ranked as the prime sin that incites Allah's wrath in Islam. The Qur'an warns and advises people not to fall into this kind of intellectual poverty:

"..Whoever joins other gods with Allah, Allah will forbid him the garden, and the fire will be his abode. There will for the wrong-doers be no one to help." (Maida, 5:72).

"But it has already been revealed to you, as it was to those before you. If you were to join (gods with Allah), truly fruitless will they be your work (in life), and you will surely be in the ranks of those who lose (all spiritual good)." (Zumar, 39:65).

"Allah forgives not that partners should be set up with Him; but He forgives anything else, to whom He pleases; to set up partners with Allah is to devise a sin most heinous indeed." (Nisaa, 4:48).

Other religions of revelation were the same as Islam in their original form but they were subsequently distorted, moving away from the basics. Among them the manipulation exercised on Christianity is highly remarkable. The belief in the unity of Allah in Christianity was terribly changed at the end of the fifth century and the belief in the absolute unity and oneness of Allah was replaced with that of the Trinity. However, religiously sophisticated people of our time do not support this unreasonable belief and dissociate themselves from the church. Therefore, the papacy today has started scholarly work in order to have Christianity revert to properly expressing its original belief in the unity of Allah.

Allah is "One." And this statement is clear enough to indicate that there is no probability to have a second god. The poet articulates the Oneness of Allah with these words: "It is only Him that exists. He is One on His own; He is the only One!"

Hence, the belief in the unity of Allah should be clear enough not to regard a second being as possible. Islam requires and enjoins such a kind of belief in the unity of Allah. This is the first step in coming under the religion of Islam. Many doors of Allah's mercy, blessing, grace, and beneficence are unfolded to those who take a worthy step in this way. Thus, Bilal-i Habashi (may Allah be pleased with him) endured the severe torture by the idolaters to have him return to idolatry, and with a great ecstasy of faith he replied to them by uttering the words "*Ahad, Ahad* (One, One.) (Allah is One!)" In return for his forbearance he was given the honor of being the chief muezzin (caller to prayer) of the Prophet.

Even a scrap of deficiency in the matter of faith cannot be recovered by many virtuous acts. This may be likened to the position of somebody who appreciates many favors towards him, but cannot bear any insult towards his honor. So, blasphemy is nothing but a violation of the Glory of Allah. It is a villainy committed against Allah's Majesty. It is for this reason that it is regarded as unforgivable. Therefore, faith is the primary act that Allah demands and then comes pious work.

During the battle of Uhud a courageous man named Amr bin Sabit came into the presence of the Prophet (ﷺ) to embrace Islam, but when he witnessed the intensity of the battle he asked the Prophet (ﷺ) whether he should join the battle first or pronounce his faith in One Allah. The Prophet told him:

"- Pronounce your faith first, join the battle afterwards!"

Amr bin Sabit followed what the Prophet (ﷺ) told him. After the battle, when the Prophet (ﷺ) saw his body among the martyrs he said:

"He worked little, but gained a lot!.." (Ramazanoglu Mahmud Sami, *Uhud Gazvesi*, 35).

Unity requires pronouncing Allah to be the one sole and unique without a partner. It is the denial of duality. It is a palace of faith that offers humans the most excellent throne. Yunus Emre puts this point into words so nicely:

We need the palace of unity,
And announcement of good tidings,

Wangle out of the idea of duality,
And your ego, o, the servant!

As unity is an attribute that belongs to the Glory of Allah, favoring it with Allah is effectual in having one's prayers answered. The Prophet (ﷺ) used to advise his companions to favor Allah's attributes, especially the Unity, so that their prayer could be accepted.

Ubade bin Samit narrates from the Prophet (ﷺ):

"Let those who awake in the night invoke these words: 'There is no deity apart from Allah. He is One and has no partner. Dominion is in His hands, and all praises belong to Him. He is Almighty. He is exempt from any unworthy thing, and He is Great. All due strength and vitality for prayers and devotions are from Allah'."

The Prophet (ﷺ) proceeded:

"If the person says 'O my Lord! Please forgive me!', or if s/he invokes another prayer, or if s/he makes ablution and says his/her prayers his/her prayers are answered." (Bukhari, Tahajjud, 21).

The Prophet (ﷺ) also said:

"Whoever feels that s/he needs Allah's help, let him/her make ablution first and then make two units of prayer. Let him/her praise Allah and pronounce the formula calling Allah's benediction on the Prophet, and then invoke a prayer as follows:

"There is no deity, but the Clement and the Generous Allah. The Allah of the great universe is exempt from any unworthy thing, and all praises belong to Him. Oh, my Lord! I beseech You to incur the occasions for me to have Your forgiveness, and save me from all sorts of sins. And I wish to gain safety from all sorts of wealth and favors. Please let none of my sins and shortcomings remain! O, my Lord, the most Compassionate and the most Merciful, Let me perform the actions that You approve." (Tirmizi, Witr, 17).

*

THE UNIQUENESS OF ALLAH: Allah is not to be equal to anything. He does not bear resemblance to any creature. He is, therefore, exempt from any anthropomorphic attribute.

One of the controversial points in the distorted religions today has to do with this point. These religions have gone astray leaving aside such attributes of Allah as being transcendent, being beyond imagination and perception, and they have attributed many anthropomorphic features to Allah in their books in accordance with their own imagination. They have even attributed features such as forgetfulness, exhaustion, repentance, oversight, and confusion. According to them, for example, Allah gives orders regarding a flood, but He later forgets them. Just then He sees that everywhere is covered with water! Only by then does He remember his order and after making sure that all creatures are in the ark He hastily closes the door of the ark Himself. Yet again, according to their books the Prophet Jacob wrestles with Allah and he subjugates Allah. In addition to these unreasonable expressions, it is a known that the Jews called Uzair a son of Allah, and the Christians called Christ the Son of Allah (Tauba 9: 30). Allah says in the Qur'an regarding their attempt to believe in their own imagination:

"No just estimate have they made of Allah, such as is due to Him: on the Day of Judgment the whole earth will be but His Handful, and the heavens will be rolled up in His right Hand: Glory to Him! High is He above the Partners they attribute to Him!" (Zumar, 39:67).

".. There is nothing whatever like unto Him, and He is the One that hears and sees (all things)." (Shura, 42:11).

$$\text{قُلْ هُوَ اللهُ أَحَدٌ اَللهُ الصَّمَدُ لَمْ يَلِدْ وَلَمْ يُولَدْ}$$
$$\text{وَلَمْ يَكُنْ لَهُ كُفُوًا أَحَدٌ}$$

"Say: He is Allah, the One and Only; Allah the Eternal Absolute; He begets not, nor is He begotten; and there is none like unto Him." (Ikhlas, 112:1-4).

When the Prophet heard someone praying "O, my Lord! You are One and Only, You do not beget nor are You begotten, You are not to be equal. I appeal for Your Mercy. Please, forgive my sins, You are all-forgiving and all-merciful!", he said:

"He was forgiven. He was forgiven. He was forgiven!" (Abu Daud, Salaat, 179).

Yunus Emre, who knows this good news, takes refuge in Allah with the following words:

Allah the Almighty, Allah the Almighty,
There is none like unto You!
Please forgive our sins,
You are the most Merciful!..

SELF-EXISTENCE OF ALLAH: Allah is ever Self-existent and Eternal. The attribute of Self-existence and eternity is one of the divine names of Allah, meaning that He is self-existent with no beginning and end, and that He is free of any need from creation. Rather, everything needs Him for existence. The Qur'an says:

"O you men! It is you that have need of Allah: but Allah is the One free of all wants, worthy of all praise." (Fatir, 35:15).

"... Allah is free of all needs from all creation." (Ankabut, 29:6).

As these Divine messages clearly put, Allah does not need any agent for His existence. That is why it is stated that Allah is permanently self-existing.

If a person does not perceive this Divine attribute of Allah, and if s/he does not have a complete faith in this regard, his/her faith is ranked as insufficient and void, because by doing so s/he reduces Allah to the level of creation.

Thus, Allah is exempt from the attributions that belong to all else besides Him. However, those hearts having mature faith constantly invoke the Divine name of "Self-Existent and Eternal", and with the blessing of this invocation they, heart and soul, bind themselves to the bond of Allah and annihilate themselves in Allah. Namely, the servant's enjoyment of the invocation of the Divine names of Allah is to do with how much s/he is independent of all else besides Allah.

A companion of the Prophet prayed as follows:

"O, my Lord! All praises be to You, You are the most Beneficent, and there is no deity, but You, You are the Creator of the skies and the earth who has Glory and Kindness. You are the **Living**, the **Self-**

Subsisting, and **Eternal**. O my Lord, I beseech you by means of Your names!.."

When the Prophet (ﷺ) overheard this praying person, he asked those around him:

"Do you know by what means is this person praying?"

They replied: "Allah and His Prophet know better!"

The Prophet (ﷺ) answered:

"I swear by the Allah who sustains my life that this person prayed to Allah by means of His greatest names. The prayers and wishes by means of these greatest names are answered." (Tirmizi, Daawaat, 63).

*

The established attributions of Allah are as follows:

LIFE: Allah has life, and this feature of Him is existent with Himself. He is the Ever-living as the famous name "*Hayy*" indicates. He is alive, everlasting, and He has an absolute life.

And so, all lives come to being as reflections of this attribution of Allah, and they are relative. Therefore, the life of a creature is a contemporary and material one that comes about as a result of the union of the body and the spirit. Thus, it is taken back from every earthling in due course. The attribution of Ever-living *(Hayy)* is associated with Allah's Being, because His Excellency is to do with Him being alive, permanent, and having an absolute life. In short, the life of Allah is not the negation of death, and it belongs only to Allah. This is pointed out in the Qur'an:

"And put your trust in Him Who lives and dies not..." (Furqan, 25:58).

Abu Musa (may Allah be pleased with him) narrates:

"The Prophet (ﷺ) rose among us and uttered these five sentences:

"Allah is always alive, never slumbers, and slumber, in fact, does not go with Him. He reduces or increases the sustenance that He provides. The prayer made at night reaches Allah before the one made at daytime, and the prayer made at daytime reaches Allah before the one made at night. His curtain is the Divine Glory. If Allah was to uncover this curtain, His face would burn out all creation." (Muslim, Iman, 293).

It is said in another saying of the Prophet (ﷺ):

"Whoever prays asking Allah's forgiveness by saying three times 'I appeal for mercy from the Allah who is Ever-living and Everlasting", s/he is forgiven." (Ahmad bin Hanbal, Musnad, III, 10).

Allah states:

"He is the Living (One): There is no god but He: Call upon Him, giving Him sincere devotion. Praise be to Allah, Lord of the Worlds." (Mumin, 40:65).

The Prophet (ﷺ) used to make the following prayer when something worried him.

"O, my Lord, the Ever-living, the Everlasting! I appeal for your help that comes out of your Mercy." (Tirmizi, Daawat, 91).

Ali (may Allah be pleased with him) narrates:

"When the battle of Badr started I fought for sometime. Then I came to the Prophet (ﷺ). I wanted to see what he was doing. And I found him in position of prostration saying these words:

'O, my Lord, the Ever-living, the Everlasting! I take refuge in You, I appeal for your help!'

I left him and went to fight again for sometime. Then I came back to see him again. He was still in the position of prostration and he was still saying:

'O, my Lord, the Everliving, the Everlasting! I take refuge in You, I appeal for your help!'

I went back to fight again, and after a while I returned once again. He was still in the same position, and he kept his position until Allah granted us victory."

With regard to the following verse of the Qur'an, **"Know you (all) that Allah gives life to the earth after its death! Already have We shown the signs plainly to you, that you may learn wisdom."** (Hadid, 57:17)

Ibn Abbas said:

"Bringing the earth back to life is an object lesson that we can observe. However, the following meaning is also pointed to in the above verse. Allah mellows the black and hard hearts in matters of faith and He leads them to return to their Creator. He mellows dead hearts through learning and wisdom."

*

KNOWLEDGE (WISDOM): Allah has knowledge, and His knowledge (wisdom) is all-encompassing. There is nothing beyond His knowledge. He is accordingly the One who knows the past and the future. Nothing remains hidden from His knowledge. Everything is known by and readily observable to Him. And all the wisdom (science) that humans have acquired are only small particles' of this attribute of Allah. It is said in the Qur'an:

"**From Allah, verily nothing is hidden on earth or in the heavens.**" (Âl- Imran, 3:5).

"**Say: Whether you hide what is in your hearts or reveal it, Allah knows it all: He knows what is in the heavens, and what is on earth. And Allah has power over all things.**" (Âl- Imran, 3:29).

"**And He is Allah in the heavens and on earth. He knows what you hide, and what you reveal, and He knows the (recompense) which you earn (by your deeds).**" (Anam, 6:3).

"**He knows that which is in front of them and that which is behind them, while they encompass out of His knowledge nothing except what He wills...**" (Baqara, 2:255).

That is why we say: "Allah knows best!" for man's knowledge is even less than a pinhead in the ocean of the immense universe. It is stated in the Qur'an:

."**.. Of knowledge it is only a little that is communicated to you.**" (Isra, 17:85).

Therefore, many doors of science are kept open for human beings to investigate, but there are also walls of mystery that defy penetration or until Allah permits. The reason behind this is to let the servant know his/her powerlessness, and understand his dependence on Allah, and thereby resign himself/herself to the wisdom of Allah. It is said in the Qur'an:

.".. **It is possible that you dislike a thing which is good for you, but Allah knows and you know not."** (Baqara, 2:216).

In fact, human beings get distressed about the things that initially seem bad. S/he cannot see the mercy behind them. And s/he is sometimes wrapped up in many things coming in a shape of goodness, and s/he cannot see the evil hidden in them.

It is narrated that there used to be a righteous man belonging to an Arab tribe. The tribe used to take heed of the advice of the man and direct themselves in accordance with his instructions. One morning, when they woke up, they found all their dogs dead. They went straight to the man to tell him what happened. After a short time of meditation the man told them:

"– Their death may hopefully bring you salvation!"

The following night all of their cocks died as well. They went to the man again. He answered them in the same way:

"– Their death may hopefully bring you salvation!"

Upon hearing him one among them asked:

"– O, master! Dogs are our keepers, and the cocks are our *muezzins* (caller to prayer). What sort of salvation can their death bring to us?

The righteous man answered:

"– It is Allah who knows all secrets. Surely, He must have hidden a great truth in this event that we cannot figure out now."

And the following night no one's light was on. Everybody was wondering what kind of nuisance they would again be exposed to.

Yet, when they woke up in the morning they realized why such mysterious events had been taking place. That night the enemy had raided and looted the surrounding region. The enemy came close to that tribe, but as there was no dog and cock to be heard, and also no light to be seen they passed by without noticing them. Thus, the tribe had escaped great looting and slaughter. (Silk's-Suluk).

So, we see that an event seeming to be a source of distress turning into a favor! Ibrahim Haqqi of Erzurum puts this point into words as follows:

Do not question why this is so,
It fits where it is.
Watch what happens in the end;
Let us see what our Lord brings in the end,
He does the best!..

The Prophet (ﷺ) says:

"When the servant is taken ill, Allah sends him two angels and orders them: '– Go and find out how the servant welcomes the illness he suffers from.'.

If they find the servant thanking and praising Allah, they transmit his attitude to Allah who knows the best. And Allah, who sends the angels to have them witness the deeds of the servant, says:

'– If I take the life of this thankful servant, s/he deserves a place in paradise. Yet, if I cure him/her s/he deserves to have a better flesh and blood, and I forgive his sins'." (Muwatta, Ayn, 5).

This saying of the Prophet (ﷺ) acknowledges that the events that seem to have no outward benefit for us are divine trials, and they may have great rewards behind them.

In the history of humanity there are events that at first seemed to occur in the form of wrath, but turned into the form of grace in the end. However, the contrary also happened. For example, the people of the Prophet Hud mistook the clouds of wrath for that of rain. Only when the stones began to fall down instead of rain did they understand the fact. Yet, it was too late for them!..

Therefore, it is the duty of the servant to surrender himself/herself to Allah being conscious that Allah knows the best. And this surrender may only be actualized by the knowledge of Allah or mystical contemplation as no science can eliminate the evil consequences that ignorance may bring in this matter. It is only the knowledge of Allah that may eliminate evil consequences. In fact, there are a good many unlettered people who were given distinguished rewards through the knowledge of Allah.

For this reason, Yunus Emre tells that the fundamental science is the knowledge of Allah:

Twenty nine syllables,
You read them from A to Izzard,
You say A, o master,
What does it mean?
Science means knowledge,
It means self-knowledge,
If you do not know your self,
Why do you study science?

Allah divulges the position of humanity over against His wisdom:

".. **Nor does anyone know what it is that he will earn on the morrow**..." (Luqman, 31:34).

"**Say: As to the knowledge of time, it is with Allah alone**..." (Mulk, 67:26).

Knowledge is in the vision of Allah. Namely, the absolute knowledge belongs to Him. His knowledge encircles everything. Allah's knowledge is like a mirror. The things that are reflected in the mirror may differ, but the mirror covers all things reflected in it, and it does not change.

Allah's knowledge is exempt from being the result of a thought or an idea. The delicate order and harmony of the universe to which no will or intellect can deny, is the most fresh evidence of the endless knowledge of Allah. It is evident that a human being can reach to even a minor invention in years and through the cooperation of many different individuals. For example, the communication by cellular phone today is the result of an accumulation of knowledge beginning centuries ago and of many different experiences of humanity. Other developments and advancements are of this sort as well. Whereas all these inventions and the as yet unmanifest endless mysteries are the features that Allah placed in the order of the universe instantaneously with His divine knowledge. Allah, in the Qur'an, reminds human beings of this fact:

"Should He not know, -He that created? And He is the One that understands the finest mysteries (and) is well-acquainted (with them)." (Mulk, 67:14).

*

ALLAH, THE ALL-HEARING: Allah is the All-Hearing. His hearing is not like ours. There is no voice hidden to Him. As it is has been described He hears the sound of an ant walking on a stone. And all creatures that have the capability of hearing can only hear through the reflection of Allah's attribute of the All-Hearing. They can hear nothing when deprived of this capacity. There are many examples of it.

Allah repeatedly cites His attribute of **All-Hearing** along with that of **All-Seeing**, and reminds human beings of His Divine sight, and thereby warns them not to go astray from the right path.

*

ALLAH, THE ALL-SEEING: The attribute of the All-Seeing is also an attribute of Allah in accordance with His Divine nature. He duly sees everything, He is the All-Seeing. There is nothing hidden to His sight. Again, as it is described, He sees a black ant on a black stone at night.

Jalal al-Din Rumi explains why the human beings are notified of the attributes of the **All-Knowledge**, the **All-Hearing**, and the **All-Seeing**:

"Allah notifies you of His attribute of the All-Knowing lest you attempt to introduce subversive activities on earth."

"Allah notifies you of His attribute of All-Hearing so that you keep your mouth closed to unpleasant and nasty words."

"Allah notifies you of His attribute of the All-Seeing lest you perform evil and secret acts."

Thus, Allah lets the servants know their responsibilities in this matter as follows:

"And pursue not that of which you have no knowledge; for every act of hearing, or of seeing or of (feeling in) the heart will be enquired into (on the Day of Judgement). (Isra, 17:36).

Niyadhi Misri puts into words this responsibility with the following words:

An eye that has no ability to see,
Is nothing but an enemy to the head it stays on.
An ear that takes heed of no advice,
Deserves pouring lead through it.
A tongue that has no familiarity with invoking Allah's names,
Do not call that flesh as tongue.

The heedless servants of Allah will be addressed as follows:

"O the servant! Did you acknowledge Us in the earthly life, or not? If you did not, why did not you try to acknowledge Us? If you did, you were supposed to behave accordingly."

The noble Nahshabi who quotes the above statement says:

"O fearless person! Do what you do without the presence of other people so that it becomes clear whether you fear Allah, or the people! If you fear Allah, you fear Him everywhere!.."

"The real followers of the path of virtue and piety are, everywhere and every time, aware of the fact that they are under the observation of Allah."

The second caliph Omar was patrolling the streets of Madina at night-time when he stopped all of a sudden to hear the dispute coming out of a house between a mother and her daughter. The mother was telling the daughter:

"– Add some water to the milk that we are going to sell tomorrow!"

The daughter replied:

"– Mum, did not the caliph forbid to add water to milk?"

The mother told her daughter off saying:

"– How can the caliph know that we add water to milk at this time of the night!.."

However, the girl who feared Allah did not accede to the fraud her mother wanted, and she told the mother:

"- Mum, let us suppose that the caliph does not see, what about Allah? It is easy to hide this fraud from people, but how would it be possible to hide it from Allah who is the All-Seeing?.."

The caliph, Omar, was moved by the words of this Allah-fearing girl. He was so affected by the behavior of this pious girl that he later managed to help to arrange for his son to marry her. Omar bin Abdulaziz, who was to become the fifth caliph, was the offspring of this noble lady and his son.

Therefore, the whole issue is to manage consciously to realize that we live under the observation of Allah. It is said in the Qur'an:

"No vision can grasp Him, but His grasp is over all vision: He is above all comprehension, yet is acquainted with all things." (Anam, 6:103).

*

THE WILL OF ALLAH: Allah wills and acts as He wants. When He intends a thing, His command is just "Be!", and that thing happens. His actions are never to be questioned:

"To Him is due the primal origin of the heavens and earth: when He decrees a matter, He says to it: "Be," and it is." (Baqara, 2:117).

"He is the Irresistible (watching) from above over His worshippers, and He is acquainted with all things." (Anam, 6:118).

"Say: O Allah! Lord of Power (and Rule), You give power to whom You please, and You strip off power from whom You please: You endow with honor whom You please, and You bring low whom You please: in Your Hand is all Good. Verily, over all things You have power." (Âl-i Imran, 3:26).

As these verses point out that Allah is the Absolute Actor. Any occurrence and act depend on His Will. In a word, *a thing that He decrees occurs, and a thing that He does not decree does not occur!*

Therefore, the deeds that Allah approves occur in accordance with His Will. And the deeds that Allah disapproves, again, occur with His divine permission, but this time they are in the position of trials for us.

Thus, as the above verse states, every happening requires the condition of "If Allah pleases or permits." This condition covers all creation, both bodily and spiritual beings, as well as the prophets. An example of this occurred in the life of the Prophet (ﷺ):

A group of Bedouins came to the Prophet (ﷺ) asking him some questions. As he was not very knowledgeable about their query and thinking that he might get a revelation about it later in the day, he asked them to visit him again the following day by telling them:

"Come to see me tomorrow and get your answer then!"

Yet, as he did not say "so please Allah or Allah-willing" while speaking to them no revelation was sent down by Allah for a fortnight. And after this long wait the first revelation was of the following verse:

"Nor say of anything, 'I shall be sure to do so and so tomorrow' without adding, 'so please Allah!' And call your Lord to mind when you forget, and say, 'I hope that my Lord will guide me ever closer (even) than this to the right road.'" (Kahf, 18:23).

As this verse illustrates, human beings are not always able, or do not have the necessary capacity, to act as they wish because their will and power are deficient. So, the servant is supposed to know his/her limitations and s/he, duly observing the rights of Allah, must not go too far. So that Allah explains that He may forgive the sins and villainies of His servants, but not the denial of Allah or attributing partners to Him as well as infringing on the rights of his fellows. Namely, Allah will forgive anyone whom He pleases and will not forgive anyone who has displeased Him. This is declared in the Qur'an as follows.

"To Allah belongs all that is in the heavens and on earth. He forgives whom He pleases and punishes whom He pleases; but Allah is Oft-Forgiving, Most Merciful." (Âl-i Imran, 3:129).

Friends of Allah commit their will to the will of Allah through perceiving this attribute. As in other subjects they annihilate themselves in Allah. They duly know that any will of Allah is perfectly placed and they guide their surroundings in this direction.

Sheikh Sunbul Sinan (may Allah be pleased with him) asked his disciples the following question:

"O my sons! What would you do, if Allah gave you the right to mastermind the world?"

They each gave different answers. One said:

"– I would exterminate all unbelievers!"

Another said:

"– I would eradicate all who drink!"

Another one said:

"– I would exterminate all smokers!"

Among the disciples there was a learned scholar named Mustapha Muslikhiddin Affendi. He was keeping quiet. The sheikh faced him and asked:

"– O my son! What would you do?"

Mustafa Muslikhiddin Affendi answered decently:

"– O master! What is wrong -Allah forbid!- with the way Allah is already masterminding? I would keep the things as they are."

Sheikh Sunbul Sinan rejoiced and said: "The thing now found the center it should be in." And from that day forth Mustafa Muslikhiddin Affendi was called as the center of masters and he succeeded the sheikh.

Ibrahim Haqqi of Erzurum declares his commitment to Allah by the following words as if he summarizes this point:

All His acts are superior,
All His acts are well-matched,
And all his acts are favorable;
Let us see what He does,
He does the best!

Upon my word He has done the best,
Upon my oath He has done the best,
Upon my word He has done the best;
Let us see what Allah has done,
He has done the best!..

THE OMNIPOTENCE OF ALLAH: Allah is the Omnipotent and the Almighty. There is no hardship for Him. Allah summarizes this attribute in the Qur'an as follows:

.".. **Allah has power over all things**." (Baqara, 2:20).

In another verse it is said:

"**Verily, when He intends a thing, His command is 'be', and it is!**" (Yasin, 36:82).

And when Allah commands a thing, that thing is bound to happen. Therefore, we should not fall into the error of thinking about the Omnipotence of Allah with our weak mind as we have limited power. Allah's endless power is exempt from any of the limitation and impotence humans are subject to. Therefore, there is no being who is not impotent before His endless power. Our power is only as much as He ordains.

History has witnessed the defeat of many who rose against this Power. Among them were Nimrod, Croesus, Abu Jahil, and many others. They left the world empty-handed. Allah took their lives bringing them into derision. In particular, the death of Nimrod, who claimed to be a divine being, is a striking one, providing a message regarding the Divine Power. Nimrod died from a mosquito bite. The termination of Abraha and his soldiers who attacked the Ka'bah, counting on the elephants he had, by the birds of Abâbil is again a striking one.

Jalal al-Din Rumi says:

"Though this world is too great and endless in your view, it is not even a particle before Allah. Open your eyes and look around; what an earthquake, a hurricane, and a flood does to the world and its contents!"

Truly, the Power of Allah sometimes makes itself manifest in extraordinary ways that we are not used to. For example, the positive quality of fire, water, wind, and other natural elements are sometimes transformed into a destructive quality by the Divine Power. In this regard, one is supposed to see the Divine Will in the background of the events taking place in the nature. Those who cannot see it are stuck with a blind perspective. Jalal al-Din Rumi warns those heedless people:

"Do not forget that this world is a straw before Allah. The Divine

Will sometimes elevates it and sometimes lowers it. It sometimes makes the world sound, and sometimes unsound. It sometimes carries the world to the right, and sometimes to the left. It sometimes makes it a rose garden, and sometimes a thorn garden..."

These facts are frequently touched upon in the Qur'an:

"Know you not that to Allah belongs the dominion of the heavens and the earth? And besides Him you have neither patron nor helper." (Baqara, 2:107).

Yunus Emre, the sultan of the sagacious people and the lovers, puts into words our impotence before Allah:

If I take my way without You,
I cannot be helped to take a step!
You are my power in my body,
To take my head away!..

THE WORD OF ALLAH: Allah has a word. He does not need a voice, letters, words, and sentences to line up. Namely, Allah's speech is exempt from both letters and sound; His speech never has any resemblance to that of humans. And humans can speak through receiving a share from that of Allah. Yunus Emre voices this point so perfectly:

Oh the Knower of the essence of the words
Come and say from him this word comes through?
The one who does not understand the essence of the word,
Thinks that it comes from me!

Allah Almighty communicates His orders, prohibitions, and other wills to angels, prophets, and human beings, and even to all other creation through the attribution of Divine Word. Essentially, as His creation comes through His word of "Be!" creation, in a way, depends on this attribute of Allah. A minute manifestation of this attribute is to be seen in the ability to talk given to human beings. Yunus Emre says in this regard:

A word may stop the war,
A word may have the head cut off,

A word may turn the poisonous soup
Into honey and butter!

All the Divine holy books are sent down through the attribute of the Divine Word. Revelation was sometimes sent down by the Angel Gabriel, and sometimes directly, hidden behind many veils. This is a kind of communication with Allah. It is said in the Qur'an:

"It is not fitting for a man that Allah should speak to him except by inspiration or from behind a veil, or by the sending of a messenger to reveal, with Allah's permission, what Allah wills: for He is Most High, Most Wise." (Shura, 42:51).

".. And to Moses Allah spoke directly." (Nisaa, 4:164).

Allah spoke to Moses directly not by means of a tongue or voice, but by means of His attribute of the eternal Divine Word. Seventy people who were accompanying Moses to witness the occasion and the Angel Gabriel did not hear or sense this Divine speech. Moses lost consciousness in the face of this Divine transfiguration. He felt beyond the limits of time and space not remembering where he was, in this world or in the Hereafter. He strongly wished for the sight of Allah, but he was told by Allah: "You can never see Me!"

However, when Moses unconsciously insisted to see Allah he was told to look at the mountain and in case he sees the mountain remain he would be able to see Allah as well. According to narratives, radiance came to the mountain behind many veils, and the mountain exploded, and Moses lost consciousness. When he regained consciousness he appealed for mercy, feeling that he had gone too far. If Moses had not lost consciousness then, he would have been blown up together with the mountain as well.

On the other hand, the Angel Gabriel, one of the great angels, told the following words to the Prophet (ﷺ) on the night of the Prophet's miraculous journey to heaven when they together reached the lotus tree in the seventh heaven:

"– O Prophet! I am allowed only to this point. Beyond this point you will go alone. If I take just one step more, I will burn to a cinder!"

It is the Prophet Muhammad (ﷺ) who was given the generous opportunity in this respect and he had the honor of having ascended to the heavens. On the night of the ascension, the Prophet (ﷺ), sultan of the universe, was honored with a special union and communication in a way that we cannot perceive.

As the attribute of the Divine Word has no association with other words, it is exempt from any limitation. The Divine Word that are reflected to us in this world, in fact, are an endless ocean of meaning. This is told in the Qur'an as follows:

"Say 'If the ocean were ink (wherewith to write out) the Words of my Lord, sooner would the ocean be exhausted than would the Words of my Lord, even if we added another ocean like it, for its aid." (Kahf, 18:109).

"And if all the trees on earth were pens and the ocean (were ink), with seven oceans behind it to add to its (supply), yet would not the Words of Allah be exhausted (in the writing). For Allah is Exalted in Power, full of Wisdom." (Luqman, 31:27).

All words in this world are reflections of the attribute of the Divine Word. Thus, Allah has His Great Names cited by countless tongues. Allah endowed all creation, including the ones that are thought to be inanimate, with a language from His attribute of the Divine Word. It is said in the Qur'an:

"The seven heavens and the earth, and all beings therein, declare His Glory: there is not a thing but celebrates His praise; and yet you understand not how they declare His Glory! Verily He is Oft-Forbearing, Most Forgiving!" (Isra, 17:44).

Yunus Emre perceives the mystery of this verse:

Rivers of paradise
Flow splashing the words Allah, Allah
The nightingales of Islam
Sing out saying the words Allah, Allah

Branches of the Tuba tree swing
Read the Qur'an by their tongues
Rose of the paradise
Smell saying the words Allah, Allah

CREATION (GENESIS): It is the attribute by which Allah creates. It means creation from nothingness; and this type of creation only belongs to Him. The countless worlds are His production. And other factual attributes of Allah are included in the attribution of creation.

It is said in the Qur'an:

"He who has made everything which He has created most good: He began the creation of man with (nothing more than) clay." (Sajda, 32:7).

"It is He who has created for you all things that are on earth; moreover His design comprehended the heavens, for He gave order and perfection to the seven firmaments; and of all things He has perfect knowledge." (Baqara, 2:29).

"The same who produces for you fire out of the green tree, when behold! You kindle therewith (your own fires)!" (Yasin, 36:80).

"Do they not look at Allah's creation, (even) among (inanimate) things, how their (very) shadows turn round, from right and the left, prostrating themselves to Allah, and that in the humblest manner?" (Nahl, 16:48).

The attribute of creation differs from other attributes of Allah. Allah knows through the attribute of Knowledge. And through the attribute of Power, He makes things exist or annihilates them. And through the attribute of Will He decides to make things exist or to annihilate them. And then comes the attribute of **Creation** through which things are created.

The mysteries of the universe are hidden in the attribute of Creation. Therefore, everything bears witness to the existence of Allah.

*

To sum up, Allah is known by His servants mainly through the above attributes. All these attributes and all other countless divine attributes are not existent now and then, in accordance with the requirements of time and space, but existent all the time.

No attribute of Allah has an opposite to it in Allah's Person. Namely, Allah is alive, but He is exempt from death. He exists, but His existence is exempt from extinction. He has Knowledge, but His

Knowledge is exempt from ignorance. He supplies the needs, but He is exempt from being needy. All attributes of Allah follow this line.

On the other hand, Allah is exempt from having human organs regarding all attributes, and not even an atom of the attributes of Allah exists in humans. It is only the reflections that exist in humans. Namely, our ability to talk comes from a particle of the reflection from Allah's attribute of the Word. Thus, Allah's life does not bear resemblance to our life. His Sight is not like ours.

In a word, the content of all attributes of His Exalted Being present an endlessness and infinity. And all the attributes are eternal in the past and in the future. Namely, no attribute of Allah is limited. Accordingly, His Knowledge, Power, Word, Creation, and all other attributes are exempt from any kind of similitude and explanation. When it comes to our makings they are both limited and transient. Thus, humans, who cannot properly know themselves, cannot know the attributes of Allah as required. Namely, as we cannot perceive the factual being of Allah we cannot either perceive the factual characteristics of the attributes of Allah.

On the other hand, a superior being or an attribute cannot be compared or associated with an inferior one. If that sort of association is established, it is only done to devalue the superior one. For example, when a cat is associated with a lion, this association points out that cat's superiority over fellow cats in terms of strength. Yet, if a lion is associated with a cat, this association shows the cowardice and impotence of the lion. Thus, comparing Allah with the creatures is a blindness and a villainy. Moreover, it is a defamation that does not go with the supremacy of Allah. That is why such an act is called polytheism, and the actor is called a polytheist. For instance, polytheists make the mistake of associating the boundless attributes of Allah such as the All-Hearing and the All-Seeing in parallel with their own capacity to hear and see in view of their own framework and they, subsequently, reduce their beliefs regarding the attributes of Allah to the impotent stones they themselves give shape to. However, those who comprehend the truth that his human attributes are a scrap of reflection from Allah's attributes live in the season of nothingness by this spiritual knowledge and they, feeling the delight of faith, say:

"There is no being, but Allah."

They mentally and emotionally have sound knowledge of the fact that **"My Lord! You are what you are!"**

In this way, they, being exempt from any suspicion and delusion, and having a sound heart reach their Lord, and they find a place in the book of saints.

One of the dervishes asked Bayazid-i Bastami:

"O master! What are the great names of Allah?"

Bayazid-i Bastami answered:

"– O my son! Are there any minor names of Allah? Do not be unwary; All names of Allah are great. If you want your request to be answered by Allah, stop being occupied with the vanities of life! Allah's names are not reflected in unwary hearts. It is the enlightened hearts which Allah attends through many names."

II. BELIEF IN THE ANGELS

Angels are benevolent non-material beings. That is why we cannot see them in their actual form with our eyes. Yet, they have the ability to be seen in whatever form is deemed best. However, they were allowed to be seen by some of the great prophets in their non-materialized form. Their nature requires no food, drink or sleep. As they are created to spend their entire existence in the service of Allah they are not given a soul (*nafs*). Therefore, their nature does not allow disobedience to Allah. They are uncountable in number. It is said that the rain drops are brought down by the angels and each angel can have just one turn until the Day of Judgment. That is why rain drops or snowflakes do not come into collision while coming down.

Angels have different levels in accordance with different responsibilities. Mawlana Jalal al-Din Rumi says in this regard:

"Each angel has a different value or degree as the difference between the new moon and the fullmoon."

"Each angel has a share from the Divine Light. And they are endowed with the Divine Light according to their levels."

There are four prominent angels whom we may call at the level of "prophets" of angels. They are Jibra'il (*Gabriel*), Mika'il (*Michael*), Izra'il (*Azrail*), and Israfil (*Israfil*).

Gabriel was given the duty of bringing revelation to the prophets. Mika'il is responsible for natural events. Azra'il is responsible for ending our life. Israfil will blow the trumpet at the time of the end of the world and on the Day of Judgment.

Angels are, in a manner of speaking, like the spirit that is given to us. As we cannot see our spirit, so we cannot see them. As we cannot deny the existence of our spirit we cannot deny the existence of angels. It is said that to deny the existence of angels is like denying the existence of prophets as an angel transmitted the divine truth to humanity. Thus, the Qur'an warns those who deny Jibra'il, the angel of revelation:

"Say: Whoever is an enemy to Jibra'il –for he brings down the (revelation) to your heart by Allah's Will, a confirmation of what went before, and guidance and glad tidings for those who believe." (Baqara, 2:97).

As we have already seen, angels, apart from divine service to Allah, have other duties as well. Some help humans in difficulty on the command of Allah. This type of angel, helping the men of faith, have often been observed in the history of Islam. The companions of the Prophet, veterans of the Battle of *Badr*, testified to this fact as follows:

"During the hot hours of the Badr battle we have witnessed the deaths of enemies even without our swords touching their bodies."

Allah declares this fact in the Qur'an saying:

"Remember your Lord inspired the angels (with the message). 'I am with you: give firmness to the Believers: I will instill terror into the hearts of the unbelievers: smite you above their necks and smite you all their finger-tips off them.'" (Anfal, 8:12).

"If you could see, when the angels take the souls of the unbelievers (at death), (how) they smite their faces and their backs, (saying): 'Taste the penalty of the blazing fire!'" (Anfal, 8:50).

Some angels are occupied in protecting us. They are called Angels of *Hafaza*; and some angels are recording all that we do. They are called the Honorable Recorders (*Kirâman Kâtibîn*). And the angels *Munkar-Nakir* are engaged in questioning the person immediately after his/her death. There are also angels who pray for humans to be forgiven by Allah and not to go astray.

III. BELIEF IN THE BOOKS OF ALLAH

From Adam (a.s), the first man and the first prophet and onwards, Allah has sent His commandments and prohibitions through revelation, first in the form of pages (scrolls) and later in the form of books since more guidance was needed as society expanded and problems increased. There are four major holy books: the Taurat (*Torah*), the Zabur (*Psalms*), the Injil (*Gospel*), and the Qur'an. Adam was given 10 pages (or scrolls); Seth was given 50 pages; Idris (Enoch) was given 30 pages; and Abraham was given 10 pages. As for the major books, the Taurat was given to Moses; the Zabur was sent to David; the Injil was sent to Jesus, and finally the Qur'an was sent to Muhammad (ﷺ), the sultan of the universe.

Holy books are like letters from Allah to His servants. They deal with how humans should spend their lives and provide a prescription for eternal happiness. They are reflections of Allah's attribute of the eternally pre-existent Word of Allah to the world and perception of human beings. So, the holy books also present a miracle of the word as well as the message they contain.

The Qur'an, which is the last holy book, abrogated the previous ones. The reasons for this were twofold. *Firstly*, long before the revelation of the Qur'an, the holy books in their original form had either been lost or corrupted or verses had been concealed. Secondly, changing human needs required a new, complete and final message. However, the original and the primary message of all the scrolls and books regarding the cardinal principles of faith are the same. A poet puts this fact into words very nicely.

*The meaning of four books is
There is no god but Allah*

Allah says in the Qur'an:

"To every people have We appointed rites and ceremonies which they must follow: Let them not then dispute with you on the matter..." (Hajj, 22:67).

The great characteristic of the heavenly religions is that they are without doubt based on Divine revelation. However, today this feature remains only with Islam since the books of the religions previous to Islam were exposed to human error in preservation and through interpolation and distortion of the original meaning. As a matter of fact, Islam was sent primarily due to this distortion. At the same time, the Qur'an, as the final revelation, covers the essence of the previous ones and it is the perfection and completion of what humanity needs for peace and happiness here and in the Hereafter. As it is the final one, it is under the protection and authority of Allah. The Qur'an puts forward the challenge that it will never be distorted or replaced:

"If you are in doubt as to what We have revealed from time to time to Our servant, then produce a Surah like thereunto; and call your witnesses or helpers (if there are any) besides Allah, if your (doubts) are true." (Baqara, 2:23).

As this verse states, the Qur'an has remained unaltered through the centuries. It covers the guiding principles for our salvation as follows:

1. *Fundamentals of faith and pious deeds.*

2. *The nature of the life of man:* Stages of creation; birth, life, and finally death. And also man's nature: immature drives of the ego; mature drives of the spirit; and methods of purification of the ego.

3. *The complex system of the universe:* Seven layers of the heavens; sun, moon, stars, natural events, rain, alternation of the day and night, creation between the earth and the sky and their features.

4. *Historical information:* Positive and negative status of nations both in the world and in the Hereafter; Divine vengeance; the lessons from prophets and their peoples; and lessons from the past.

5. *An ocean of contemplation and remembrance that proceeds from pre-eternity to future eternity.*

IV. BELIEF IN PROPHETS

Prophets are the guides for leading to, finding and remaining on the straight path.

As humans are prone to go astray from the straight path, Allah protected them from being further misled by sending prophets. Thus, Allah, through the holy books and prophets, informs humans about their responsibilities and limitations, and made them accountable; and Allah gave this opportunity to every people.

It is said in the Qur'an:

"For We assuredly sent amongst every people an apostle (with the command), 'serve Allah, and avoid evil'...." (Nahl, 16:36).

The purpose of religion is to help humans eliminate or reduce the negative drives of the self, and help them enhance the positive ones. However, in order to actualize this target humans need a "perfect example." This is one of the reasons why Allah sent prophets to humanity, to be perfect examples for humans.

Allah says in the Qur'an in this regard:

"We sent not an apostle, but to be obeyed, in accordance with the Will of Allah..." (Nisâ, 4:64).

Prophet Muhammad (ﷺ) is the zenith of perfection. That is why Allah says in the Qur'an:

"You have indeed in the Apostle of Allah a beautiful pattern (of conduct) for any one whose hope is in Allah and the Final Day, and who engages much in the praise of Allah." (Ahzab, 33:21).

So, everybody is responsible for the belief in Allah and being a good servant. Though Allah promised His messengers paradise in the Hereafter, they too, were held responsible for fulfilling the mission of prophethood. This is told in the Qur'an as follows:

"Then shall we question those to whom Our message was sent and those by whom We sent it." (Araf, 7:6).

As Prophet Muhammad (ﷺ) was duly conscious of this responsibility, he asked his companions of over a hundred thousand during his Farewell Sermon before his death:

"O people! You will be asked about me tomorrow; what would your words be?"

The companions answered him en masse:

"– You have accomplished your mission to convey the message of Allah. You have advised and preached to us!"

Upon their words the Prophet (ﷺ), the light of existence, said:

"O my companions! Have I conveyed the message?..
Have I conveyed the message?..
Have I conveyed the message?.."

The Prophet (ﷺ) had their testimony affirmed by repeating his question three times and then pleaded for Allah's testimony:

"Be witness O Lord!..
Be witness O Lord!..
Be witness O Lord!.." (Bukhari, Ilm, 37).

As every people has been sent a prophet, the number of prophets have been numerous. It is said in the Qur'an:

"Of some apostles We have already told you the story; of others We have not..." (Nisâ, 4:164).

According to some narrations, the number of prophets is one hundred and twenty four thousand. The Qur'an mentions by name only the twenty-five most prominent. Some of them were given a new *shariah* (canonical law), but many continued the previous prophet's *shariah*.

Prophets were given the following three major missions:

1. Recite the verses of Allah to their people,

2. Lead people to purify their *nafs* (ego),

3. Study the Divinely revealed Book and learn wisdom to lead people to the straight path.

The existence of prophets is essential for our well-being. They combine many models of good personalities in one body; and they harmoniously lead the souls of human beings to their Lord.

They were prepared and chosen by Allah. Thus, they have different features endowed by Allah. These features are as follows:

Truthfulness: Prophets always maintain the feature of righteousness. Their actions are in complete accord with their words. It is impossible for them to lie. Their truthfulness was even confirmed by those who did not believe in them. Here are a few examples of many regarding their feature of honesty:

Heraclius, the emperor of Byzantium, in order to learn about the Prophet Muhammad (ﷺ), questioned Abu Sufyan, who was at that time without belief. One of the questions was:

"– Has he ever dishonored his word?"

Though Abu Sufyan was then opposed to the Prophet (ﷺ), he answered favorably regarding the Prophet (ﷺ):

"– No! He always abides by his word!"

Ubay bin Khalaf was a zealous enemy of Islam; so much so that he, before the emigration to Madina, used to tell the Prophet (ﷺ):

"– I am breeding a strong horse, and I will one day kill you while riding that horse."

And the Prophet (ﷺ) used to answer him:

"– I will -Allah willing- kill you!"

While the battle of Uhud was going on Ubay bin Khalaf was looking for the Prophet (ﷺ) by saying:

"– If I cannot find him today, I will be doomed!"

When he came close to the Prophet (ﷺ) the Companions wanted to behead him. Yet the Prophet (ﷺ) called to them:

"– Let him come to me!"

When he came near, the Prophet (ﷺ) got a spear from the hand of a Companion and threw it to him. The spear glanced off Ubay's neck, but it was enough to cause him to tumble from his horse. He was so shocked that he hastily ran back to the line of his army screaming, "– I swear that Muhammad has killed me!.."

The idol-worshippers who looked at his injury said:

"– This is only a scratch!"

Still that did not calm him and he said:

"– While in Mecca Muhammad told me: 'I will definitely kill you!' I swear that I will die even if he spits at me!.."

Ubay kept howling. Abu Sufyan told him off saying:

"– You are not supposed to howl about this tiny scratch."

Ubay answered:

"– Do you know who has done this to me? It is Muhammad. I swear by Lât and Uzzâ that if this scratch is distributed to the people of Hijaz they would all perish. Muhammad told me in Mecca: 'I will definitely kill you.' I then got convinced that I would be killed by him. As he said that, I would surely be killed by him even if he spat at me."

Eventually, Ubay, who was an enemy to the Prophet (ﷺ), died a day before returning to Mecca.

This event is an important object lesson. Even an ardent idol-worshipper who knew the Prophet (ﷺ) quite well believed how powerful his words were.

Trustworthiness: Prophets are the most trustworthy of humanity. Even non-believers give credence to what they say. Thus, even the idol-worshippers regarded Prophet Muhammad (ﷺ) as worthy of confiding in; they called him Muhammad the trustworthy, and they entrusted him with their belongings more than their kinsfolk. So much so that the Prophet (ﷺ) had the deposits of some idol-worshippers with him even up to the time of his migration to Madina. Though he was in danger of his life he asked Ali , his nephew, to stay in Mecca to hand them over to their owners.

Intelligence: Prophets are distinguished humans in terms of intelligence and awareness. They have strong mental faculties, good judgement, and persuasiveness. These features are observed differently in each prophet. Prophet Muhammad's (ﷺ) life has many examples of this feature.

Before the revelation the Ka'bah was renovated by the the tribes of Mecca. Yet, a controversy occurred about who would have the honor of placing the Black Stone in the corner of Ka'bah. As they were about to clash, one among them made a suggestion:

"– Stop fighting! As we cannot solve this matter among us let us appoint the first person entering the gate as a judge!"

As the person entered, a smile covered their faces because the one entering was Muhammad, "the Trustworthy."

After the Prophet (ﷺ) learned about the dispute, he selected a representative from each tribe. He then spread his robe on the ground and asked them to place the Black Stone on it and the representatives each to hold a corner of the robe. Thus, each tribe was able to have the honor of carrying the Black Stone. Then, he himself, placed the Black Stone in its place while they were holding the robe. By thus displaying a good example of foresight and intelligence, the Prophet Prophet (ﷺ) averted a probable fight.

On the other hand, the wisdom that he exhibited in the battles for Islam and the foresight, particularly in the battle of Hudaybiya, the victory in Mecca and Hunain and the way he dealt with the people of Taif, and the justice displayed are all lofty and beyond the reach of any human.

Communication: Prophets convey the Divine commandments to humans as they are ordered. In their convenance they neither add to nor subtract from the transmission.

Innocence (purity): Prophets are saved from every kind of disobedience and sin. However, as they are to be aware that they are also weak beings and lest they claim to be a deity they sometimes make small human mistakes. There is another aspect of wisdom in that as well. If they were to be infallible in every respect, humans would have in their minds an excuse for not following their example by thinking that they would not be capable enough to abide by the divine orders and prohibitions. Thus, prophets are not to be thought of as from among the angels, and the Qur'an touches on this subject in these respected verses:

"Say 'If there were settled, on earth, angels walking about in peace and security, We should certainly have sent them down from the heavens an angel for an apostle.'" (Isra, 17:95).

"Nor did we give them bodies that ate no food, nor were they exempt from death." (Anbiyaa, 21:8).

*

In addition to these five qualities of the prophets there are three additional qualities of Prophet Muhammad (ﷺ). These are as follows:

1. Prophet Muhammad (ﷺ) is the beloved of Allah. He is superior to all others. He is the most honored of humanity. Nadjib Fadhil Kisakurek, the Turkish poet describes the Prophet (ﷺ) with these words:

Your aroma was filtered in time immemorial,

You are honey, existence is the honeycomb...

2. Prophet Muhammad (ﷺ) has been sent to all humanity and the jinn. Namely, he is the prophet of the two dominions. And the religion he brought is permanent until the end of the world. Other prophets were sent to a certain people for a certain period. Therefore, while the miracles of all other prophets were valid for their own periods, the miracles of Prophet Muhammad (ﷺ) have no time limit. Among them the Qur'an is the major one that will remain until the end of the world.

3. Prophet Muhammad (ﷺ) is the last prophet of Allah. However, taking into account the saying of the Prophet (ﷺ): "I was a prophet when Adam was between the water and the soil" he is the "first" on account of creation as he was created to be a prophet for both the world of humanity and jinn.

Apart from all these qualities, Prophet Muhammad, (ﷺ) was granted the high station of *"Makam-i-Mahmud"* and the greatest intercession. For this reason, the merciful Prophet (ﷺ) will ask forgiveness from Allah for the sins of his nation on (ummah) the Day of Judgment and this intercession will be accepted. The words of the Qur'an,

.".. **If they had only, when they were unjust to themselves, come unto you and asked Allah's forgiveness, and the Apostle had asked forgiveness for them, they would have found Allah indeed Oft-returning, Most Merciful.**" (Nisa, 4:64), indicate how important and effective the Prophet Muhammad's intercession would be on the Day of Judgment.

The following account of the Prophet (ﷺ) also gives good news to our hearts:

"On the Day of Judgment people will go to Adam and request him to ask Allah for their forgiveness saying:

"– Please ask Allah for our forgiveness!"

Adam answers:

"– I am not in that position; you had better go to Abraham! He is the close friend of the Lord..."

When they go to Abraham he tells them:

"– I am not in that position; you had better go to Moses! He is the one who spoke to Allah..."

They go to Moses. He tells them:

"– I am not in that position; you had better go to Jesus! He is the spirit and the word of Allah..."

When they go to Jesus he tells them:

"– I am not in that position; you had better go to Muhammad!"

Then, they come to me and I tell them:

"– Yes, I am in that position."

Then I ask permission to enter the presence of Allah and permission is given. I am then inspired by some words of praise that I now do not know; I praise Allah with these words and prostrate. By then I am told:

"O Muhammad, raise your head! Say now; Your words will be heard! Ask now; Your requests will be granted! Ask for forgiveness now; Your intercession will be accepted!"

Then I say:

"O my Lord! I want my nation, I want my nation!.."

77

Allah says:

"O Muhammad! Come and take everyone who has faith in his heart as much as a mustard seed out of hell."

I come out and act as I am told. Then I return to thank Allah with the words of praise as I earlier did. And I prostrate again. And Allah says again:

"O Muhammad, raise your head! Say now; Your words will be heard! Ask now; Your requests will be endowed! Ask for forgiveness now; Your intercession will be accepted!"

I speak again:

"O my Lord! I want my people, I want my people!.."

Allah says:

"O Muhammad! Come and take everybody who has faith in his/her heart as much as a mustard seed out of hell."

I come out and act as I am told. Then I return to thank Allah with the words of praise as I earlier did. And I prostrate again. And Allah says again:

"O Muhammad, raise your head! Say now; Your words will be heard! Ask now; Your requests will be granted! Ask for forgiveness now; Your intercession will be accepted!"

I speak again:

"O my Lord! I want my community, I want my community!"

Allah says:

"Come and take everybody who has faith in his/her heart even much smaller than a mustard seed."

I come out and act as I am told. Then I return to thank Allah for the forth time with the words of praise as I earlier did. And I prostrate again. And Allah says again:

"O Muhammad, raise your head! Say now; Your words will be heard! Ask now; Your requests will be granted! Ask for forgiveness now; Your intercession will be accepted!"

I, this time, say:

"O my Lord! I ask your permission for everyone who had said 'There is no deity, but Allah!..'"

Allah says:

"I swear by My Grandeur and Highness that I will take everybody who had said 'There is no deity, but Allah' out of hell." (Bukhari, Tawhid, 36).

*

In short, prophets had unsurpassed features and they became guides for humanity, and their people were ordered to believe in and follow them: Allah, Most High, orders:

"(Say O Believers): 'We believe in Allah, and the revelation given to us, and to Abraham, Ismail, Isaac, Jacob, and the Tribes, and that given to Moses and Jesus, and that given to (all) Prophets from their Lord: we make no difference between one and another of them: and we bow to Allah (in Islam).'" (Baqara, 2:136).

"Those were the (prophets) who received Allah's guidance: follow the guidance they received..." (Anam, 6:90).

Those who obey this divine command gain happiness and salvation both in this world and in the Hereafter. They get an honorable position in both worlds. Allah says:

"All who obey Allah and the Apostle are in the company of those on whom is the Grace of Allah, of the Prophets (who teach), the Sincere (lovers of Truth), the Witnesses (who testify), and the Righteous (who do good): Ah! What a beautiful Fellowship!" (Nisâ, 4:69).

Those who disobey this divine command are the unfortunate ones in both worlds:

".. So travel through the earth, and see what was the end of those who denied (the Truth)!" (Nahl, 16:36).

"Any who denies Allah, His angels, His books, His Apostles, and the Day of Judgment, has gone far, far astray." (Nisâ, 4:136).

In the past, indeed, many unwary people who were deceived throughout history by the transitory glitter of this world have gone astray from the bright horizons that the Prophets of Allah pointed out, and they were doomed. And they even led their people to destruction. They foolishly fell for the dreadful debris of this world and they became wretched. They, having no comprehension about the wisdom and mystery of creation, imitated the behavior of animals, and in the end they, facing the Divine Wrath, were destroyed.

It is stated in th Qur'an:

"But how many (countless) generations before them have We destroyed? Can you find a single one of them (now) or hear (so much as) a whisper of them?"

"Do they not travel through the earth, and see what was the end of those before them? They were superior to them in strength: they tilled the soil and populated it in greater numbers than these have done: there came to them their Apostles with Clear (Signs), (which they rejected, to their own destruction): it was not Allah who wronged them, but they wronged their own souls." (Rum, 30:9).

Allah says about these negligent people who persisted in infidelity in spite of countless Divine signs and warnings:

".. So away with a people that will not believe!" (Muminun 23:44).

In short, all prophets are blessed personalities who guided humanity on the basis of the unity of Allah. Denying a single one of them whose prophethood is established by the Qur'an takes the person out of the circle of faith. For example, a person who denies the prophethood of Jesus is not considered to be a believer. All prophets communicated the same principles, and it was all the religion of Islam. The Last Prophet, Muhammad (ﷺ), is the master of all prophets. He will band his people together under the "banner of praise" on the Day of Judgment. This banner will also cover the previous prophets accompanied by their people who believed their prophets found the straight path. Namely, all the prophets and their people who believed in them until their communicated orders were abolished by Allah will take their place among the "People of Muhammad."

"And Peace on the apostles! And Praise to Allah, the Lord and Cherisher of the Worlds." (Saffat, 37:181-82).

V. BELIEF IN THE HEREAFTER

Almighty Allah has ordained five stages for human life. The first stage is the realm of souls; the second is the period spent in the mother's womb; the third stage is the temporal life in this world; the fourth stage is the period spent in the intermediate stage and the grave; the fifth stage is the Hereafter and eternal life either in heaven or in hell. The temporal life was granted to mankind as a test: Salvation and eternal happiness depend upon deeds and conduct of humankind in this temporal life. Belief in the Hereafter is one of the principles of six articles of faith enabling men to become aware of the fact that there is a reward or a punishment in return for these deeds and acts and thus men have responsibilities during this temporal life. Important significance was attributed to the belief in the Hereafter to the extent that it is mentioned in many verses in the Qur'an together with the belief in Allah.

The Almighty Allah says:

"…. whoever believes in Allah and the Last Day and does good deeds will have their reward with Allah, and there shall no fear come upon them nor shall they grieve." (Baqara, 2:62)

In praise of the qualities of believers: "Those who believe in Allah and the Last Day ask thee for no exemption from striving with their goods and persons. And Allah knows well those who do their duty, (Tawba: 9:46)" The verses draw attention to the characteristics of belief in Allah and the Last Day.

The Hereafter that will begin after death is a new, real and an eternal life. The respected verse states:

"What is the life of this world but amusement and play? But verily the Home in the Hereafter, - that is life indeed, if they but knew." (Ankabut, 29:64)

Because of knowing this anyone would put every moment to good use and seize every opportunity and never remain unwary of Allah for a moment. Their life turns into a life of worship full of good deeds. They are in a state between awe and hope regarding their fate and final destination. Their hearts cry and eyes shed tears because of the fear of Allah and worry of the reckoning on the Day of Judgment.

It is narrated that a pious man came to a market. He was going to buy a few items he needed. He had calculated the cost of what he planned to purchase and decided that he had enough money. However, when he went to the market he realized that the money he had was not enough to finish the shopping. Thus, that pious man started to cry and continued while the people around him were surprised seeing him in that situation. They tried to comfort him by telling him that crying for not having sufficient money was not correct behavior. After a while this pious man recovered from his state and addressed the astonished people while sobbing:

"Don't assume that my tears are shed for this world! I have realized that my calculation at home did not correspond to the account in the market! How then can the calculation of the account in this world be suited tomorrow to accord with that in the Hereafter!"

No doubt, tears that are shed for the sake of worship and serving Allah in this life would bring a smile in the Hereafter. Therefore, the renowned poet Yunus Emre takes his place in the front row of those who shed tears for the afterlife and invites everyone to join the same rank:

Upon remembering that day (the Day of Judgment)
Let's shed tears for this day
It is a day of giving up on all
Let's shed tears for this day

The earth cracks on that day.
All of the dead resurrect
Entire wrongdoings are questioned
Let's shed tears for this day

The sky splits off on that day
Man endures so much
Everybody is frightened
Let's shed tears for this day

Horror of that day
Turns the innocents to old men
What a pity to the sinner
Let's shed tears for this day

That day is the moment of crying
Men and women become naked
Let all hearts get burned
Let's shed tears for this day

Oh Yunus! Step in the straight path
What can a brother do?
Remedy can only come from Allah
Let's shed tears for this day

In a different poem, Yunus moans:

May the balance of account be lawful
May the unlawful receive punishment
Wrongdoers will be treated as they deserve
What should I do, what shall I say?

When the life on this earth is completed, one of the Archangels, Israfil would blow a "horn" *(the Sur)* and with the primordial sound coming from *the Sur* human beings will be resurrected and then they will gather at the place of resurrection.

Resurrection of men on the final day is a simple act for Almighty Allah who created things that didn't exist before. The Qur'an speaks of this fact as follows:

"Man says: "What! When I am dead, shall I then be raised up alive? But does not man call to mind that We created him before out of nothing?" (Maryam, 19:66-67)

"Does man think that We cannot assemble his bones? Nay, We are able to put together in perfect order the very tips of his fingers." (Qiyama, 75:3-4)

"Doth not man see that it is We Who created him from sperm? Yet

behold! He (stands forth) as an open adversary! And he makes comparisons for Us, and forgets his own (origin and) Creation: He says, "Who can give life to (dry) bones and decomposed ones (at that)? Say, "He will give them life Who created them for the first time! For He is Well-versed in every kind of creation! The same Who produces for you fire out of the green tree, when behold! Ye kindle therewith (your own fires)! "Is not He Who created the heavens and the earth able to create the like thereof?" - Yea, indeed! For He is the Creator Supreme, of skill and knowledge (infinite)! Verily, when He intends a thing, His Command is, "be", and it is! So glory to Him in Whose hands is the dominion of all things: and to Him will ye be all brought back." (Ya Seen, 36:77-83)

"It is He Who brings out the living from the dead, and brings out the dead from the living, and Who gives life to the earth after it is dead: and thus shall ye be brought out (from the dead)." (Rum, 30:19)

"Say: "(Nay!) Be ye stones or iron, or created matter which, in your minds, is hardest (to be raised up),- (Yet shall ye be raised up)!" then will they say: "Who will cause us to return?" Say: "He who created you first!" Then will they wag their heads towards thee, and say, "When will that be?" Say, "May be it will be quite soon!" (Isra, 17:50-51)

"O mankind! If ye have a doubt about the Resurrection, (consider) that We created you out of dust, then out of sperm, then out of a leech-like clot, then out of a morsel of flesh, partly formed and partly unformed, in order that We may manifest (our power) to you; and We cause whom We will to rest in the wombs for an appointed term, then do We bring you out as babes, then (foster you) that ye may reach your age of full strength; and some of you are called to die, and some are sent back to the feeblest old age, so that they know nothing after having known (much), and (further), thou seest the earth barren and lifeless, but when We pour down rain on it, it is stirred (to life), it swells, and it puts forth every kind of beautiful growth (in pairs)." (Hajj, 22:5)

These verses, as words of Almighty Allah, who takes life and brings the dead to life, demonstrate resurrection will no doubt take place. In the face of such an inevitable fact one should take into account the following declaration: "You will die as you have lived; you will be resurrected as you have died." Then one should be prepared for this day.

As Yunus said:

O friends! o brethren!
I fear that I will die
Yet I am prepared to get what is deserved
Thus I don't mind dying

Then, Almighty Allah says:

"Then shall anyone who has done an atom's weight of good, see it! And anyone who has done an atom's weight of evil, shall see it." (Zalzala, 99:7-8)

"The Day whereon neither wealth nor sons will avail, but only he (will prosper) that brings to Allah a sound heart." (Shuara, 26:88-89)

Inspired by these verses the renowned poet Arif Nihad composed the following lines:

They said: "No wood exists in the hell;
The passenger will take his own wood!"
Then I realized that one who goes to the paradise
Will take his rose and lily with him!

Yunus also draws attention to the fact one should be prepared while heading to the Day of Judgment:

Tomorrow the work will not be finished
If it is not completed today on this earth!

In other words, the Hereafter is an indispensable place for both the good and bad people because nothing is more natural than rewarding the good and punishing those who deserve it. Had there been no prisons or other institutions for criminals and wrongdoers in this temporal world, life would have been unbearable. Even for this reason only, it is possible to believe in the existence of the Hereafter.

It is a simple observation to notice the reciprocity in the following examples: a man tends to punish even the smallest insect for a bite on his body. On the other hand a man tends to appreciate even the kindness of an offer of a cup of coffee and the memory of this appreciation can last for years. Therefore, it is simply unacceptable blindness to expect that unlawful deeds and actions of a man throughout his lifetime will remain unreciprocated before the Almighty Allah. There is the persecution of the oppressor; complaints of the oppressed; blasphemy of the unbeliever and faith of the believer in our life on this earth. Had there been no rewards and punishment for these events and behaviors, not only the Divine program that brought all beings under the control and command of men but also the creation of men would have been meaningless. All of these would have been in conflict with the attribution of Almighty Allah, who is Just and Fair. As Almighty Allah is far away from having any flaws, He is also far away indeed from falling into any such deficiency. Thus, in order to emphasize the day of reckoning, reward and punishment, Almighty Allah states:

"Does man think that he will be left uncontrolled, (without purpose)?" (Qiyama, 75:36)

"Did ye then think that We had created you in jest, and that ye would not be brought back to Us (for account)?" (Muminun, 23:115)

"We created not the heavens, the earth, and all between them, merely in (idle) sport." (Dukhan, 44:38)

"The Unbelievers say, "Never to us will come the Hour": Say, "Nay! But most surely, by my Lord, it will come upon you; - by Him Who knows the unseen, - from Whom is not hidden the least little atom in the heavens or on earth: Nor is there anything less than that, or greater, but is in the Record Perspicuous." (Saba, 34:3)

"Allah! There is no god but He: of a surety He will gather you together unto the Day of Judgment, about which there is no doubt. And whose word can be truer than Allah's?" (Nisa, 4:87)

"O ye who believe! Believe in Allah and His Messenger, and the scripture which He hath sent to His Messenger and the scripture which He sent to those before (him). Any who denieth Allah, His

angels, His Books, His Messengers, and the Day of Judgment, hath gone far, far astray." (Nisa, 4:136)

"He questions: "When is the Day of Resurrection?" At length, when the sight is dazed, and the moon is buried in darkness. And the sun and moon are joined together,- That Day will Man say: "Where is the refuge?" By no means! No place of safety! Before thy Lord (alone), that Day will be the place of rest. That Day will Man be told (all) that he put forward, and all that he put back." (Qiyamah, 75:7-13)

Neither in the Qur'an nor in the Prophetic traditions (hadith), is any information given regarding the timing of the Day of Resurrection. However, a number of minor and major signs of the day of judgment are mentioned in these primary sources. We can summarize the available information as follows:

a. Minor Signs:

1. Learning and knowledge will decrease while ignorance will increase. Alcohol consumption and fornication will take place explicitly.

2. Murders for simple reasons and even for no reason at all will rise.

3. Justice and competence will disappear; no attention will be paid whether something is lawful or unlawful, legitimate or illegitimate.

4. Rebellion against parents and (slavish) obedience to (the unnecessary demands of) women will increase.

5. Cheating and corruption will spread and everybody will start complaining about these ills.

6. Respect and compassion for people will decrease significantly and warnings will remain unnoticed.

7. Migration to cities will soar and buildings will spring up. Incompetence and wicked people will enjoy respect and they will hold power and authority.

8. Gambling, fortune telling and tools for gambling will become more varied and popular. People will not notice the passing of time.

9. Wasting money, goods and resources will increase; people will prefer material and worldly interests to the happiness in the Hereafter.

b. Major Signs:

1. The emergence of a smoke lasting forty days,

2. The emergence of the Antichrist (Dajjal),

3. The emergence of an animal called Dhabbatu'l Ard,

4. The rising of the sun from the West,

5. The spreading of Yajuj and Majuj in the world,

6. The descent of Jesus (a.s) to the earth,

7. The rising of a strong fire in the Hejaz region and,

8. The sinking of three places in the East, the West and in the Arabian Peninsula.

The Day of Judgment would start when Israfil, one of the archangels, blows his trumpet and resurrection would take place when he blows the same horn: trumpet for the second time. This is described in the Qur'an as follows:

"The Trumpet would (just) be sounded, when all that are in the heavens and on earth will swoon, except such as it will please Allah (to exempt). Then will a second one be sounded, when, behold, they will be standing and looking on!." (Zumar, 39:68)

In addition to this explanation and information about the signs of the Day of Judgment, there is a classification regarding Israfil's blowing of a trumpet. According to this classification, there will be three blows:

1. Blow of Space *(Nefhatu'l-feza):* With this blow the whole world would remain motionless.

2. Blow of Thunderbolt *(Nefhatutu's-saika):* With this blow everything would perish. No hills would remain and the earth will become absolutely flat and straight. Everything except the Almighty Allah would perish at this blow.

3. Blow of Resurrection and Judgment: Almighty Allah would command all beings to "rise up" and everybody will rise. (Tefhim IV, 591)

Allah, Most High states:

" The trumpet shall be sounded, when behold! From the graves

(men) will rush forth to their Lord! They will say: "Ah! Woe unto us! Who hath raised us up from our beds of repose?.".. (A voice will say:) "This is what (Allah) Most Gracious had promised. And true was the word of the Apostles." (Ya Seen, 36:51-52)

According to some scholars, the unbelievers and those who rebelled against Almighty Allah will face punishment and pain in their graves. However, the pain in the grave is little compared to the pain in hell and therefore the period spent in the grave is regarded as a time of sleep. When they awake from this sleep, those who sinned or died as unbelievers will face a great pain and thus they will start panicking and shouting for help by saying "shame on us, what on earth is happening to us" (Ömer Nasuhi Bilmen, Tefsir, VI, 2943)

Those who are condemned to punishment will utter "shame on us, what a pitiful situation we are in." According to these views, punishment in the grave will be lifted during the course of a forty-year gap between the first and the second blow to the horn and the deceased will be in a state of sleep. For this reason, when they awake from their sleep on the Day of Judgment and realize that they would face the punishment, they will start lamenting saying:

"Who woke us up from our sleep?"

What is important to remember here is not when the Final Day will come but whether everybody is prepared for death as his or her personal last day and for the life in the Hereafter.

The world is a deceitful mirage whereas the Hereafter is an endless life. We should come to our senses before death claims us so that that we will not face punishment and become helplessly regretful. There is no doubt that every human being will inevitably come across Azrail (Angel of Death) at an unknown time and place. There is in no place to hide from death. Therefore man should be aware of the wisdom in following the verse **"Hasten ye then (at once) to Allah"** (Dhariyat, 51:50) and take refuge in Allah as the only shelter.

Sincere believers are those who start investing in their life after death from today before waiting for their personal final day (death).

There will be no fear and no sadness for such people on the terrifying Day of Judgment.

The renowned poet Yunus utters the following wish on the Day of Judgment:

Oh (The Almighty Allah), may you please make us
Among those who enter the Divine house of paradise!
And among those who see Your Beauty
Upon arrival to Your presence

VI. BELIEF IN DESTINY

The Will of Almighty Allah is present in all beings. Nothing can take place, which is devoid of His Will and Power. Not even a drop of dust can move from its place or a tiny fly can move its wings without His will. Since Almighty Allah has universal Knowledge and Wisdom, He knows what has happened in the past and what will happen in the future. The predestination of something that would happen in the future is "destiny *(qadir)*" and when the predestined event comes true that is the Divine Decree *(qadha)*.

One cannot grasp the meaning of destiny properly with human knowledge and measurements. For this reason, it has been misused many times. There is nothing to be gained in trying to have a deep knowledge of the concept of destiny because human understanding of it is limited. The Qur'an shows this very clearly and doesn't allow any effort to be spent for having a deeper knowledge of destiny:

"With Him are the keys of the unseen, the treasures that none knoweth but He." (Anaam, 6:59)

As it is impossible to describe the nature and look of color to a blind person, similarly, human understanding with its limited capacity and vocabulary fails to grasp the mysteries and qualities of destiny. Only those who have Allah-given knowledge can have a tiny bit of understanding of it. The following story mentioned in the Qur'an illustrates this point very clearly.

Almighty Allah sends Moses (a.s) to Khidir (a.s) who had Allah-given knowledge so that Moses (a.s) can learn from him. This knowledge reflects a light from the Preserved Tablet *(Lauh-i Mafuz)* which is beyond the realm of causes and motives. Moses (a.s) and Khidir (a.s) set out on a journey. They experience manifestations of the Divine. When the occurrences in the story involving Khidir (a.s) are carefully analyzed by reason, one can see that puncturing a hole in the ship literally means an injustice to its owners whereas if one looks at the same event in its reality, this means protecting the ship from being taken by the attackers and it remains as a source of income and survival for the poor.

Again, although the killing of a child in the story is apparently a murder, in reality it is the protection of the life of the devout parents in the Hereafter. Again looking outwardly, it is not logical to erect a wall for those who have driven Khidir (a.s) and Moses (a.s) away; this was in fact the protection of a trust that belonged to two innocent orphans.

However, the mysteries and wisdom can only be discovered through a Allah-given knowledge. Therefore the mystery of destiny cannot be grasped by reason alone. Understanding the meaning of destiny is beyond the capacity of the human intellect. It for this reason the Prophet Muhammad (ﷺ) ordered us to believe in destiny and banned us from having quarrels and bickering about its nature. When he came across a group where there was an intense debate about the concept of destiny, the Prophet (ﷺ) said:

"Are you commissioned to have a debate on destiny? Or was I sent to you for this purpose? Your predecessors perished because of their discussions on this issue. You should never debate this question."

What is crucial at this point is not to concentrate on the detailed knowledge of destiny but to understand the main message and the subtlety. The Almighty Allah divided the behavior He attributed to human beings into two:

1. Compulsory/Necessary Acts
2. Optional/Voluntary Acts

1. Compulsory/Necessary Acts

Compulsory acts take place without our desire and will and these are totally the results of predestination and Divine decree. It is impossible to act or change the course of such events. Birth, death, resurrection, sleeping, getting hungry, our physical structure, the length of our lives and similar facts are parts of the compulsory or inevitable dimension of destiny. These occurrences and acts are also called absolute destiny (*qader-i mutlaq*) and human beings are not held responsible for these inevitable acts and deeds. Human eyes cannot see, and their ears cannot hear when such inevitable acts will take place. The renowned Sufi poet Rumi illustrates this shocking and puzzling state as follows:

"When the time comes for the happening of predestined acts, fishes throw themselves out of the sea. Birds flying in the sky rush towards the traps prepared to catch them on the ground."

"Escape from such destiny and the Divine decree is only through involvement in still another destiny and Divine decree."

The Qur'an speaks of the inevitable occurrence of the predestined acts as in the following verse:

"..And the command of Allah is a decree determined." (Ahzab, 33:38)

One should not however think of natural disasters etc. as destiny and decree. Destiny in a sense signifies the balance and stability in the universe and expresses the divine measure of this equilibrium as Almighty Allah explains in the Qur'an:

"Verily We have created everything according to a measure" (Qamar, 49)

It if for this that criticizing the result and wisdom of destiny means to be ignorant and even stupid. Whatever happens according to predestination is appropriate and expedient. For example, the movement of the sun is set up in such a perfect manner that nobody feels any doubt about its movement or gets worried whether the sun comes closer to the world and burns it or moves distant to endanger life on it. Both Muslims and non-Muslims believe that the sun rises from the east and sets in the west every single day without any defect and lapse. Likewise, if one realizes the wisdom and reason behind other positive or seemingly negative out-comes of events he would say without exception that, "whatever the outcome is, it is the perfect one." This means confirmation and valida-tion of the Divine plan. Even the most radical unbelievers unconscious-ly feel convinced when they see how beautiful and harmonious the events take place and order in the universe is established. They admire the course of events. Each and every mystery human beings discover, as much as permitted by the Divine will, pull reasonable people, even if they are unbelievers, to the wonders of the Divine plan in the eternal val-ley and astonish them, let alone supporting criticism about the wisdom of these mysteries. Those who produce unreasonable arguments and talk nonsense about the existing mechanism of destiny are ignorant of the mystery of the sacred decree and devoid of wisdom and reason. Those people who cannot distinguish between good and evil, right and wrong, reality and falsehood are the victims of ignorance.

It is obvious on the other hand that the nature of destiny and the decree of Allah are unknown. This mysteriousness is indeed a blessing for man who is a mortal being because life becomes unbearable if he knows what will happen to him, either good or bad. In such a case, his life functions such as eating, drinking and working etc. will come to a standstill. Human beings live with a hope of life and never give up functioning even when they are on the verge of death simply because Almighty Allah kept destiny and His decree secret and unknown. This is a mighty blessing and a perfect Divine order, which enables man to carry on his life in this world.

When it comes to the question of evil, no evil emanates from the will of Almighty Allah. However, He allowed the emergence of evil acts as requirement of examination in this world. Almighty Allah limited the happening of evil acts and this limitation is a blessing for mankind because he does not permit all kinds of evil occupying human life. We may not be aware of this fact, but his limitation and visa so to say pro-tects mankind from material and spiritual harms. Otherwise, had men not enjoyed this level of protection, mankind would have succumbed to many other sins following the evil and with his self-indulgence.

Because man, whether consciously or unconsciously, aspires to evil as much as he aspires to good deeds. Almighty Allah underlines this tendency in the Qur'an:

"The prayer that man should make for good, he maketh for evil; for man is given to hasty (deeds)." (Isra, 17:11)

"If Allah were to hasten for men the ill (they have earned) as they would fain hasten on the good, - then would their respite be settled at once..." (Yunus, 19:11)

The more mankind contemplates and evaluates their self the better they will grasp the meaning conveyed in these verses. In order to understand the Divine protection that mankind enjoys we can give the following examples that show the Divine wall against evil and harmful happenings.

Let's look at a liar's behavior and words: In order to convince somebody he would say "I am telling you the truth, if I am lying may my eyes turn blind." When he tells lies he doesn't become blind and his trial and test time in this world continue as normal. Similarly, many people make promises and utter words such as "If I do this may my head break off and may my hands be broken; if I act like that may you see my death." These wishes may be genuine and serious at the time of their utterance. However, many people do things or commit acts in conflict with their promises that require the happening of all these harmful wishes. Despite the fact that they fall into situations which they don't wish, neither their heads are broken off nor are their hands broken nor do they meet their death. There are numerous similar examples of this kind in human life. In these circumstances, Almighty Allah erects a wall of protection as a result of His compassion and mercy between man and the evil acts he wishes for if he does something he is not supposed to do. The evil things cannot take place because Almighty Allah protects mankind. The aforementioned verses express this intelligence and wisdom.

In the light of this reality, Gnostics and pious believers accept positive and seemingly negative outcomes of destiny and the Divine plan being aware of the Mercy and Compassion of Almighty Allah. The following poems expresses such surrender to the Divine will:

Whatever comes to me from you is pleasant,
Whether it is a rose or a thorn,
Whether imperial dress or burial clothes,
Both Your grace and distress are pleasant.

Almighty Allah himself commands us to be in such a state of acceptance and submission in the following verse:

"Say: "Nothing will happen to us except what Allah has decreed for us: He is our protector": and in Allah let the believers put their trust." (Tauba, 9:51)

How beautiful a poet has said:

Know that the evil doesn't come from an enemy, nor good comes from a friend
Trust all that happens to Almighty Allah; know that all comes from Him.

The Qur'an also reveals to us that Almighty Allah has great Compassion and He shows it to whomever He wills:

"If Allah do touch thee with hurt, there is none can remove it but He: if He do design some benefit for thee, there is none can keep back His favor: He causeth it to reach whomsoever of His servants He pleaseth. And He is the Oft-Forgiving, Most Merciful." (Yunus, 10:107)

To put it in a nutshell, peace of heart and mind is hidden in submission to the Divine decree. Any act or deed other than the acceptance of the outcome of destiny is futile and brings no benefit. The renowned Sufi poet Rumi expresses this very eloquently:

"You will face a disaster wherever you go with the hope of safety from evil and of finding comfort; and the trouble which is destined to happen to you will happen and find you.

"You should be aware that no corner of this temporal world is devoid of traps and dangers. There is no other way to find happiness other than discovering Him in the heart and taking refuge in His spiritual presence. This is the only way to reach salvation and comfort. Don't you see that even those who live in the safest places in this temporal and transient world and those who are thought to be the most powerful also finally die"

"You should try to take refugee in the Mercy and Protection of The

Almighty Allah rather than trying to be in safety in temporal traps. He turns the poison into a cure for you if He wishes and He turns water to poison if He wishes so."

2. Optional/Voluntary Acts:

Almighty Allah endowed mankind with a partial and relative will in order to differentiate human will from His Divine will. Man will be rewarded for good deeds as a result of his choice or will be punished if his will leads him to evil deeds. Almighty Allah provides the mechanism that enables man to go in whichever direction he decides to take. The involvement of Almighty Allah is limited by such a degree of interference. He is involved in this process as a Creator and doer of acts. The real performer of an act is the man. However, man sometimes cannot perform an act despite his intending to carry it out because Almighty Allah gets involved in this process as a Creator and sometimes prevents the man from acting as he likes.

As we have explained earlier, it is not appropriate to try get more detailed knowledge about destiny except understanding the basic wisdom of it. Almighty Allah has the only key that opens the mysterious gate of destiny. The nature of destiny is beyond the realm of human understanding. Only some of those who are rewarded with paradise are allowed to solve the mysteries of the nature of destiny. Therefore, any attempt to open the door leading to the mysterious nature of destiny means going too far. While the nature of destiny is kept secret and mankind is not informed of what will happen in the future some ignorant people say, "my destiny is written badly." By saying this, these people interpret the concept of destiny to escape the responsibility of their acts and deeds. Trying to escape one's responsibilities and acting in conflict with the purpose of creation is both vulgar and banal.

Almighty Allah's knowledge recognizes no limits and no borders. He knows all that has happened and all that will happen in the future. And the knowledge of what will happen is as clear to Almighty Allah as what has happened in the past. As our cognition functions in a temporal and time-bound world, we tend to think that the future events known to Almighty Allah are predestined and fixed by Him. This is the result of our intellectual incompetence and its limitation by our inability not to be able to contemplate outside the bounds of time. When the curtain of time is lifted everything will be seen clearly. Thus, the Prophet Muhammad (ﷺ), during his Night Journey *(Miraj)* witnessed the eternal world and while he was explaining his experiences he said:

"I heard the sounds of a pen which was writing destiny" (Hakim, Mustadrak, II, 405)

While recalling his observation of the eternal world he said:

"I saw how Abdurrahman Ibn Auf was taken to paradise"

During this experience the Prophet (ﷺ) was taken out of the boundaries of time and experienced a different aspect of reality during the night of ascension. Almighty Allah has eternal knowledge of the naked truth of reality, because He is not bound by time and place.

So, when we think of our impotency to understand the nature of time we will be able to see that Allah has provided His servants with a willpower in proportion to their responsibilities. If it were not so, the most Beneficent and the most Compassionate Allah would not burden His servants with such responsibilities and judge them on that basis. The fact that Allah holds His servants responsible for their deeds and that they will be judged accordingly proves that Allah has already granted freedom of will to His servants

Mawlana Jalal al-Din Rumi calls out to those who do not understand this point:

"If the servant submits to predestination, he gets the reward for it from Allah. Predestination is as tasty as a sweet for the servant who submits to it; it makes the face of the servant to smile."

"If you go wrong the pen writes wrong. If you are on the right track the pen brings happiness."

"A thief told the police when caught: 'Well, what I have done has been predetermined by Allah.' Upon this the police replied: 'Well, what I am doing is also predetermined by Allah. You misbehave and then blame predestination; this cannot be the mentality of a wise person.'"

"In short, Satan leads the servant to evil, and the soul leads to good. If these were not made optional for the servant why should the two, Satan and the soul, compete?"

"We humans have a hidden capacity to choose. See how this capacity interacts when we are faced with two diverse ideas. You make a judgment about 'which is best for you', and make up your mind to prefer one to another! And nobody directs you in your determination. Would you be able to do so, if you did not have the capacity to choose?"

"The belief that we are forced in our acts is a great mistake. Such a belief means denial of one's own intellect as well." The proponents of the fatalistic view act in accordance with their intellect, but they deny the role of the intellect. O brother! If the human being did not have the willpower and the capacity to choose, would there exist such an expression as "this is evil, that is good" or "this is nice, that is bad?" Even animals have perceptions in proportion to their senses and capacity. Yet, one needs to be wise to comprehend this fact!"

"If humans were not given free will, would you not look for healing directly from Allah, instead of from the doctor? Illness is a good lesson to teach you what free will means."

"If you think you do not have free will, why do you plan to do such and such today and tomorrow? Do you think one can make plans without free will?"

"O those who favor the fatalistic view! When you claim that 'the servant has no free will' while aiming at eliminating the deficiency of power on the side of Allah, do not you realize why Allah holds His servants responsible for their acts? By holding such a view you also ascribe a humanly attribute of ignorance to Allah. Do you think Allah, the Creator of the universe, tyrannizes over His servants by holding them responsible for what they can bear? Gather yourself together, and try to comprehend the wisdom behind why Allah holds His servants responsible for what they should do and should not do!"

"Look at your own world; If you think it is only Allah who has free will, why do you hold the thief who steals your goods responsible for his act. Why do you regard some as your enemy and have a bitter grudge against them? How come you assign such sin and crime on those who have no free will? So, there must be free will! Otherwise, there would be no need for prisons!"

There is another point to be made here:

Overvaluing free will, and seeing the intellect above everything is also a sign of ignorance. Thus, one comprehends how incompetent man's individual will is in the face of Allah's Absolute Will in proportion to the knowledge or wisdom he has acquired. After all, man's individual will, which is only a fragment, is hardly found in the servants who annihilate themselves in Allah. So, the words and acts of those saintly people who are said to be disclaiming man's individual will should be viewed in this context. They do not utterly rule out man's individual will, but regard it as almost non-existent in the face of Allah's Absolute Will. Especially, for those servants who annihilate themselves in Allah to become "Allah's eye and hand" in this world, man's individual will is like the fire of a candle melting under the light of the sun to finally disappear. The following example draws attention:

A rumor spread about Muhammad al-Noor al-Arabi, a saintly servant who lived in the latter period of the Ottomans, that he denied man's individual will. The Sultan, Abdulhamid II, summoned him to his special circle of learning so that he could be asked to explain what he really believed. Muhammad al-Noor al-Arabi explained his views when in the circle as follows:

"I have never disclaimed man's individual will. However, I said that it was almost non-existent for some individuals; because the pioneering saints always feel the presence of Allah their individual will does not have any chance to come into the open. Therefore, they act depending on the Will of Allah who is the Absolute Controller, not depending on their own will. For example, we are now in presence of the Sultan. We do what we are told. If we are told to come, we come; if we are told to leave, we leave. It is not possible for us to use our individual will against the will of the Sultan that is above us. Whereas, look at the careless people and other creatures outside, they are very much independent and free in their will."

When we go deep into these basic principles we face many problems to be explained. However, the root of the matter is as follows:

Man possesses a free will. This free will or power has been given to him by Allah. Though Allah is found together in the formation of every desire, He is pleased only for the good. A teacher's objective is to have his student equipped with knowledge and prepared. Yet, if the student does not endeavor in this direction, there is nothing for the teacher to do. Likewise, a doctor's mission is to heal his patient. Yet, if the patient does not follow his prescriptions, it is only the patient who should be responsible for the negative outcome. The patient, in this case, can put no blame on the doctor.

Therefore, as our actions are the outcome of our individual will, we cannot excuse ourselves on the pretext of predestination.

Such an excuse of the one who does not worship or follow the precepts of religion is nothing but blindness. Allah provides the one who wishes to worship with facilities, and He does not help the one who does not wish to worship.

Excusing ourselves for our sins by taking shelter in predestination in this manner is an unjust, unwise, and indecent act.

*

So, the statement of witness that "There is no god but Allah" covers all these precepts, and those who completely approve this principle of faith with their heart and tongue are considered to be believers.

It is unwise to be unaware of the contents and the meaning of this confession of faith. Those saints of Allah who have mature souls live their lives worthy of the Highness of Allah that they deeply feel. Their lives are like a rosary. They wrap themselves up with the light of Allah. They always try to annihilate themselves in Allah. Muhammad Asad al-Arbili, one of those saintly servants of Allah who achieved this position, said:

"I am still working to perfect my faith. I am still trying to say the confession of faith properly; because it is not so easy to say "There is no god but Allah" when still having worldly idols in your heart. And even if said, it is doubtful that it is acceptable in the sight of Allah."

Thus, the declaration of faith with the words "There is no god but Allah" requires a good perception of its essence. Confession of faith with no insight does not bring the expected intent, though it is not too far from bringing benefit. Nevertheless, the confession of faith when consciously expressed provides the soul with eternal rewards.

*

The Prophet (ﷺ) once delivered a sermon saying:

"If one utters the words 'There is no god but Allah' heartfelt and without any additional things to throw it into confusion, paradise is necessary for him."

Ali, (the nephew and son-in-law of the Prophet (ﷺ) and later Caliph) asked:

"O Messenger Of Allah! What does 'without additional things to throw it into confusion mean?"

Allah's Messenger (ﷺ) answered:

"It is the love of this world; it is losing one's heart to this world." (Ihya).

Another saying of the Prophet (ﷺ) in this regard is as follows:

"No servant of Allah who says "There is no god but Allah" **ends up without having the doors of the heavens** opened to him; so much so that his words of confession of faith go up to the throne of Allah as long as he refrains from committing great sins." (Tirmizi, Daawat, 126).

Therefore, one needs to refrain from committing sins. The Prophet (ﷺ) says:

"When a servant commits a sin he gets a black stain on his heart. When she repents this black stain disappears; otherwise it installs itself there. When the servant commits another sin he gets another black stain on his heart; and finally his heart gets as black as soot." (Tirmizi, Tafsir, 83).

Confession of faith does not influence the heart of such individuals. So, the following four points are to be refrained from:

1. Disputation with foolish people.

101

2. Excess of sins.

3. Communing frequently with members of the opposite sex who can be married.

4. Associating with those whose hearts are religiously dead.

The greatest wish of Satan is to impose himself on the heart. If the heart engages in remembrance of Allah, then Satan cannot approach it, and then Satan goes down. Yet, if the heart moves away from the remembrance of Allah, then Satan easily approaches it.

It is said in the Qur'an:

"Has not the time arrived for the believers that their hearts in all humility should engage in remembrance of Allah and of the Truth?" (Hadid, 57:16).

An individual who is away from the remembrance of Allah and overcome by his ego is like a jewel fallen into mud. The struggle against the ego is actualized by purifying oneself from the negative conditions and bringing goodness in one's essence. Those who can manage this kind of purification get blessings from Allah. Allah says:

"But those will prosper who purify themselves." (Ala 87:14).

It is without doubt that this kind of purification begins with the confession of faith.

Abu Ali Daqqaq says:

"When the servant says, "There is no deity" his heart is cleaned as a wet cloth cleans the mirror. Then when he says "but Allah" the light of Allah begins to emanate into a very clean heart. In this case it is clear that all the efforts of Satan go to waste."

Hasan al-Basri describes what Satan thinks as follows:

"– I stir up sins for the people of Muhammad, but their repentance causes me to fail. In this case, I cause some wrong things to appear which are seemingly good. In this way, many of them do not refrain from them as they do not regard them as sinful and they do not repent for them either." And Hasan al-Basri warns believers about Satan saying:

"So, those deeds which are thought not to be sinful are heresies; namely those acts committed by conforming to the carnal mind, and considered to be within the boundaries of religion."

Wahb bin Munabbih says:

"Fear Allah! You curse Satan in the presence of people; but when you are on your own you obey him, and you make friends with him."

TWO ASPECTS OF FAITH

The Confession of Witness (*Kalima-i shahadet*) has two parts. The first is about confirming the Existence and Oneness of Allah; the second is about confirming Muhammad (ﷺ) as His Messenger and servant.

Faith takes root in the soul by internalizing these two parts in unity. Therefore, only one part is insufficient. One should be wary about the unity of the two parts, and duly perceive the importance of believing in the prophethood of Muhammad (ﷺ).

One of the verses in this regard says:

".. **He that obeys Allah and His Apostle, has already attained the highest achievement.**" (Ahzab, 33:71).

The essence of the universe, which came into being as the product of the love that Allah showed towards His creatures and that of humanity is made up of the light of Muhammad (ﷺ).

Therefore, the essence of Muhammad (ﷺ) is the mirror image of the reign of love. The light of love which sustains the creation caused the sky and the earth to come into being. Allah addressed the Prophet Muhammad (ﷺ) with the words "O my beloved!" and thus made him the zenith of creation. So high a zenith that Allah uttered the name Muhammad along with His name and imprinted it on the tablet of decrees in the beginning with the formula of

"There is no god but Allah, and Muhammad is His messenger."

Prophet Adam (a.s.) appealed for the Mercy of Allah for Muhammad's sake as he saw the above formula imprinted on the sky when he was sent down on earth upon falling from paradise. Allah then forgave him and said:

103

"– O Adam! He is the most beloved of creation to Me. When you make supplications, do them for his sake. I have forgiven you now as you prayed for his sake. Had it not been for him, I would not have created you." (Hakim, Mustadrak, II, 672; Bayhaki, Dalail, V, 488-489).

Allah confirms this honor, championship, and distinction that He bestowed on Muhammad (ﷺ) in the Qur'an:

"And raised high the esteem (in which) you (are held)." (Inshirah, 94:4)

Some exegetes interpret this verse as follows:

"O My Messenger! Your name is mentioned along with Mine in the formula of confession of faith."

Confession of faith begins with "There is no Deity." It means removing all other deities from the heart.

This is explained in the Qur'an as protecting the heart from passions and impulses:

"Seest you such a one as takes for his Allah his own passion (or impulse)?.." (Furqan, 25:43).

And after removing all other deities from the heart comes the words of "but Allah." This means filling the palace of the heart that was purified of all other besides Allah with the light of Allah.

And through the following words of the declaration of faith "Muhammad is His messenger" the love of the Prophet (ﷺ) is placed in the heart. And the individual who thus receives the mystery of the formula finds a place among those lovers of Allah and His Prophet, and joins the ranks of the fortunate ones.

That is why the formula of faith, or the articulation of the Oneness of Allah and Muhammad being His messenger and servant, is the opening confirmation from one's heart and tongue, and thereby is the basic condition of Islam to join the community of faith.

Our Lord created the universe, the Qur'an, and the human according to the requirements of His Names and Attributes, and He decorated them in accordance with Divine Order and Power. This universe of existence, which travels from the pre-eternal to the eternal, has a delicate arrangement and impeccable order, and it is a school of perfect unity. Imprinted at the gate of this school of unity, and in the sky and earth is:

لَا اِلَهَ اِلَّا اللّٰهُ مُحَمَّدٌ رَسُولُ اللّٰه

"Behold! Verily, there is no god but Allah."

There is no particle that does not remember Him and that does not reflect His Power.

As there is a connection and familiarity between the Creator and the creation, every particle is granted Divine love as much as its capacity permits. And the greatest share in this regard is imparted to the human being; because he is at the zenith of creation.

The human being is endowed with enormous Divine knowledge and spiritual truth. His/her soul is adorned the spirit of religion. Therefore, belief in Allah began with the commencement of humanity and it will, for the most part, keep going forever. However, there will always be a minority of those who are scatter-brained who disbelieve and follow their carnal passions. It is said in the Qur'an:

".. **His light should be perfected, even though the unbelievers may detest (it)."** (Tauba, 9:32).

If the jewel of remembrance of Allah finds room in the servant's heart, the servant worships only Allah, and the spirit of the following verse shows up:

"For, believers are those who, when Allah is mentioned, feel a tremor in their hearts..." (Anfal, 8:2).

Thus, the true fact takes root. The Prophet (ﷺ) says on the importance of this position:

"Just as a dress gets worn out and old so does faith in the heart become worn out and old. In that condition, renew your faith with the declaration of unity!"

If the remembrance of Allah is not engraved in the heart, the servant cannot help control his inclination towards carnal passions. Allah says about these people:

"Seest you such a one as takes for his god his own passion (or impulse)? Could you be a disposer of affairs for him?" (Furqan, 25:43).

That means the declaration of bearing witness should keep us from the swamp of carnal passions, and lead us to follow the ethics of the Prophet (ﷺ). Otherwise, we can acquire no enlightenment and reward from his side.

It is narrated that someone who did not follow the morals of the Prophet (ﷺ) dreamt he saw the Prophet (ﷺ). The Prophet (ﷺ) was not paying attention to him. In this sad state, he asked:

"– O Messenger of Allah! Are you displeased with me?"

"– No!"

"– Why are you not paying attention to me?"

"– I do not know you!"

"– How can you not know me, O Messenger of Allah? I am from your people. Scholars say that you recognize your people easier than a mother recognizes her son..."

"Certainly! However, I cannot recognize anything in you of my morals. Besides, no call for blessings and peace upon me came from you. Behold, I recognize my people to the degree that they follow my morals."

When this person woke up sadly he repented for what he was, and began to follow the ethics of the Prophet (ﷺ). He engaged in pronouncing the formula calling Allah's benediction on the Prophet (ﷺ). After sometime he dreamed of the Prophet (ﷺ) again. This time the Prophet (ﷺ) told him:

"– I now know you and I will intercede with Allah for you."

The Prophet (ﷺ) is the dearest of the dear, and he is worthy of love in every respect, and he is a supernormal creation. He is the most pleasant and virtuous of all, and he is the most gracious and unique guide of mankind. It is he who transformed a society that had been burying new-born babies alive under the hot desert sand into a tender-hearted society, and taught them the book of Allah and its wisdom. Considering

106

him superior to all others, and loving him incomparably is a sign of complete faith. The Prophet (ﷺ) says in this regard:

"You are not regarded a complete believer unless you love me more than you love your own self, parents, wife and children!.." (Bukhari, Iman, 8).

The above saying is quite fair an awakening and warning. For those who are away from this love the ways to spiritual enlightenment and development are closed. The seed of love comes into leaf only in his soil of love. He is the source of blessing for the soul. His soil of love transforms fossilized souls into pure jewels.

The prophets and the saints who are enlightened with the light of Muhammad (ﷺ) are witnesses for him as the moon is for the sun. That is why, in every heart that says:

أَ شْهَدُ اَنْ لاَ اِلَهَ اِلَّا اللهُ وَ أَ شْهَدُ اَنَّ مُحَمَّدًا عَبْدُهُ وَ رَسُولُهُ

"I bear witness that there is no god but Allah, and Muhammad is His servant and messenger", a Divine light is kindled as a light reflected in a mirror. So much so that, such hearts enjoy ineffable pleasure through the manifestation of this light.

The condition of Bilal Habashi who enjoyed this pleasure is an exemplary one:

Bilal Habashi was a lonely man having no relative or whatever to hold on to. He was simply a slave. Yet, one day he was honored with the light of faith. The sufferings he was exposed to afterwards as he held to his faith were so hard to bear that his resistance became an example for the Muslims in their struggle for their faith.

He saw the face and the light of the Prophet (ﷺ), and tasted his love. His entire existence was almost a part of the Prophet (ﷺ). Yet, his master, who had no blessings from the Divine light put him to torture by having him held down bared to the flaming desert. His master had his naked body whipped. Blood gushed from his black skin. And the unconcerned crowd around called to him:

"O dirty slave! Turn to us and save your soul!"

Yet, he roared like a wounded lion and shouted out the declaration of faith.

Upon this, the crowd kept beating him again and again. Having been unable to vent their anger they lashed his neck and dragged him through the streets of Mecca. Still, Bilal Habashi took shelter in the love of the Prophet (ﷺ). He was not feeling any pain, but his heart was filled with the love of the Messenger. His heart was as large as the world. Whereas in the material world he was in a miserable position; he had nothing at all.

So, the love and fondness of Bilal (may Allah be pleased with him) advanced him from being a simple slave to being the sultan of hearts. He became the *muezzin* (caller to prayer) of the Prophet (ﷺ). Insomuch that the love he felt for the Prophet (ﷺ) was on his lips at his last breath and he said while passing:

"– Rejoice, rejoice!.. I am flying to the Prophet (ﷺ)..."

So, we have to take notice of the meaning of the following saying of the Prophet (ﷺ):

"The individual is with the one he loves most." (Bukhari, Adab, 96).

We have to make effort to benefit from the facts that the following verse reveals:

"So take what the Apostle assigns to you, and deny yourselves that which he withholds from you. And fear Allah; for Allah is strict in punishment." (Hashr, 59:7).

The first part of the declaration of witness, which is the fundamental pillar of Islam, encapsulates being a sincere servant of Allah. The second part means following the guidance of the Prophet (ﷺ) so as to be a sincere servant of Allah.

The following conditions are prerequisites for this declaration finding room in the heart:

1. The heart should be in communion with the Lord.

This can be achieved by remembrance of Allah. It is said in the Qur'an:

اَلاَ بِذِ كْرِ اللهِ تَطْمَئِنُّ الْقُلُوبُ

" ... for without doubt in the remembrance of Allah do hearts find satisfaction." (Rad, 13:28).

The word "heart" does not only consist of flesh, it is also the center of sentiment and conscience. And the word "remembrance" in the above verse does not mean only repetition of the names of Allah in words. It means perception of Allah from within one's heart. Only in this way does the heart find satisfaction and develop spiritually. And the happiness that Allah bestows on humans comes about only in this way.

Those hearts, which have already achieved this target, are always fascinated by the Divine Beauty. They admire the beauty of existence, and they are conscious that this is nothing but the manifestation of Divine Perfection.

2. Increasing the love of the Messenger of Allah in one's heart leads to embracing those in favor of Islam and deservedly detesting those opposed to the religion.

Love or fondness is a prerequisite to being a sincere believer. Through fondness, worship and good manners it becomes an enjoyment and blessing for the believer. One's outlook towards existence changes positively. One, thereby, realizes the mystery of the rising sun in the morning and the setting sun in the evening. One feels how adept is the artist who draws wonderful paintings; but what about the riot of colors in nature changing every moment of the day... Varicolored violets, lilies, roses... How can they get all these colors from this black soil?.. In short, when one sets eyes on himself and the universe with fondness he is bound to get carried away by the wonders in it.

The greatest achievement after faith is to enter upon a spiritual training that will guide one to the love of Allah and the Prophet (ﷺ).

3. One should be in communion with the saintly servants of Allah and imitate their style of worship and conduct.

According to the findings of psychology "active or dynamic characters have the characteristic of spreading." Namely, character and conduct are invasive as contagious illnesses are. The companions, who were once people of ignorance, became the most virtuous people in the world through the inspiration, enlightenment, and spiritual energy they received through being in the circle of the Prophet (ﷺ).

In fact, even the dog of the Seven Sleepers (*Ashab al-Kahf*) named *Kithmir* got a blessed achievement in the name of being in communion with pious people. The Qur'an talks about the story of the Seven Sleepers and their dog as an exemplary event.

4. One should treat creatures gently for the sake of Allah.

Allah mostly inspires His servants with His names "the most Beneficent and the most Compassionate", among His other names. Namely, He inspires compassion in His servants. One who loves the Lord treats His creatures kindly and mercifully. Even killing a poisonous snake should be done in a delicate way so as to not cause it needless agony.

These are manifestations of the declaration of faith that is the key for paradise; namely, they are the teeth of the key of paradise.

It is narrated from Wahb bin Munabbih:

He was once asked:

"Are not the words لَا إِلَهَ إِلَّا اللهُ "There is no god but Allah" the key to paradise?

He answered:

"Yes, but a key has teeth on it. If you have a key with teeth, only then is the door of paradise opened to you. Otherwise, it is not opened." (Bukhari).

THE WEIGHTIEST STATEMENT ON THE BALANCE (ON THE DAY OF JUDGMENT)

The Prophet (ﷺ) said:

Surely, Allah will pick out in public one individual from among my people and ninety-nine files which are big enough to be seen by everyone will be opened and Allah will then say:

"– Can you deny any of these? Have my recording angels done you an injustice?"

The individual will answer:

"– No, My Lord!"

Allah will say again:

"– Yes, You have rewards in our sight. No injustice will be done to you today."

And a paper which bears the statement وَ أَ شْهَدُ اَنَّ مُحَمَّدًا عَبْدُهُ وَ رَسُوُله اَشْهَدُ اَنْ لَ اَلَهَ الاَّ اللهُ "I bear witness that there is no god but Allah, and Muhammad is His servant and messenger" on it will be unfolded, and it will say:

"– Come get ready for the judgment!"

Then the individual will say:

"– O my Lord! What sense does this single paper make in the face of so many files?"

Upon this, he will be told:

"– No injustice will be done to you today."

On one side of the balance will be placed the files while on the other side will be that single piece of paper having the declaration of witness. And the paper will outweigh the files; for nothing can outweigh Allah's name." (Tirmizi).

In this valued sacred hadith it states:

"The most excellent remembrance is, لَ اَلَهَ الَّ للهُ 'There is no god but Allah'; and the most excellent prayer to be said is 'Praise be to Allah'." (Ibn Maja, Adab, 55; Tirmizi, Nasai).

Declaration of faith is the grass roots of faith. The more it is said, the more it makes the faith strong and perfect.

A sacred hadith says:

"– The Prophet Moses (a.s.) said:

"– O my Lord! Teach me something which I can praise and worship you with."

Allah answered:

"– Say, لَ اَلَهَ الَّ للهُ There is no god but Allah!"

The Prophet Moses (a.s) said:

"– O my Lord! I wish you suggest something special for me."

Allah answered:

"– O Moses! If the sevenfold heavens and sevenfold earths are placed on one scale of the balance while the other has the statement لَا اِلَهَ اِلَّا اللهُ "There is no god but Allah" on it, the statement outweighs them all." (Nasai).

King Solomon was passing by a locale having a magnificent army of jinn and humans in his company. There was a valley of ants there. The chief of the ants said when he saw Solomon (a.s) and his army:

"– O ants! Go to your nests; Do not let Solomon (a.s) and his army run over you unconsciously! The reign of Solomon (a.s) is a great one; you will be run over! "Get back to your nests!"

The Prophet Solomon (a.s) who was Divinely bestowed by Allah with the ability to understand the language of animals heard the words of the chief and answered.

"– No, my reign is a transitory one! And my worldly life is limited. **Yet, the happiness gained through saying the declaration of unity once, is boundless!**"

Regarding the recitation of the declaration collectively, Tabarani mentions the following saying of the Prophet (ﷺ) that Imam Ahmad narrates from Shaddad bin Aws:

The Prophet (ﷺ), one day, gathered the companions together and asked them:

"– Are there People of the Book (Christians and Jews) among you?"

"– No, Messenger of Allah!" they said.

Upon this, the Prophet (ﷺ) asked them to close the doors and said:

"– Raise your hands and remember Allah with the words "There is no god but Allah." لَا اِلَهَ اِلَّا اللهُ

Shaddad bin Aws reports what happened then in this gathering of remembrance as follows:

"We remembered Allah with the words 'There is no god but Allah.' Then the Prophet (ﷺ) said the following prayer:

"– O my Lord! You ordained me as your messenger for this statement. You ordered me to pronounce it. You promised me paradise upon my pronouncement. You do not break Your word!"

Then, the Prophet (ﷺ) told the companions:

"– *Pay attention! I am going to make you happy! Be happy; Allah has forgiven you.*" (Ahmad bin Hanbal, Tabarani).

In another honored hadith it again states:

"The Declaration that there is no Allah but Allah is so valuable in the sight of Allah. It has a god place in the sight of Allah. Whoever says it truly and sincerely, Allah puts him in paradise. And whoever says it just vocally, not from his heart, his blood and property are saved; but he will be judged for that in the Hereafter." (Jam al-Fawaid, I, 23).

Again the Prophet (ﷺ) says:

"*Announce good news to people who succeed you! Whoever pronounces* لَا اِلَهَ اِلَّا اللّٰه '*There is no god but Allah' sincerely and whole-heartedly, he will enter paradise.*" (Jam al-Fawaid, I, 18).

One who pronounces the statement, لَا اِلَهَ اِلَّا اللّٰه 'There is no god but Allah' is supposed to move away from any carnal and worldly passions that lead him to heedlessness, and is to progress to such an extent, that the heart is filled only with the light of Allah; and also with Divine wisdom and mystery; and in this state he continues to contemplate the Grandeur of Allah and his weakness. Expounding on this point it has been declared:

"*One who knows himself also knows his Lord.*"

From this secret there is something very important to understand.

Allah's sight is directly exposed to the heart filled with the love of Allah. One of the disciples (derish) asked Bayazid al-Bastami:

"– Suggest to me a type of worship that brings me closer to Allah!"

Bayazid al-Bastami advised him as follows:

"Love the saintly servants of Allah! Try to make a conquest of their hearts; for Allah looks into their hearts 360 times a day. Let Allah find you there during these visits!.."

DECLARATION OF FAITH AT THE LAST BREATH

Being able to say the Declaration of Faith that is, لَا اِلَهَ اِلَّا اللهُ "There is no deity but Allah" (*Kalimah-i-Tauhid*) at one's last breath is a great good fortune of fate. The verbal declaration should have made a conquest of our heart so that we may be able to say it at our last gasp. It etches in our heart only by living in accordance with its requirements. If the servant is ignorant of Allah's commands, there would be a great distance between him and the declaration of faith and if the servant does not overcome his ignorance, the distance becomes wider, and then the mere verbal pronouncement of the declaration of faith will have no effect on him. This is a great disappointment. Therefore, every moment of our lives should be organized in accordance with the requirements of the Declaration of Faith for our eternal happiness. The following event that took place in times of the Prophet (ﷺ) is an exemplary one in this regard:

There was a young and pious man named Alqama among the companions of the Prophet (ﷺ). He never showed unhappiness when given some task. This feature of his was also praised by the Prophet (ﷺ). Yet, when he was about to die, he was not able to pronounce the Declaration of Faith. The Prophet (ﷺ) was then informed about his condition. As the Prophet (ﷺ) liked him he immediately went to see him and asked what had happened. The young man answered:

" – O Messenger of Allah! I feel that I have something like a lock on my heart."

The Prophet (ﷺ) asked the people around whether it was a hindrance for him to pronounce the Declaration of Faith. And when they inquired about it, they came to know that he had mistreated his mother and she was angry with him. The Prophet (ﷺ) summoned the mother as he liked the young man due to his good service and asked her:

"If someone makes a big fire, and intends to throw her son into the fire, would you approve what she was about to do?"

The distressed mother replied:

" – No, O Messenger of Allah! I would not approve!"

The Prophet said:

" – If so, you should forgive his failures towards you; absolve him of your motherhood rights!" (Tanbih al-Gafilin, 123-124).

The suffering mother forgave her son upon witnessing the special compassion and mercy that the Prophet (ﷺ) demonstrated for her son. She gave up her rights on him. The young man then was able to pronounce the Declaration of Faith without feeling guilty, and yielded up his soul.

There are many occasions resembling this one in which we unconsciously do a disservice to our religion and the after-life. The Qur'an and the Traditions of the Prophet (ﷺ) are hidden in the declaration of faith. Let our Lord save us from heedlessness! And let us be able to pronounce the declaration of faith. As the Prophet (ﷺ) has said:

"Whoever is able to pronounce "There is no deity, but Allah" as his last testament in this world he enters paradise." (I. Canan, Kutb al-Sitta Muhtasar, II, 204).

THE GREAT INTERCESSOR

The Declaration of Faith serves as a great intercessor for its servants in the sight of Allah. It effectively serves until the servant is redeemed.

A holy Hadith states :

"There is a pole made up of Divine Light under the heavens. When the servant says "There is no deity, but Allah" this pole begins to shake. Upon this, Allah says to this pole:

"– Keep still!"

The pole answers:

"– The servant who pronounced the Declaration of Faith has not been forgiven yet. How can I keep still?"

Allah says again:

"– I have, in fact, forgiven him."

And the pole then keeps still." (Bazzar).

The Prophet (ﷺ) says again:

"There is no trouble for the people of the Declaration of Faith in their graves and on the Day of Judgment. I almost hear the words "Thanks be to Allah who removed sorrow and disturbance from us" by those people as they arise from their graves shaking off the soil on them." (Fadail al-Amal, 478).

'There is no god but Allah' means constant awareness of it and feeling it deep in the heart. The declaration 'There is no god but Allah' that is pronounced truly and sincerely is superior to all other forms of worship. The messages and invitations of all prophets are encapsulated in this declaration. It is the backbone of all true religion. Allah says:

"Not an apostle did We send before you without this inspiration sent by Us to him: that there is no god but I; therefore worship and serve Me." (Anbiyaa, 21:25).

Allah's mercy upon His servants to forgive them is boundless. As stated in the Qur'an, He may forgive all sins apart from attributing a partner to Him. Again, as stated in the sayings of the Prophet (ﷺ), Allah will punish those who rebelled against Him and those who are insistent on not uttering the Declaration of Faith. The Prophet (ﷺ)says:

"If one says the Declaration of Faith and does not choose the world over religion, Allah's rage is not put into effect for him. When one who chooses the world over religion and still says "There is no deity, but Allah", Allah tells him 'You are not sincere in what you say!" (Fadail al-Amal, 481).

Abu Hurayra narrates:

I, once, asked the Messenger of Allah (ﷺ):

"Who will most benefit from your intercession on the Day of Judgment?"

He answered:

"I was expecting that you would be the first to ask me this as I knew your interest in my tradition. The one who will most benefit from my intercession is the one who says 'There is no deity, but Allah truly and sincerely from his/her heart..." (Bukhari).

Baraa reports:

During the battle of Uhud someone with armor on his face came to the presence of the Prophet (ﷺ) to embrace Islam, but when he witnessed the intensity of the battle he asked the Prophet (ﷺ):

"– O the Messenger of Allah! Shall I join the battle first or pronounce my faith in One Allah?"

The Prophet (ﷺ) told him:

"- Pronounce your faith first, and then join the battle!"

Amr bin Sabit followed what the Prophet (ﷺ) told him, and fought courageously. The Prophet (ﷺ) said when he saw his dead body among the martyrs:

"He worked little, but gained a lot!.." (Ramazanoglu Mahmud Sami, Uhud Gazvesi, 35).

THE VIRTUE OF THE DECLARATION OF FAITH

The Messenger of Allah (ﷺ) says:

"There is a curtain between Allah and every creature. However, there is no curtain for the words 'There is no deity, but Allah' and the blessing offered by a father for his son." (Tirmizi).

It is said:

There are five types of darkness and five types of illumination in return:

a. Love for this world is a darkness; and piety is the light for it.

b. Sin is a darkness; repentance is the light for it.

c. The grave is a darkness; pronouncing "There is no deity, but Allah" frequently is the light for it.

d. The after-life is a darkness; pious deeds are the light for it.

e. The bridge to paradise is a darkness; and an absolute faith is the light for it.

One who manages to get hold of these lights achieves eternal happiness.

The Messenger Of Allah (ﷺ) says:

"Allah will command on the Day of Judgment: 'whoever pronounced 'There is no deity, but Allah, and he has even a scrap of faith in his heart, let him out of the hell! Whoever pronounced 'There is no deity, but Allah', or remembered Me, or feared Me somewhere, let him out of hell!" (Hakim).

The Prophet (ﷺ) says:

"If one of you makes ablution and then says 'I bear witness that there is no deity, but Allah, and Muhammad is His messenger and Servant', the eight gates of paradise are opened for him/her, and s/he enters through any gate s/he wishes." (Muslim, Taharat, 17; Abu Dawud, Ibn Maja).

The Declaration of Faith is the light of the heart. It is again the light of the human face.

The Prophet (ﷺ) says:

"Make your children begin to talk with the words 'There is no deity but Allah'. Inspire them to say 'There is no deity but Allah' at the last gasp; for whoever pronounces 'There is no deity but Allah' as his first and final statement in this world, he is not held responsible for any sin even if he lives a thousand years." (Bayhaki).

However, having the declaration of faith conduct one's life is so important; for the condition at the last gasp will take place according to their degree and performance in this regard. It is narrated that Prophet Abraham (a.s.) once asked the Angel of Death:

"– O Angel of Death! How do you make yourself seen while taking someone's life? I wish to see how you are seen then."

The Angel of Death answered:

"– O Prophet of Allah! Can you bear that?"

When Prophet Abraham(a.s.) replied:

"– Yes, I can."

The Angel of Death said:

"– Avert your face then!"

When Prophet Abraham (a.s.) turned his face back to him again the Angel of Death was in an awesome appearance. He was a terror to behold. Upon this sight, Prophet Abraham (a.s.) lost consciousness. And when he regained consciousness he saw the Angel of Death as he first saw him and said:

"– For an evil person, it is enough to see your face, even if nothing else!" (M. Sami Ramazanoglu, Ibrahim Aleyhisselam).

No wonder for a person who lived as a complete believer the appearance of the Angel of Death would not be awesome.

The servant is examined on many occasions in this world. And if his belief is strong he passes these examination, but if not he fails them.

Thereby, humans face many difficulties, sufferings, misery, and pain in their struggle for faith and virtue. In this way, the pious and impious ones are singled out. Therefore, having faith in Allah is not enough. One needs to advance his station by adorning his faith with pious deeds so as to pass the many examinations of life.

Allah, in the following verse, declares how interrelated belief and these tests are:

"Do men think that they will be left alone on saying, 'We believe' and that they will not be tested. We did test those before them, and Allah will certainly know those who are true from those who are false."(Ankabut, 29:2-3).

With reference to the above declaration of the Qur'an, faith is a favor, and examination is its measure by which the servant is required to pay a price so as to save his/her faith. Namely, Allah demands a price so that His servants could understand the value of faith by testing them in proportion to their capacity. It is said in the Qur'an:

"Allah has purchased of the believers their persons and their goods; for theirs (in return) is the Garden (of Paradise)..." (Tauba, 9:111).

Therefore, one has to sacrifice their souls, goods, etc. heart and soul in the cause of Allah for a perfect faith. In fact, the troubles, sufferings, and pains of the world that believers are exposed to are recorded as prices paid in this world to be compensated for in the after-life.

On the other hand, the disbelievers efforts to persecute those who strive to live in accordance with their religion will certainly lead them to a painful end in hell; for they deserve hell for two reasons. First, they do not have faith, and second, they tyrannize believers.

In short, the price of faith, namely the price of being a perfect believer is to keep the heart clear of the inclination to submit to beings other than Allah. This means making an effort to successfully pass our examinations. Therefore, fleeing from any act or behavior that may damage our chance for cultivating and maintaining perfect faith is a requirement. Not observing this requirement leads to immediate destruction and a circumstance in which no repentance will be of avail.

ACTS DAMAGING THE DECLARATION OF FAITH

1. Surrendering oneself not to Allah, but to other beings.

Allah says:

"Assuredly Allah did help you in many battle-fields and on the day of Hunain: behold! Your great numbers elated you, but they availed you naught: the land for all that it is wide, did constrain you, and you turned back in retreat." (Tauba, 9:25).

That is why the servant should follow the principle "You do we worship, and your aid we seek."

2. Disregarding divine commandments and prohibitions, and conforming to carnal passions. Namely, disobeying Allah and His messenger.

Allah says in this regard:

"Say: 'Shall I seek for a judge other than Allah? When He it is who has sent unto you the Book, explained in detail.' They know full well, to whom We have given the Book, that it has been sent down from your Lord in truth. Never be then of those who doubt."

"The Word of your Lord does find its fulfilment in truth and in justice: none can change His Words: for He is the one Who hears and knows all."

"Were you to follow the common run of those on earth, they will

lead you away from the Way of Allah. They follow nothing but conjecture: they do nothing but lie."

"Your Lord knows best who strayed from His Way: He knows best who they are that receive His guidance." (Anam, 6:114-117).

"O you who believe! If you listen to a faction among the people of the Book, they would (indeed) render you apostates after you have believed!"

"And how would you deny faith while unto you are rehearsed the Signs of Allah, and among you lives the Apostle? Whoever holds firmly to Allah will be shown a Way that is straight." (Al-i-Imran, 3:100-101).

"O you who believe! If you obey the unbelievers, they will drive you back unto your heels, and you will turn back (from faith) to your own loss."

"Nay, Allah is your Protector, and He is the best of helpers."

"Soon shall We cast terror into the hearts of the unbelievers, for that they joined companions with Allah, for which He had sent no authority: their abode will be the fire: and evil is the home of the wrong-doers!"

"Allah did indeed fulfill His promise to you when you with His permission were about to annihilate your enemy, until you flinched and fell to disputing about the order, and disobeyed it after He brought you insight (of the booty) which you covet. Among you are some that hanker after this world and some that desire the Hereafter. Then did He divert you from your foes in order to test you. But He forgave you: for Allah is full of grace to those who believe." (Al-i Imran, 3:149-152)

PRAYER (SALAT / NAMAZ)
*The First Pillar of Islamic Worship,
the Pole of Religion, the Light of Faith,
and the Vehicle of Ascension for Believers*

*Successful indeed are the believers who are humble in their prayers"
(Muminun, 1-2)

The life of man is full of signs that indicate the search for truth in order to reach the Creator of the universe. These signs are the consequence of our natural inclinations to believe and worship. These are innate and set in the nature of mankind. Those then who remain deprived of the (Divine) Reality and truth, and go astray by deifying a powerless being who cannot satisfy their true natural needs, as has been seen both in the past and present, end up following unreasonable and illogical paths. Thus, today, many millons of people deify such creatures as the cow, and many of them, as in the deviated religions, have an anthropomorphic view of the Transcendent Lord, the Cherisher and Sustainer of the Universe.

This points out that man is in need of being a servant and is in need to carry out the requirements for fulfilling that purpose. Thus, Allah says in the Qur'an:

"I have only created the Jinn and humankind, that they may serve Me." (Zariyat, 51:56).

This means that because of this destiny, man is a servant and since he is living in the secret of servanthood, he is in a state of need. Therefore, man is supposed to reach salvation and success to the degree that he is able to channel this natural inclination in to pursuing the honor and dignity of mankind. And he is, thereby, charged to praise and worship his Lord. Ultimately, all superior features and degrees that man is endowed with are based on the condition of accomplishing this task. It is stated in the Qur'an:

"Say: You have no value before My Lord if you do notworship Him" (Furqan 25:77).

Thus, Allah in this verse, and in many verses of the Qur'an, states that man needs to do good deeds as well as having faith. Therefore, the believers who aim to enter the presence of Allah with a sound heart commit themselves to the sublime springs of acts of worship called righteous deeds and with a willing heart, they travel towards the ocean of union with their Lord. And prayer is, without doubt, the biggest and most important worship that leads the servant to the ocean of union with the Lord. Because prayer is the core and the zenith of all practices in terms of content, scope, and degree.

All creation in the universe; the sun, green meadows, and trees glorify Allah. Birds, mountains, and stones all praise Allah in ways that are unknown to us. Plants glorify Allah by standing; animals glorify Him by bowing down, and inanimate objects glorify Him by lying down. And the heavenly creatures follow the same pattern. Some angels glorify Allah by standing, some by bowing down, and some by lying down. However, the prayer that Allah offered man as a vehicle for ascension covers all these acts of worship. Thereby, those who are true in their prayers gain countless rewards and spiritual manifestations since this act of worship covers the totality of worship that beings of this-world and other-worlds can perform.

Süleyman Çelebi puts this special characteristic of prayer into words so elegantly:

Whoever performs this prayer,

Acquires merit in Allah's sight...

As it covers every form of worship,

Union with Allah is included in this kind of worship...

The Prophet (ﷺ) says in this regard:

"Prayer allows the person to attain Allah's approval and also the love of the angels. It is the way of the prophets. It is the light of wisdom. It is the foundation of faith. It makes one's sustenance blessed with increase and fertility. It gives comfort to the body. It is a weapon over the enemies. It keeps Satan away. It is an intercessor between the worshipper and the Angel of Death. It is a candle and a carpet in the tomb. It is an answer to the angels of Munkar-Nakir (the angels that question the dead person right after death). It is a bosom friend until the Day of Judgment. It is a shade over the worshipper on the Day of Judgment. It is a crown on the head. It is a dress on the body. It is pioneering light. It is a curtain stretched between him and others. It is a proof for the believers before Allah. It is a weight on the Scale. It makes the passage on the bridge to Paradise very easy. It is a key to Paradise. Because prayer is praising, honoring, glorifying, reciting and requesting. In short, a prayer on time embodies all virtuous acts." (Tanbih al-Gafilin, 293).

That is why prayer is a meeting point with Allah, and it is a gift to the people of Islam as a small ascension(as compared to the Mir'aj of the Prophet (ﷺ). As stated in the Qur'an:

".. **Bow down in adoration, and bring yourself the closer (to Allah)!**" (Alaq 96:19) one is supposed to enter the presence of Allah through prayer.

In a true prayer all else besides Allah is removed, and all worldly concerns are wiped out. The worshipper and the worshipped come together in a meeting place. One can thus travel to the bottom of the Divine secrets. Prayer was enjoined on the Prophet (ﷺ) after the meeting on the Night of Ascension(Lailatul-Miraj) without the mediation of Archangel Gabriel, and therefore, it is attributed as a personal union with Allah. That is why the Prophet (ﷺ) said:

"Prayer is the light of my eye." (Nasai, Ahmad bin Hanbal).

What is gained through prayer such as perfection, serenity, relief, tranquility and intimacy, can be attained with no other practice, but prayer. The rank of prayer in the world is like the rank of seeing Allah in the Hereafter. Because, in no act of worship may the servant come closer to Allah than in prayer. The finest taste and spiritual manifestation can be acquired through prayer. It may be said that all other acts of worship are steps to prepare the servant for prayer. That is why the Prophet (ﷺ) described prayer as:

"The pillar of religion and the light of the heart, the key of happiness, and the ascension for believers."

. Prayer, with its all Divine character, is an extraordinary act of worship divided between the servant and Allah. It is like surah *Al-Fatiha* (the first chapter of the Qur'an).

The first four verses: (1- **In the name of Allah, the Most Gracious, Most Merciful.**

2- **Praise be to Allah, the Cherisher and Sustainer of the Worlds.**

3- **Most Gracious, Most Merciful.**

4- **Master of the Day of Judgment**) belong to Allah;

And the fifth verse "**You (do) we worship, and Your aid (do) we seek)**" belongs to both Allah and the servant. This brings together the servant's commitment to Allah, and also Allah's function as the deity for the servant. Namely, the servant is supposed to devote his acts of worship to only Allah by being conscious of the fact that Allah is the Unique One to worship. The rest of surah belongs to the servant. It is said in a tradition supplementing the Qur'an (Hadith-i-Qudsi): related by the Prophet (ﷺ) as if spoken by Allah:

"I divided the prayer between Myself and My servant; one half is Mine, and the other is his/hers." (Muslim, Salat, 38-40).

So, prayer is an appeal to the Lord by His servant. It is an invocation. Allah says in the Qur'an:

".. **Establish regular prayer for celebrating My Praise.**" (Taha, 20: 14).

And again the secret of the verse "**Then do you remember Me; I will remember you!..**" (Baqara, 2:152) emerges in prayer rather than in another act of worship.

Thus, during the invocation of prayer, the union with Allah is actualized as stated in a Hadith-i-Qudsi related by the Prophet (ﷺ) as if spoken by Allah:

"I am with the one who invokes Me..." (Bukhari, Tawhid, 15).

However, in order that one could duly utilize this union attaining to the lerel of *(ihsan)* is required. The Prophet (ﷺ) says in this respect:

"Ihsan(Beneficence) means to pray as if you see Allah! Even though you cannot see Him, He sees you!.." (Muslim, Iman, 1).

So, a prayer which is done in this way is regarded as "light of the eye" (joy).

Those who do the prayer in this way please Allah and His Prophet (ﷺ).

Therefore, prayer is like a glorious tree that shows Prophet Moses (a.s) the path. It is a consolation for broken-hearts; it is a joy for the hearts tired of the preoccupations of this world; it is a spiritual sustenance; it is a cure for souls; and it is a language of enlightenment. The Prophet (ﷺ), when the pressure of worldly duties grew strong, used to ask Bilal (the companion first assigned to give the call *(adhan)* for prayer) as follows:

"O Bilal! Comfort us by calling to stand for the prayer."

This is because there is no other act of worship like prayer. The person doing the prayer can engage himself with nothing, but prayer. Prayer breaks his connection with any other engagement. It gives one the opportunity to experience in true prayer, the indescribable pleasure of union with Allah. No other act of worship can provide this pleasure. For example, during the worship of fasting one can be in the market as a buyer, or a seller... The person who does the pilgrimage is also in the same position. Yet, the person who prays can neither be a seller nor a buyer. He can only do the prayer. Namely, he is in presence of Allah both physically and spiritually.

Perfect believers pray five times a day as enjoined in the Qur'an:

".. **Prayers are enjoined on Believers at stated times.**" (Nisa, 4:103).

They also do supererogatory prayers, and they, step by step, find a place among the virtuous servants of Allah, and in the end, by getting endless beneficence and mercy reach the home of peace as required by Allah's decree of "**Come back you to your Lord!**"

Muslims who follow this line are in position of "**Then do you remember Me; I will remember you!..**" (Baqara, 2:152).

They enjoy the declaration of **"Remembrance of Allah is the greatest (thing in life)!"** (Ankabut, 29:45).

This statement includes both meanings of "remembrance of Allah, namely, prayer is the greatest thing" and also "Allah's remembrance of the servant is greater than the servant's remembrance of Allah." So, prayer is the primary act of worship that makes the servant come close to Allah.

PREPARATION FOR PRAYER

In order to perform prayer it is, of course, essential to prepare for it perfectly. In the sayings of the Prophet (ﷺ), ablution (*wudhu*) is said to be the first reqirement for prayer.

Ablution is the first requirement, because prayer contains spiritual, physical, and natural beauty. The statement by Imam Azam (Abu Hanifa) in that he felt that his sins were washed away when he made ablution is such a nice account in that it explains the importance of a perfect preparation for prayer. The spiritual intuition and insight of Imam Azam, in this regard, is a famous one. He once said to a youngster who was making ablution:

"– O my son! Please leave 'this and that' sin..."

And the youngster responded:

"– How do you know that I commit 'this and that' sin?"

Imam Azam replied:

" –I know them through the water coming down from your ablution..."

On the other hand, brushing teeth with *miswaq* (a stick of wood made into fibers at one end, used as a toothbrush), which is a custom (sunnah) of the Prophet (ﷺ), is also important. The Prophet (ﷺ) says in this matter:

"The prayer that is made after brushing the teeth with the *miswaq* is seventy times stronger than the one without it." (Ahmad bin Hanbal, Musnad, VI, 272).

"The toothbrush (miswaq) not only cleans the teeth, but also pleases Allah." (Bukhari, Sawm, 28).

As it is known, the act of prayer is in the first place done by the tongue through such means as pronouncing the profession of Allah's Unity, the affirmation of "Allah is Great", praising Allah, and other recitations. Therefore, the mouth, from where Divine prayers come out, should be kept clean in prayer. This will, obviously, provide serenity to hearts as well.

Though toothbrush and toothpaste clean the teeth as well, extra medical benefits are gained by using *miswaq*. As stated in the sayings of the Prophet (ﷺ), *miswaq* protects by preventing tooth decay and stomach problems in addition to many other benefits.

*

One of the important aspects of preparation for prayer is, in view of the saying of the Prophet (ﷺ) *"a few acts of worship based on knowledge are better than many acts of worship done in ignorance"*, to know its prerequisites, traditions, and necessities.

Then again, we should try our best to be ready for prayer by purifying our hearts from enmity, malice, and other moral weaknesses as we clean our outer organs. We should remain vigilant about the tricks and traps of Satan and satanic people who keep us away from this preparation.

Wise people understand and put into practice, the verse "**And keep your garments free from stain!**" (Muddathir 74:4) meaning:

"Purify yourself inwardly and outwardly for the prayer, which means being in the presence of Allah; have good moral qualities!"

It is said in one of the sayings of the Prophet (ﷺ):

"Thin down the middle of your back and your stomach for the prayer!" (Jamiu's-Sagir).

Here, thinning down the middle of one's back refers to keeping away from forbidden acts, and thinning down one's stomach refers to not overeating.

PREREQUISITES OF PRAYER: PIOUS
REVERENCE (KHUSHU)

The outward prerequisites of prayer are regulated by Islamic jurisprudence *(Fiqh)*. A prayer that does not observe the regulations set by Islamic law is not acceptable. However, a prayer that is not done in pious reverence is not a respected one. Therefore, a prayer should combine the outward regulations and the inner ones that adorn the heart. Adornment of the heart can be accomlished by actualizing the secret of purification. It is said in the Qur'an:

"But those will prosper who purify themselves." (A'la (87:14).

This spiritual cultivation is so important for prayer. Allah does not mention the obligatory (fardh), the necessary, (wajib), and the number of units of prayer, but rather repeatedly states the importance of pious reverence, sincerity, and peace of mind. The importance of these states covers our entire life. So, the spiritual side of prayer is the most important component that the praying person should observe. It is said in the Qur'an:

"The believers must (eventually) win through: those who humble themselves in their prayers..." (Muminun, 23:1-2).

The Prophet (ﷺ) says:

"Whoever makes ablution accordingly, and prays in time, and bows down and prostrates in pious reverence, his prayer arises as a luminous light and calls to the praying person: ' –May Allah save you as you observed my details!' And whoever does not make ablution accordingly, and does not pray in time, and does not bow down and prostrate in pious reverence, his prayer arises as a dark object and calls to the praying person: ' – May Allah waste you as you wasted me!' Thus, the prayer, following Allah's decree, goes to a place and then comes back to slap the face of the praying person." (Tabarani).

*

Bahaaddin al-Naqshiband was once asked:

"– How does a servant achieve pious reverence in prayer?"

He answered:

"- There are four prerequisites for that:

1. Legitimate earning,

2. Remaining vigilant during ablution for prayer,

3. Feeling the presence of Allah as one begins prayer by saying "Allah is Great!"

4. Feeling the presence of Allah all the time; remaining in peace and tranquility, and obeying Allah after prayer."

*

Pious reverence in prayer is so important that the servant is treated by Allah accordingly. The Prophet (☀) says:

"When a person completes his prayer, one tenth of its reward is given to him; or he is given one ninth; or one eighth; or one seventh; or one sixth; or one fifth, or one fourth, or one third, or half..." (Abu Dawud, Salat, 124).

"A person cannot get one sixth, or even one tenth, of the reward for his prayer. He only gets the part he does in pious reverence." (Abu Dawud, Nesai).

Namely, the servant gets reward for only the prayer he does in pious reverence.

Those who do prayers in sincerity mean to perform prayers adequately and thereby to commit themselves to Allah. They engage themselves only with prayer, and perform prayer in order that they may renlize spiritual accomplishments. They fix their eyes on the point to which they prostrate, and sensing that they are under Divine scrutiny, they go into rapture in spiritual pleasure.

This is, of course, the condition of the sincere servants with a sound heart. Namely, pious reverence is the fruit of sincerity. Then, sincerity provides the servant with pious reverence, and it advances him to high degrees before Allah as well as providing Divine protection. The Prophet (☀) says in this regard:

"Good news is for those who are guided into the right way. It is just because of them strong troubles vanish." (Fadail-i Amal).

In order for sincerity and pious reverence to take root in the heart and thereby bring spiritual benefits the following points should be observed:

1. *Peace of Heart:* The soul should be covered up with only the spirit of the prayer, praise of Allah, and the verses. One should break with worldly engagements. A soul that cannot break with the engagements of the world cannot concentrate on the prayer. It can never be aware of his/her presence before Allah. If the servant manages to overcome this forgetfulness, and manages union with Allah, and also benefits from the meanings of the recitations, then s/he acquires peace of mind/heart. Thus, men of Allah used to struggle to compensate for not only the prayers they did not perform properly, but also the ones they were not able to perform in peace of mind. However, this does not mean that everbody must act in the same way, but it demonstrates the importance of a sound heart in prayer.

The cause for peace of mind is spiritual endeavor. It is the desire to rise spiritually. And this endeavor is actualized by comprehending that intimacy with Allah can only be attained through prayer.

2. *Perception:* One should perceive what he recites. This is the second important thing after peace of mind. And perception acts as a bridge in order that peace of mind in prayer be kept at other times as well.

3. *Reverence:* One should be aware of his being in the presence of Allah, and keep pious reverence both physically and spiritually. Namely, reverence means maintaining peace of mind, perception, and regulations in prayer. Maintaining these manners enhances the merit of the prayer and a prayer having these manners intercedes for the praying person on the Day of Judgment.

One should take into consideration the following warning:

"If you want your prayer to be an ascension, do not think that your worship is an excellent one in the face of the Grandeur of the Lord, and the blessings that Allah endowed you with! Do not ever think that your worship is enough to thank Allah! Think about the Prophet (ﷺ) who used to say: 'O my Lord! I was not able to duly thank You; please forgive me!'"

4. *Awe and Fear:* The praying person should feel the awe and dread which come out of reverence. Awe and Fear provide the praying person with an awareness of Allah's Power and Highness, and thereby earnestness and piety come out. Piety arises from the awe of Allah, and protecting the heart from unawareness. These are the most effective way of enhancing the rank of the servant before Allah. It is said in the Qur'an:

".. **The most honored of you in the sight of Allah is that (believer) who has Taqwa (god-fearing)**..." (Hujurat 49:13).

Abu Zarr narrates:

The Prophet (ﷺ), one day, had gone out in the autumn. The leaves of trees were falling down. The Prophet (ﷺ) then said:

"O Abu Zarr! There is no doubt that if a Muslim prays just for the sake of Allah with all his sincerity, his sins fall off him as these leaves fall off the trees." (Ahmad, Targib).

5. *Hopeful Expectation:* One is supposed to expect the Mercy of Allah during prayer, and appeal to Allah after the prayer as well. If one fears only, this condition makes the person sorrowful, and it may one day play havoc with our spiritual balance. Therefore, hopeful expectation eliminates this danger.

6. *Modesty:* This is a complementary virtue to the above mentioned merits. The servant who sees himself in the presence of Allah feels ashamed of his/her indecent behaviors, and therefore avoids them. Thus, he becomes aware of his lapses and oversight in prayer. He does not get obsessed with relying on his worship. The Prophet (ﷺ) says in this regard:

"No one should ever rely on his sins being forgiven just because of his worship (prayer)." (Fadail-i Amal, 251).

Thus, one cannot guarantee that his sins would be forgiven because of prayer, and one should always remain ashamed of his indecent behavior as forgiveness is a Blessing and a Mercy from Allah. It is a requirement of His Compassion. Otherwise, we are unable to pray and thank the Lord adequately. However, prayers that are done in a humble and vigilant manner please Allah through His Beneficence and Blessing.

In short, one who does not combine the rhythm of the body with

135

the awe of the heart cannot attain to the essence of prayer. One needs to strive to capture the essence of prayer both physically and spiritually. Those things that damage the union of body and spirit should be cleared away and the mind should be kept free of all kinds of distraction. The Prophet (ﷺ), for example, says in this matter:

"When prayer and a meal overlap have the meal first!" (Bukhari, Muslim).

Muslim scholars are particular about the union of body and spirit in prayer, and they metaphorically point out that the prayers of the following three groups of people are not accepted:

1. Hunter

2. Porter

3. Merchant

Here, the hunter represents that person who pries about with his eyes during prayer; here, the porter represents the person who does not ease himself to avoid freshening his ablution though he really needs to do so; and the merchant, here, stands for the person who does not clear his mind and heart of worldly dealings. These three metaphorical groups of people cannot steep themselves in prayer, and cannot attain awe and tranquility. They perform prayers just for the sake of doing, and this is not acceptable before Allah as the parts of the body should be ready for prayer as well. Thus, when the Prophet (ﷺ), who saw a person passing his hand through his beard said:

"– If there were awe in this person's heart, all parts of his body would remain quite still." (Tirmizi). This saying of the Prophet (ﷺ) points toward the union of body and spirit in prayer.

The following sayings of the Prophet (ﷺ) call attention to this point:

"When you rise up for prayer, do your prayer, keeping all parts of the body very still! Do not weave as Jews do. Because keeping the body immobile is a requirement for a sound prayer." (Tirmizi).

"Seven things are from Satan in prayer (i.e., Satan likes them): bleeding of the nose, napping, misgivings, yawning, itching, looking around, and playing with something..." (Tirmizi).

These things encroach upon the spirit of prayer.

Conversely, if the praying person seems outwardly in awe, but inwardly away from awe, this is called hypocritical awe. And the heart should be kept away from such a condition.

The epilogue in this matter of awe is the words of the prayer of the Prophet Abraham (a.s), which Allah has provided us with in the Qur'an:

"My Lord! make me keep up prayer and from my offspring (too), O our Lord, and accept my prayer!" (Ibrahim, 14:40).

Hatem-i Asam suggests the following points about performing prayer properly:

"Prepare for prayer in the best way. Then put the Ka'bah in between your eyebrows; and the bridge (*sirat*) to paradise under your feet; and paradise to your right; and the hell to your left! Enter the presence of Allah with awe and hope, thinking that Azrail (angel of death) is about to take your life, and this is your final prayer in this world! Begin to pray consciously saying "Allah is Great"! Start reading the Qur'an slowly and think of the meaning! Make your soul bow down in reverence and prostrate in humbleness. Make your body follow the external requirements for prayer, but let your soul always remain in the state of prostration and do not allow separation from this union for one breath.."

Al-Gazzali discusses having the love of the Messenger of Allah (ﷺ) while in the sitting position (*tahhiyat*) in prayer and gives an important example. In prayer it is necessary for the heart to be at peace as made clear in the following teaching.

He says:

"It is required to imagine the Prophet (ﷺ) in between the eyes of the heart while saying, (O Prophet, may the Peace and Blessings of Allah be upon you!) in the first and final sitting."

This particular greeting by Allah to His Prophet at the time of the Prophet's ascension (mi'raj) to the heavens with the words "O Messenger! May the Peace and Mercy of Allah be upon you both in this world and the Hereafter" is such an exceptional exaltation for him.

Prayer, is like the ascension of the believer, providing those who think deeply on it with benefits from Divine Grace.

Therefore, one should try to benefit from the spirit of sending blessings on the Prophet (ﷺ) in prayer. It means a remembrance for us of the Prophet's ascension to the Heavens. His ascension is the mysterious transfiguration of the love of Allah towards the Prophet (ﷺ). The Declaration of Faith that is cited right after sending blessings on the Prophet signifies how honorable a gain is the belief in One Allah and being a servant to Him, and also signifies the requirement of sending greetings on the Prophet (ﷺ) whenever his name is mentioned. So, the prayer with all these contents is like a window shutter opened to us from the true essence of Islam. Lovers of Allah come close to Allah through this window shutter, and they watch the High transfigurations and realities as they observe the Divine mystery. Therefore, one cannot reach perfect faith without realizing the mystery in sending blessings on the Prophet (ﷺ) alongside citing the name of Allah by chanting the formula of the Declaration of Faith.

Thus, Allah enjoins believers to send blessings on the Prophet (ﷺ) as a reflection of fondness for the Prophet (ﷺ) in a verse in which it is said that Allah and the angels send blessings to him as well:

"Allah and His angels send blessings on the Prophet: O you that believe! Send blessings on him, and salute him with all respect." (Ahzab 33:56).

Thus, those who worship and pray get carried away and do not care about worldly concerns. They take no account of worldly pleasures.

Jalal al-Din Rumi says about those people who can manage to pray in this framework:

"Those people go out of this world as soon as they enter prayer as a sacrificial animal does when slaughtered."

Then Rumi calls to the praying person:

"You pray standing as a candle in the niche of a mosque indicating the direction of Mecca. Be wise and know the meaning of the first recitation while beginning prayer as (Allah is the Greatest-اَللهُ اَكْبَر) It means: (O our Lord! We sacrifice ourselves in your presence! And by putting our hands to our ears we put everything behind us, and we direct ourselves to You!)

The recitation of اَللهُ اَكْبَر 'Allah is the Greatest' while beginning prayer is like the recitation of 'Allah is the Greatest' while slaughtering a sacrifice. By saying (اَللهُ اَكْبَر) 'Allah is the Greatest' while beginning prayer you are supposed to slaughter your sensuality."

"At that moment your body is like Ishmael and your soul is like Abraham (a.s). When your soul says 'Allah is the Greatest' your body gets rid of all sensuality and passions. And when you say الرَ همن الرحيم بِسم الله 'In the name of Allah, the Most Beneficient, and the Most Merciful', they get sacrificed."

"Those who pray stand in line as they would do on the Day of Judgment; they begin to account for their actions and appeal to Allah."

"Standing in prayer while weeping corresponds to standing before Allah on the Day of Judgment after arising from the grave. Allah will question you and ask: 'What have you done in your worldly life? What have you earned and what have you brought to Me?'"

"Such questions come to mind in Allah's presence in prayer."

"While standing in prayer the servant feels ashamed, and then bows down as he cannot manage to stand because of the shame he feels. While bowing down he glorifies Allah by saying 'Glory to my Lord, the Great'."

"Then Allah orders the servant: 'raise your head and answer the questions!'"

"The servant raises his head ashamedly, but he cannot bear that condition and this time he prostrates."

"Then he raises his head again, but he cannot bear that condition and he prostrates again."

"Then Allah says: 'Raise your head and answer. I will question you about what you have done in your earthly life.'"

"Allah's Word to him is so forceful that he cannot bear to stand.

139

And therefore he sits with his knees bent. Allah says: 'I provided you with favor and benefaction, how did you make use of them? Did you return thanks for them? I provided you with material and spiritual wealth; what did you earn with them?

"Then the servant turns his face right; and greets the soul of the Prophet (ﷺ) and the angels. And tells them: 'O masters of the spiritual world! Please intercede with Allah for this poor servant.'"

"The Prophet (ﷺ) answers to the greeting person: 'The time for help and comfort is over. It should all have been done in worldly life. You have not performed good deeds there, you have not worshipped, you have wasted your time!'"

"Then the servant turns his face left. He asks for help from his relatives. They answer: 'Do not ask help from us. Who are we? You are supposed to answer your Lord on your own!'"

"The servant who cannot find help from any side gets disappointed. Having abandoned all hope to find help he resorts to Allah, to seek refuge in Him and opening his hands in prayer he says: 'O my Lord! I have abandoned any hope from anybody. You are the First, the Last, and the Unique for the servants to appeal to, and the last to turn to. I seek refuge in Your Eternal Mercy and Compassion.'"

Rumi continues;

"See these pleasant signs of prayer and be aware of what you would be facing. Gather yourselves together and try to benefit from your prayer both physically and spiritually! Do not put your head like a bird collecting grain on the ground!.. Take heed of the saying of the Prophet: **'The most wicked thief is the one who steals from prayer.'**" (Hakim, Mustadrak, I, 353).

"If one prays in pious reverence and beseeches Allah in awareness of His Love, Allah pays him a compliment saying that 'I am at your service.'"

The Prophet (ﷺ) says about the degrees of prayer in terms of pious reverence:

"Two people pray separately at the same place and at the same time. However, there is as huge a difference between them as between the sky and the earth." (Ihya).

Therefore, the Qur'an points out that true believers are those who justly do their prayer in pious reverence: "**And those who guard (the sacredness) of their worship.**" (Maarij, 70:34).

It is again said in the same chapter of the Qur'an:

"**Those who remaining steadfast to their prayer.**" (Maarij, 70:23).

Those who spiritually experienced think that:

"The intent of this verse is to express the spirit of prayer as solely outward manifestation of prayer cannot remain permanently. But it is the spirit that bows down and prostrates. Permanent prayer means remembering Allah all the time."

Mawlana Jalal al-Din Rumi, also, interprets this verse metaphorically:

"The servant keeps his state at prayer and also afterwards. In this way he spends all his life in pious reverence and decency; and also watches his mouth and soul. This is the way of the lovers of Allah."

Rumi goes on:

"The prayer that keeps us away from evil acts is done five times a day. Whereas the lovers of Allah always remain in prayer for the love in their soul and the Divine fondness that kindles their lungs does not calm down with praying five-times a day."

"The prayer of the lover of Allah is like the condition of a fish in water. As a fish cannot live without water, the soul of a lover of Allah cannot find peace without constant prayer. Therefore, the expression that "visit me not much!" is not for the lovers of Allah. The soul of the true lovers always remains thirsty."

"If a lover stands apart from his desire even for a moment, it feels like thousands of years to him. And if he spends thousands of years with his dearest one it feels like just a moment to him. That is why a lover of Allah always remains in prayer and it is by this that he meets Allah. If he misses even a unit of prayer, it feels to him like missing thousands of units of prayer."

"O wise and smart ones! It is beyond the reach of the intellect to under-stand the union with Allah in prayer. It can only be understood by sacrificing the intellect for the Dearest and reviving the heart."

And reviving the heart depends on to which direction the servant goes. Rumi says about this direction as follows:

"The direction for kings is the crown and the belt; and the direction for the worldly-minded is gold and silver; and the direction for those who love material beings is idols; and the direction for lovers of spirit is the heart and the soul; and the direction for ascetics is the niche of a mosque; and the direction for the careless is unnecessary works; and the direction for the lazy is to sleep and eat; and the direction for humans is knowledge and wisdom.

The direction for the lover is eternal union; and the direction for the wise person is the Face of Allah; and the direction for the worldly-mind-ed is possessions and rank; and the direction for dervishes is the provi-sions of religious orders; and the direction for passion is worldly desires; and the direction for the people of confinement is putting trust in Allah.

We must be aware that the direction we face for prayer is not the building of the Ka'bah, but it is the place where the Ka'bah is located. If the Ka'bah is moved to another place it cannot be the direction for prayer there."

So one is supposed to direct his heart to Allah while directing his body towards the Ka'bah. Because the direction for the heart is Allah.

On the other hand, in order to accomplish pious reverence in prayer one is supposed to have a perfect intention to perform his prayer in accordance with the following saying of the Prophet (ﷺ), "acts are judged by intentions." This means being conscious of whose presence we are in as we pray. This requires examining the desires of the heart and also divorcing all aims except the approval of Allah.

One is supposed to feel the Grandeur of Allah as soon as he begins prayer with the words "Allah is Great!" When the person raises his hands to his ears to begin prayer he is supposed to put everything behind him. The praying person should feel the delight of being in

Allah's presence in his heart. He should feel as if he has left this transitory world for the Hereafter when he begins prayer.

The praying person is supposed while standing to set his eyes on where he puts his head for prostration. He should always feel that he is in Allah's presence, and that s/he is an impotent being and therefore s/he always needs Allah. He should try to be among those servants whom Allah praises with the words "What a nice servant!"

While reciting from the Qur'an he is supposed to read properly, and also to try to understand and to contemplate the meaning of the verses as well as putting them into practice in life. The Prophet (ﷺ) says that "Recitation of the Qur'an means speaking to Allah." (Abu Nuaim, Hilya, 7, 99). Therefore, one's soul should be vigilant while reading the Qur'an.

One is supposed to say the words "Glory to my Lord, the Greatest" by contemplating its meaning and feeling the Grandeur of Allah while bowing down.

And while saying the words "Glory to my Lord, the Highest" in the position of prostration one is supposed to feel, again, the Grandeur of Allah. Being aware of the fact that the servant comes closest to Allah in the position of prostration, we should get our soul to prostrate as well as our body. Only by doing so can we attain that blessing from the secret of the verse **"Bow down in adoration, and bring yourself closer (to Allah)!"** (Alaq 96:19). Thus, the servant should enjoy his union with Allah and try to be among those lovers of Allah who long for receiving the love of Allah.

While sitting upright after every two units of prayer the servant should sit in reverence and feel how impotent he is and, therefore, he should call down Allah's mercy.

When it comes to the act of turning one's face to the right and to the left to complete prayer with the words said to the two angels "peace and mercy of Allah be upon you", this should be done feeling the joy of union with Allah through prayer and sharing this feeling by greeting the two angels on one's right and left shoulders.

If a prayer is performed in a way that pleases Allah, the greeting said to the two angels is returned by them. And Allah rewards this kind of prayer in the Hereafter as said in the Qur'an:

"Peace unto you for that you persevered in patience! Now how excellent is the final Home!" (Rad, 13:24).

*

Such requirements of prayer as pious reverence, decency, and union with Allah are not beyond the reach of humans. Spiritual enjoyment in prayer should not be considered as just a decorative element of prayer since the prayers of the Prophet (⸙), who taught us how to pray, present a nature transcending such an evaluation. Also, the prayers of his companions and those of the (chosen) friends of Allah who follow them are spiritual guides for us too.

PRAYERS BY THE PROPHET (⸙)

It is narrated that while the Prophet (⸙) was praying the people around him used to hear a voice of weeping that came out of his chest. Ali, (may Allah be pleased with him), remembers his observation in this regard:

"I saw the Prophet weeping in prayer under a tree at the Battle of Badr. Insomuch that he spent all night in that position..." (Fadail al-Amal, 299).

The Prophet (⸙) was even observed in a state in which his heart spread voices as if a stewpot boiled inside.

Aisha, (May Allah be please with her), the wife of the Prophet (⸙), says:

"We used to hear during the prayer - from time to time some voice coming out of the Prophet's chest as if a stewpot boiled inside." (Abu Dawud, Salat, 157; Nasai, Sahv, 18).

Aisha also says:

"The Prophet always used to have conversations with us. Yet, when the time for prayer came due he used to change as if he never knew us, and he used to direct himself to Allah..." (Fadail al-Amal, 303).

So, availing oneself of this blessing of prayer should be the primary aim of our souls. Though this cannot always be achieved we should endeavor in this way. In short, the mood of the Prophet (ﷺ) in prayer should be our ideal. The closer we come to this ideal, the more benefit we will receive.

It must be stated here that no acts of man are to be performed in complete perfection before many trials. So is it for prayer. Prayer is done in the form of imitation at first. The servant needs time to reach perfection in prayer as an artist needs time and experience to produce a perfect work. Therefore, those who cannot perform their prayer in a perfect way should not lose hope and keep going to reach perfection. As one needs to sift tons of earth to gain a gram of gold, one needs to try to reach perfection and peace in prayer with perseverance.

And it is a requirement to have a feeling in prayer described in the following saying of the Prophet (ﷺ):

"When you pray you do it as if it was your last prayer! Do not say a thing that you will be sorry for; do not be inclined to things that careless people desire!" (Ibn Maja, Zuhd, 15).

The companions of the Prophet (ﷺ) and those saints of Allah who followed them have always strained after this objective indicated by this saying of the Prophet (ﷺ).

PRAYERS BY THE PIONEERS OF ISLAM

Omar, (May Allah be pleased with him), the second caliph, was mortally wounded by a disgruntled fire-worshipper. He was losing blood and in critical condition and soon lost consciousness. Yet, when it was time for prayer somebody stated close to his ear:

"O Omar! It is time for prayer!" Astonishingly, he then became aroused to perform his prayer. And afterwards he said:

"One who does not perform prayer has no place in Islam!" After these words he lost consciousness and later expired.

Ali, the fourth caliph, was growing pale and shedding all worldly senses while praying. When he was struck with an arrow in a battle he began prayer for somebody to remove the arrow from his body. He felt no pain while the arrow was being removed. He was once asked:

"– O Leader of Believers! Why is your face growing pale and your body shaking when it is time for prayer?"

He replied:

"It is time to perform a worship that the earth and the sky could not bear. And I do not know whether I will be able to do it perfectly, or not."

All companions of the Prophet (ﷺ) used to have a feeling of awe and fear while praying.

Hasan (r.a), the grandson of the Prophet (ﷺ), used to turn pale while making ablution. Somebody who noticed that asked him:

"– O Hasan! Why do you turn pale while making ablution?"

He replied:

"– It is time to enter the presence of Allah, the All-Powerful, the Glorious, and the Great."

Hasan used to read a prayer while entering the mosque as follows:

"O my Lord! Here is your servant at your door. O the most Merciful Lord! Your sinful servant is before You. You ordered Your righteous servants to forgive the evil acts of sinful people because You are the Most-Generous and the Most-Forgiving. Please forgive my sins and show mercy to me by Your Generosity and Compassion!"

Zayn al-Abidin used to turn pale whenever he rose to make ablution and his legs used to shake when he was about to pray. And he used to answer those who asked him "what happens to you" as follows:

"– Do not you ever know whose presence I am about to enter?"

Once, his house caught fire while he was in prayer, but he did not notice it. On completion of his prayer he was told about it, and he was asked:

"– What made you have no notice for what had happened?"

He answered:

"– The fire in the Hereafter prevented me from feeling this worldly fire."

Muslim bin Yasar used to have the same kind of feeling during prayer. Once, while he was praying in a mosque in Basra, the mosque collapsed, but he did not notice what had happened and went on praying. On completion of his prayer he was asked:

"– The mosque collapsed, but you were indifferent to it? What makes you behave so?

"– Did it really collapse?", he asked them in astonishment.

Sufyan al-Sawri was once in a great spiritual ecstasy. He secluded himself for seven days. He ate and drank nothing. His spiritual master was told about what he was doing and asked:

"– Is he conscious of the times of prayer?"

And he was told:

"– Of course, he is conscious, and he properly performs prayer."

Upon hearing this, he said:

"– Thanks be to Allah who did not let Satan attack him."

A lover of Allah narrates:

"I prayed a late-noon prayer which Dhunnun–i-Misri led. When he, a saint like servant of Allah, said, "Allah is Great!", the word "Allah" was so powerful that I thought his soul left his body. And when he said "Great" my heart was torn into pieces."

Amir bin Abdullah used to cut all his connection with the outside world and he used to say:

"I would prefer an arrow to pierce my body rather than being aware of the talks and acts of people around me while I am praying."

Those who cannot pray as the companions of the Prophet (ﷺ) did are so alienated from the joy of prayer that they even have doubts about the transcendent nature of it. They lack the intelligence to understand that while people enjoy doing worldly and evil acts, why should they not too get spiritual pleasures from prayer. Yet, it is so difficult for those people who cannot appreciate this kind of pleasure to understand the nature of this joy. Those unwary people believe that humans can lose sight of everything in the face of engagements and conversations with their lovers, but they cannot perceive that one can take pleasure from prayer which enables the servant to have a conversation with Allah, the Most Beloved. What a blindness and deprivation this is.

147

In fact, true prayer leads the servant to perfection and knowledge of Allah. Therefore, performing prayer is regarded as an easy act by those who are strong in faith and whose hearts are adorned with the love of Allah; prayer provides them with an exceptional joy. That is why they always feel as if they are in prayer even though physically they are not. Waisal Qarani always wanted to remain in prayer. He was once visited by a friend while he was praying. His friend waited for him to finish the prayer, but upon seeing that he would not do so he said to himself:

"– O my soul! You came here to visit Waisal and benefit from his spirituality. Here is his highest condition. This is the best advice to you! Action speaks more than words! If you can manage to take a lesson from what you have seen, this is more than enough for you until the end of your life!"

It was a silent, unspoken and generous lesson for this person. And then, considering himself to have been endowed with Divine Blessings he left that place.

When it comes to those who are deprived of this position, Allah says about them in the Qur'an:

".. **And prayer: it is indeed hard, except to those who bring a lowly spirit**." (Baqara, 2:45).

It must be stated here that:

Though it may be impossible to reach the level that the beloved of Allah do, we must try earnestly as much as our hearts and souls can manage. Satan sometimes deludes us not to pray because we cannot do it in pious reverence. This is a trap. This may lead one to go astray. It is better to pray, though it may not be done in complete pious reverence, than not praying. The difference between the two is great. Those who do not pray always incur losses. Yet, those who pray, though not perfectly, may one day be endowed with Divine Bounty that guides them to perform prayers acceptable before Allah. If we can do even just one prayer of this kind we may have the face to enter the presence of Allah.

THE FIVE COMPULSORY DAILY PRAYERS

Basic duties have been declared to the Prophet (ﷺ) through the

Archangel Gabriel. However, the five compulsory daily prayers were directly presented to the Prophet (ﷺ) on the night of *Mir'aj*, the miraculous journey of the Prophet (ﷺ) to the heavens. At first, it was fifty daily prayers, but when Prophet Moses (a.s) told Prophet Muhammad (ﷺ) that:

"– O Messenger of Allah! I unsuccessfully tried this on the Sons of Israel before you. Your people cannot bear that responsibility either!"

The Prophet (ﷺ), that night, appealed to Allah five times to reduce it to five daily prayers.

Prophet Moses (a.s), again, told Prophet Muhammad (ﷺ):

"– They cannot bear the five daily ones either!"

The Prophet answered:

"– *I have no face to appeal to Allah any more!*"

And it was, then, determined to be five times a day.

However, Allah showed Mercy due to the appeal of the Prophet (ﷺ), and also announced good news to the Prophet (ﷺ) as well as reducing it to five daily ones:

"O the Prophet (ﷺ)! Allah abides by His word. You will get reward of fifty for the five." (Ibn Maja, Ikametu's-Salah, 194).

The Prophet tells his people about the five daily prayers:

"Allah said: 'I enjoined the five daily prayers on your people. There is a pledge by Me. I will surely place those who perform the five daily prayers in time into the paradise. And there is no pledge by Me to those who do not keep these prayers.'" (Ibn Maja, Ikametu's-Salah, 194).

It is stated in another saying of the Prophet (ﷺ):

"Allah enjoined the five daily prayers on His servants. Allah assures those who faithfully do these prayers of paradise on the Day of Judgment. Yet, Allah does not assure those who do these prayers lightly, without care and have defects in the manner of its performance; Allah deals with them as He wishes, either punishes them, or forgives them." (Ibn Maja, Ikametu's-Salah, 194).

The Prophet (ﷺ) asked the following question to the companions to explain to them the importance of the five daily prayers:

"– If one of you has a river next to his door, and he washed himself five times a day in this river, do you think that person can have a scrap of dirt on his body?"

The Companions answered:

"– No dirt will remain on that person."

The Prophet went on:

"Five daily prayers function in the same way. Allah deletes sins through five daily prayers." (Bukhari, Mawaqit, 6).

The Prophet (ﷺ) announced the following good news in several sayings as well:

"If deadly sins are avoided, the five daily prayers and the Friday congregational prayers are considered to be redemptions for minor sins committed between them. And this is valid for all times." (Muslim, Taharat, 14).

"If a Muslim makes ablution when the time for prayer is due, and does the prayer in pious reverence, this prayer redeems his previous sins. And this is valid for all times." (Muslim, Taharat, 7).

It must be stated here that the five daily prayers are all-important. There is a wisdom behind their being at different times of the day. The way they are divided is good for humans both bodily and spiritually. Therefore, one should be serious about performing each one of them with sincerity. Allah says in the Qur'an:

"So (give) glory to Allah, when you reach eventide and when you rise in the morning; To him be praise, in the heavens and on earth; and in the late-afternoon and when the day begins to decline." (Rum 30:17-18).

Abdullah ibn Abbas regards these verses as covering the five daily prayers and says:

"The words 'when you rise in the morning' refers to the morning prayer;

The words 'in the late afternoon' refers to the noon-prayer;

The words 'the day begins to decline' refers to the late-noon prayer;

The words 'when you reach eventide' refers to the evening and late-night prayer."

There are other verses in the Qur'an referring to the obligatory prayers.

Saphiri attaches great importance to the five daily prayers and describes the condition of those who do not offer them as follows:

"The angels call to those who give up the morning prayer as 'O the great sinner!';

'Those who give up the noon-prayer as 'O deprived one!'

'Those who give up the late-noon prayer as 'O rebel'

'Those who give up the evening prayer as 'O ungrateful one!'

'Those who give up the late-evening prayer as 'O loser!'.."

On the other hand, the ways and regulations of prayer, and also the additional prayers (*sunnah*) that the Prophet (صلى الله عليه وسلم) always performed or the ones he usually did, should be attentively observed. These are essential parts of the five daily prayers besides the optional ones throughout the day.There are many narratives attributed to the Prophet (صلى الله عليه وسلم) in this regard:

"The two units of sunnah of morning prayer is more beneficial than the world and also all the creation in the world." (Muslim, Salat al-Musafirin, 96).

"The Prophet used to pray four units before the obligatory units of the noon-prayer, and he also used to pray two units after that." (Tirmizi, Cuma, 66).

"May Allah show mercy to those who pray four units before the obligatory units of the late-afternoon prayer." (Tirmizi, Salat, 201).

"Hurry up to pray the two units of sunnah prayer after the three obligatory units of evening prayer as it is uplifted together with the obligatory units." (Rezin).

The following narrative is said to refer to the four extra units before the late-night prayer:

"There is a prayer between the call to prayer(adhan) and the call for the beginning of the obligatory units(iqamat)." (Bukhari, Azan, 16).

And the two extra units after the obligatory units of the late evening prayer is known to have been done by the Prophet routinely.

One of the most important aspects of prayer is to do it in time. Whenever the Prophet (صلى الله عليه وسلم) was asked:

"What is the most virtuous worship?"

He answered:

"The prayer that is performed in time." (Bukhari, Mawakitu's-Salah, 5).

So it is preferable to offer prayers as soon as their time is due. The Prophet (صلى الله عليه وسلم) says in this regard:

"Allah is pleased with those who offer prayers in their due time, but He forgives those who do them towards the end of the time." (Cam'u'l-Fawaid, I, 163).

*

Apart from the five daily prayers there is also the obligatory Friday (*Jumu'ah*) prayer. It is offered in congregation with a sermon on Fridays in place of the noon prayer. All adult male Muslims must take part except for travellers. It is not a must for women, but they can join. It is said in the Qur'an about the importance of Friday prayer:

"**O you who believe! When the call is proclaimed to prayer on Friday (the Day of Assembly), hasten earnestly to the Remembrance of Allah, and leave off business (and traffic): that is best for you if you but knew!**" (Jumu'ah, 62:9).

OPTIONAL PRAYERS

In a Hadith-i-Qudsi -a tradition that was communicated by Allah by inspiration to the Prophet (صلى الله عليه وسلم) and related by him as if Allah was speaking:

"Whoever bears enmity to My saintly servant I will proclaim war on him. The thing that I like most among the acts that bring My servant closer to me is his performance of the acts that I enjoined on him. At the same time, My servant keeps coming closer to Me through optional worship. In the end he attains My Love. And when I love him I become the ears that he hears with; I become the eyes he sees with, I become the hands that he holds with, I become the feet that he walks with (I become the heart that he reasons with, and I become the tongue that he speaks with). When he asks for anything from Me, I immediately grant it to him. When he seeks refuge in Me, I safeguard him. I never hesitate about anything as I do in taking the life of a believing servant: He dislikes death, and I do not like anything he dislikes..." (Bukhari, Rikak, 38).

Therefore, pious Muslims, following the tradition of the Prophet (ﷺ) offer optional prayers in times of fear, during the latter part of the night and at other times, and when they need something- in addition to performing the obligatory prayers. They are among those who are praised in the Qur'an:

".. **On their faces are their marks, (being) the traces of their prostration.**" (Fath, 48:29).

They get endless pleasure from prayer and optional prayers are offered to keep up this endless pleasure. The Prophet (ﷺ), though he committed no sin, used to pray at nights until his feet became sore, and he used to read the Qur'an until he was exhausted. So, optional prayers do not hinder obligatory prayers but, on the contrary, fortify them. The point here is to try to perform them in their proper way.

The Prophet (ﷺ) says:

"The first worship that the servant will be questioned about on the Day of Judgment is prayer. If his prayers are done properly, he will be saved. If not, he will be among the losers. If the obligatory prayers are not enough to save him, Allah will ask:

'Are there optional prayers done by My servant so that they could complement the obligatory prayers?'

Other worship will be the same." (Tirmizi, Salat, 188).

So, regarding obligatory prayers as sufficient will be a grave mistake, for it is almost impossible to perform the obligatory ones perfectly and duly. No matter how much weight we give to them we may, any time, make mistakes in our performance. Thus, we have no other chance, but optional prayers to complement our mistakes. Our deficiencies in offering the obligatory ones may be complemented by optional ones as we do not have a second chance to perform the obligatory prayers in case we miss or perform them incorrectly. However, this does not mean that we should leave out the obligatory prayers for optional ones. We should try to observe both at the same time. The practice of the Prophet (ﷺ) in this regard is a unique example before us. On the other hand, those who did not offer obligatory prayers in time should not try to supplement only the unperformed prayers, but try to offer optional prayers as unperformed prayers could be done any time of the day whereas such optional prayers as those done during the night, forenoon, the rising of sun, and late-evening are to be done only at certain times.

*

Rabia bin Ka'b al-Aslamî said:

I used to stay with the Prophet at night and wait upon him to bring water for ablution and so forth. One day he told me:

"– Wish anything you like from me!"

I said:

"– I want to be with you in Paradise."

He said:

"– What else do you wish?"

I said:

"– I only wish what I said."

"– If so, please help me by offering as much prayer as you can!" (Muslim, Salat, 226).

Another saying of the Prophet (ﷺ) in this regard is as follows:

"Nothing is more helpful to the servant to approach Allah than prostrations s/he does in solitude. Namely, it is optional prayers that s/he does on his/her own at home that bring him/her close to Allah most." (Ibn Mubarak).

Shaqeeq al-Balkhisaid:

We looked for five things and we found them in five things:

1. The fruitfulness of sustenance in forenoon prayer.

2. The light in the grave in prayer done during the night.

3. The answers to the questions asked by the two angels that question the dead in reading the Qur'an.

4. The success in passing the bridge from this world to Paradise in fasting and giving alms.

5. The shelter on the Day of Judgment in remembering Allah in solitude.

There are various optional prayers. The most important ones are as follows:

Duha Prayer (*Prayer done in the earlier part of the forenoon*)

The Prophet (ﷺ) said:

".. The words 'Praise be to Allah' is a charity; the words 'Glory be to Allah' is a charity; the words 'There is no god but Allah' is a charity; the words 'Allah is Great' is a charity; enjoining the good is a charity; detaining from evil is charity. And a dukha prayer of two units substitutes all of these." (Muslim, Salat al-Musafirin, 81).

Aisha, wife of the Prophet, told:

"Once I saw the Prophet offering the dukha prayer, and I never left it out in my life afterwards." (Bukhari, Muslim).

Awabeen Prayer (late-evening prayer)

The Prophet said:

"Whoever offers a prayer between the evening and late-night prayer, it is called the awabeen prayer." (Ibn Mubarak, el-Raqaik).

Tahiyyat al-Masjeed Prayer (prayer done to greet the Mosque)

The Prophet said:

"Let one of you pray two units of prayer when s/he enters a mosque before sitting down!" (Bukhari, Salat, 60).

Tarawih Prayer (prayer performed after the prescribed night service of worship in the month of Ramadan)

Aisha, wife of the Prophet, (*may Allah be happy with her*) said:

"The Prophet was not so wrapped up in worships in other months as he was in the month of Ramadan. And he was particularly wrapped up in worships done during the last ten days of Ramadan." (Muslim, Itikaf, 832).

The Prophet (ﷺ) says:

"Whoever spends a night of Ramadan offering prayer with a sincere belief and hope that s/he will get reward for it, his/her past sins are forgiven." (Bukhari, Iman, 27).

And the primary prayer that is done in Ramadan is the *tarawih* prayer. It is done in twenty units. And as it takes a long time one is supposed to observe it duly.

Istikhara Prayer (prayer done before lying down to sleep in the hope that Allah will decide for the best between two or more options through a dream)

Jabir bin Abdallah said:

"The Prophet used to teach us the Istikhara prayer as if he was teaching us a chapter from the Qur'an..." (Bukhari, Tahajjud, 28).

Hajat Prayer (prayer done for the fulfillment of wishes)

The Prophet says about the *hajat* prayer through which the servant seeks refuge in Allah for the fulfillment of his/her wishes:

"Whoever wishes anything from Allah, let him/her make ablution properly first, and do two units of prayers afterwards. Then call Allah's benediction to the Prophet, and finally say the following prayer:

'There is no god but Allah, the Clement, and the Gentle. Praise be to Allah, the Master of the heavens. And praise be to Allah, the Lord of the universe.

O my Lord! I wish things that come out of Your Mercy, and I wish Your forgiveness, and I also wish to reach righteousness. O the Lord, the Most Compassionate! Please do not let any sin be unforgiven, any sorrow unrelieved, and any lawful wish declined!.." (Tirmizi, Witr, 17).

Tahajjud prayer (prayer performed by becoming awake after sleep at night) and other prayers offered at night-time

Every time has a specific feature in Allah's sight. However, certain times are more valuable than others, and they are to be taken advantage of. And night-time is one of these times that the Qur'an and the sayings of the Prophet (ﷺ) describe as valuable.

The value that Allah ascribes to night-time and the secrets hidden in it are countless. Allah says: **"The night and its homing!"** (Inshiqaq, 84:17). **"And by the night when it is still!.."** (Dhuha, 93:2). The secret of the swearing of Allah by the night is a Divine window to get our hearts and souls to watch many facts.

The night is the time to prostrate before the Divine Being with love and affection for the sake of pleasing Him instead of lying down in smooth beds. Therefore, extra prayers performed at night are of great importance in achieving immediacy with Allah. Thus, one desires and performs prayers at night as much Divine Love as s/he has. It may be said that praying at night is like meeting and conversing with one's lover at night. Being awake at a time when everybody is asleep means being included in the group of love and mercy.

The Prophet (ﷺ) used to pray at night until he was footsore. He was once asked:

"– O the Messenger of Allah! Why do you strain yourself though Allah declared in the Qur'an (in chapter 48) that you were forgiven of all your sins?"

He replied:

"– Should not I be a thanking servant?" (Bukhari, Tahajjud, 6).

The Prophet (ﷺ) also said:

"The most virtuous prayer except the obligatory prayers is the one offered by becoming awake after sleep at night." (Muslim, Siyam, 202-203).

"Two units of prayer performed at night is more beneficial than anything in the world. If I thought that it would not be a burden on my people I would enjoin it on them." (Fadail al-Amal, 257).

"There is a certain moment at night. If a Muslim catches that moment to wish something from Allah, that thing is granted to him/her." (Tirmizi, Vitr, 16).

"If a man wakes up at night and also wakes his wife up to offer two units of prayer together, Allah registers their names among those who remember Allah most." (Abu Dawud, Tatawwu, 18).

"Do not ever disregard praying at night! Because it was a custom of righteous people before you. Worshipping at night brings one closer to Allah, atones for one's sins, keeps the body from illnesses, and prevents one from performing sinful acts." (Tirmizi).

"Let Allah show mercy to the man who wakes up at night to pray, and also wakes his wife up to do so. Let Allah show mercy to the woman who wakes up at night to pray, and also wakes her husband up to do so!" (Abu Dawud, Vitr, 13).

The Prophet (صلى الله عليه وسلم) told Abu Zarr:

"– Do you get prepared when you are about to set forth on a journey?"

Abu Zarr replied:

"– Of course, o Prophet"

The Prophet (صلى الله عليه وسلم) said:

"– Well, how do you think that the journey on the Day of Judgment will be? Take heed of what I will tell you; shall I tell you what you would benefit from on the Day of Judgment?"

Abu Zarr replied:

"– Yes, o Messenger of Allah!"

The Prophet (صلى الله عليه وسلم) said:

"Fast on a very hot day for the Day of Judgment. Offer a prayer of two units at night to be saved from loneliness in the grave. Make the journey to Ka'ba once in a lifetime, and give alms to a needy person for the great occasions of the Doomsday. Say just words or save your tongue from saying unjust things!" (ibn Abi'd-Dunya, Kitab al-Tahajjud).

The Prophet (صلى الله عليه وسلم) said to Abu Hurayra in this regard:

"O Abu Hurayra! If you want the company of the Mercy of Allah when in the grave and on the Doomsday, wake up at night to offer a prayer for Allah's sake. O Abu Hurayra! If you pray at the corner of your house, your house lightens as a constellation in the sky, and it becomes like a star for the people of the world." (Ihya al-Ulumiddin, I, 1023).

Abdallah bin Omar, for interpretation, let the Prophet (صلى الله عليه وسلم) know one of his dreams through Hafsa, who was the sister of Abdullah and the wife of the Prophet (﷽). The Prophet (﷽) said while interpreting the dream:

"Abdallah is a great person. Yet, it would be superb if he prayed at night!.."

From that day on, Abdallah never abandoned praying at night. (Bukhari, Tahajjud, 2).

The Prophet (﷽) said:

"The Archangel Gabriel said: 'The honor of a believer is, no doubt, related to night-time prayer...'" (Hakim, Mustadrak, IV, 360).

One of the servants whom Allah is pleased with is one who gets out of his/her gentle and warm bed in order to offer the prayer of *tahajjud*. Allah is well-pleased with that servant and says to the angels:

"– What makes this servant of Mine care about praying at this time of the night?"

The angels reply:

"– It is his/her wish to attain Your Grace and Blessing, and also fear of Your punishment."

Allah says:

"I grant him/her what s/he wishes from Me then. And I safeguard him/her from what s/he fears from." (Fadail al-Amal, 299).

Many verses of the Qur'an call the servants to remember Allah at night-time.

"And during part of the night, (also), celebrate His praises, and (so likewise) after the postures of adoration." (Qaf, 50: 40).

"And for the part of the night also praise Him, and at the retreats of the stars." (Tur 52:49).

"Those who spend the night in adoration of *their Lord prostrate and standing*." (Furqan 25:64).

Allah explains the features of those who will be saved from the Divine punishment and be placed in paradise:

"They were in the habit of sleeping but little by night. And in the

hours of early dawn, they (were found) praying for forgiveness." (Zariyat, 51:17-18).

In addition to this honoring, Allah cites those believers who remember Him at night-time as superior when comparing believers with disbelievers:

"What! he who is obedient during hours of the night, prostrating himself and standing, takes care of the hereafter and hopes for the mercy of his Lord! Say: Are those who know and those who do not know alike? Only the men of understanding are mindful." *(Zumar, 39:9).*

As Allah describes those who devoutly worship at night as such, He forewarns those unwary servants who do not behave accordingly:

"And part of the night, prostrate yourself to Him; and glorify Him a long night through."

"As to these they love the fleeting life, and put away behind them a Day (that will be) hard." *(Insan, 76:26-27).*

The second part of the night is said to be more valuable. The Prophet (ﷺ) was once asked about it:

"– In which part of the night are the worships more likely to be accepted?"

He replied:

"The worships that are done in the second half of the night..." (Abu Dawud).

However, as it is not too easy to worship at night, one is supposed to observe some points. In addition to the strong desire to worship at night, one is supposed to have a light dinner and keep early nights. It is narrated that:

"The Prophet (ﷺ) used to discourage people to sleep before the late-night prayer, and he also used to discourage them to have long conversations after it." (Bukhari, Mawaqit al-Salat, 23).

A Muslim should be in the habit of keeping early hours, and waking up early. There may be exceptions to that on condition that they should not hamper one's activity to worship at night. Omar, the second caliph, says:

"The Prophet (ﷺ), sometimes, used to speak with Abu Bakr about the affairs of Muslims until daybreak. And I used to stay with them." (Tirmizi).

These principles are necessary to remove the strain of waking up for prayer and also to untie the knots of Satan tied through sleep. The Prophet (ﷺ) says:

"When you sleep Satan ties three knots on the back of your neck. And he says to each knot 'let a long night stay with you.' When you wake up and cite the name of Allah one of the knots unties. When you make ablution another knot unties. And when you offer a prayer all of the knots untie. Thus, you wake up hale and hearty in the morning. Otherwise, you wake up asleep and downhearted." (Bukhari, Tahajjud, 12).

So, it is clear that the prayer offered at night is so valuable that it comes second only after the obligatory prayers. **However, those who do prayers at night are to be reminded that they should not be proud just because they do worship at night. If so, they lose the blessing they would get.** They should always bear the following saying of the Prophet (ﷺ) in mind:

"There are many who worship at night, yet they get nothing out of it. They just stay awake." (Ahmad bin Hanbal, Musnad, II, 373).

PRAYER IN CONGREGATION

One of the most important points about prayer is to offer the obligatory ones in congregation.

Praying the obligatory ones in congregation is a strong tradition of the Prophet (ﷺ), never omitting praying them in congregation except during the last days of his life when he was seriously ill.

The following event that points out the importance of praying in congregation is a striking one:

One of the companions of the Prophet (ﷺ) called Abdallah ibn Mektum, a blind man, once asked the Prophet (ﷺ) to be excused from attending the congregation for the obligatory prayers:

"O Messenger of Allah! You know my position; there are many

palm trees on my way to the mosque! And I cannot find a guide every time!"

The Prophet (🕮) answered:

"– Can you hear the call for prayer?"

"– Yes, I can!"

"– Then, you are supposed to attend the congregation, even by crawling..." (I. Canan, Kutub al-Sitte, VIII, 256).

The Prophet (🕮) says:

"Those who attend the mosque at dark will find a shade on the Day of Judgment when no shade is to be found." (Ibn Maja).

Other sayings of the Prophet (🕮) are to be found in this regard:

"The prayer offered in congregation is twenty seven times superior to the one offered on one's own." (Bukhari, Adhan, 30).

."... The prayer done by two persons is superior to the prayer done by one person; the prayer done by three persons is superior to the prayer done by two persons. The more their number the more lovely their prayer is to Allah." (Abu Dawud, Nasai, Imamat, 45).

"Those who offer late-night prayer in congregation are regarded to have spent the first half of the night; and those who offer morning prayer in congregation are regarded to have spent the second half of the night praying." (Muslim, Masjid, 260).

"Those who attend congregation for five daily prayers regularly will pass the bridge from this world to Paradise like a thunder. Moreover, Allah will resurrect and assemble them for judgement among the second generation of Muslims after the Prophet (🕮). Those who attend congregation night and day will get as much reward as a thousand martyrs." (Camu'l-Fawaid, 246).

"Stand in proper lines while praying in congregation, because it is a sign of perfect prayer." (Abu Dawud, Salat, 93).

Praying in congregation advances the power of one's faith. It is a mirror of the Muslim community. The community of faith is kept through attending congregational prayer.

The Prophet (ﷺ) says:

"The person who goes to mosque for prayer after making ablution at home is like the person who goes to the Ka'bah for pilgrimage after putting on ihram, a special cloth for pilgrimage." (Fadail al-Amal, 275).

This person is given a reward for every step he takes on the way to the mosque, and one of his/her sins is forgiven.

"S/he who prays in congregation from start to finish for forty days is given two titles of privilege. The first is salvation from hell. The second is distancing himself/herself from hypocrisy." (Muslim, Tirmizi).

Allah will ask on the Day of Judgment:

"Where are my neighbors?"

The angels will answer:

"O the Lord! Who are your neighbors?"

Allah will say:

"Those who regularly attend mosques."

The Prophet (ﷺ) says:

"The mosque is the home of every sincere believer. And Allah assured these servants of all kinds of easiness, mercy, and convenience on the bridge from this world to Paradise." (Tabarani).

Attending congregation is so important that the Prophet (ﷺ) seriously warned about the negative consequences of being careless about it. One of the sayings of the Prophet (ﷺ) in this regard is as follows:

"The prayers of those who do not attend congregation though they hear the call for prayer (and offer their prayer where they are) with no reasonable excuse are not accepted."

The companions asked him:

"O Messenger! What is to be regarded as an excuse?"

The Prophet (ﷺ) said:

"It is illness or fear of danger." (Abu Dawud, ibn Maja).

If a group of people cannot join congregation at mosque, they are supposed to offer their prayer together where they are. The Prophet (ﷺ) said in this regard:

"If a group of people of three in a village or countryside do not perform their prayer together, Satan will impose himself on them. Try to offer your prayer with other people, and do your best to join congregation; because the wolf eats a lonely sheep." (Abu Dawud, Ahmad, Nasai).

Attending congregational prayers for the morning and late-evening prayers is of great importance. The Prophet (ﷺ) says:

"He who offers late-evening prayer in congregation is regarded to have worshipped in the first half of the night; and he who offers morning prayer in congregation is regarded to have worshipped in all parts of the night." (Muslim).

"If people knew the virtue of the call for prayer and standing in the first line of congregation, and if they had no other chance, but drawing lots in order that they could be the one to call for prayer and stand in the first line, they would go for drawing lots. If they knew the virtue of being an early comer for prayer in congregation, they would contest among themselves. And if they knew the reward for morning and late-evening prayer, they would attend them even by crawling." (Bukhari, Muslim).

So, a believer is supposed to lend his heart to prayer, and his ears to the call for prayer. Participation in congregation begins with participation in the call for prayer. The companions of the Prophet (ﷺ) used to stop all their worldly engagements while the call for prayer was being recited in order to get ready for the mood of prayer. The hands that swung hammers and the tongues that spoke used to stop, and the roads were only for the mosque. Their hearts filled with the love of Allah used to follow the guidance described by the Prophet (ﷺ):

"When you hear the call for prayer, repeat the words said by the caller! Then pronounce the formula calling Allah's benediction on me! Whoever pronounce the formula calling Allah's benediction on me, Allah grants him ten benefactions in return. This is so great a rank in paradise that it is given only to one servant. And I myself wish to be that person. And whoever wishes my intercession, it is granted to him." (Muslim, Salat, 11).

He who goes to the mosque without enjoying the deep and spiritual meaning of prayer as described above gets no blessing out of his action. The saying of the Prophet (ﷺ) is to be remembered in this regard:

"The person gets what he intends by coming to the mosque." (Abu Dawud).

On the other hand, attending congregation grants the person a facility to keep his life under control, and acts as an agent to regiment the person's disorganized life.

The saying of the Prophet (ﷺ), "Does not the person who raises his head from the position of prostration before the leader of the prayer fear that Allah might turn his head into that of donkey?" (Bukhari, Muslim), points out that disorganized individuals can be trained through prayer and the individual thus can be prepared to duly stand in the presence of Allah. Otherwise, order and stability cannot be established in prayer.

The final word about prayer in congregation is that every believer should have his heart attached to the mosque; because among seven groups of people who are promised Divine shade by Allah on the Day of Judgment when there is no other shade that will exist is the group of believers "who have hearts clinging to the mosque."

PRAYER AS A UNIQUE REFUGE

Prayer, as the most exceptional form of worship, is also the most exceptional form of seeking refuge in Allah. Therefore, when one faces any kind of hardship, trouble, tribulation, suffering, and pain he is supposed to turn to prayer immediately. This is the tradition which the Prophet (ﷺ) often put into practice.

Hudhayfa said:

"The Prophet used to turn to prayer whenever he faced a difficulty." (Ahmad, Abu Dawud). Abu Darda said:

"The Prophet used to go into the mosque whenever a storm broke out, and would stay there until it was over. He also used to pray during the eclipse of the moon or the sun."

165

We may here elaborate on the eclipse of the moon or the sun. The day when Ibrahim, the son of the Prophet (ﷺ), died was a day when the moon was eclipsed. Due to this coincidence some of the companions said:

"– The moon eclipsed on the same day when the son of the Prophet (ﷺ) died."

Yet the Prophet (ﷺ) disapproved of this and said:

"Neither the moon nor the sun eclipses upon one's death!" (Muslim, Kusuf, 29).

On the other hand, Asma, the daughter of Abu Bakr asked Aisha, wife of the Prophet (ﷺ), during an eclipse of the sun:

"Is this a sign of rage or doomsday?"

Aisha answered:

"Yes."

Amr bin As narrates as follows:

"The sun had already eclipsed. The Prophet (ﷺ) stood up for prayer. He stood so long that we thought he would never bow down. Yet he bowed down, but he again was so long that we thought he would never raise his head again. Then he went down for prostration. Again, we thought he would never raise his head. Yet he raised his head, but he kept his new position so long that we thought he would never go back to the position of prostration. Yet he then went down for prostration. We again thought the same. Yet he raised his head again. And he did the same in the second unit of the prayer. He was crying while prostrating.

Then he appealed to Allah:

'O my Lord! Have not You assured that You would not punish them when I am among them? Have not You assured that You would not punish them as long as they ask forgiveness from You?'

The eclipse of the sun was over and it was shining again when the Prophet (ﷺ) had finished his prayer." (Nasai, Abu Dawud).

As these accounts display, the eclipse of the sun is not just an ordinary act of nature. It is to remind us of the Divine Grandeur and Power. It is also a Divine Warning and a sign of Doomsday; because having a dark sky suddenly at daytime demonstrates how both the moon and the sun bow down to Allah in accordance with the Divine Order, and also reflects the atmosphere of Doomsday. Humans are supposed to take warning by the eclipse of the moon and the sun and thereby be wary all the time; and know that everything in this world is passing, and thereby get prepared for the Hereafter; because the eclipse of the sun may not be lifted again.

These kinds of warnings by Allah can be found in other areas. For example, the fault lines on earth are of this kind of warning. Allah can take the lives of His servants without activating the fault lines. However, He displays them before the eyes of His servants as an example of the inevitable end so that they might be in constant vigilance, and thereby be prepared for the Hereafter. This is, in fact, a warning by Allah. Surely, these are not the only Divine warnings. Floods, hurricanes, incurable illnesses and so on are of this kind. A poet says in this regard:

Death has approached me,
With the excuse of a headache!

However, it must here be emphasized again that if these did not occur, humans would carelessly fall into the claw of death all of a sudden, and perish. Yet, Allah, the Most Merciful, guides His servants through many Divine Manifestations so that they might be prepared for the inevitable realities before the die is cast. Hadrat Nadr narrates:

One day it became dark at daytime. I ran to Anas to ask him:

"Has anything like this occurred at the time of the Prophet? (ﷺ)"

He answered:

"Allah forbid! We used to run into the mosques even if the wind blew a little bit faster."

They used to do so, as prayer is a shield against many calamities and harms in this world, and also a shield against the hellfire. Allah says:

"O you who believe! Seek help with patient perseverance and prayer: for Allah is with those who patiently persevere." (Baqara 2:153).

The dynasty of Pharaoh in Egypt is a very well-known one in history. It was famous for tyranny and arrogance. It was in power in Egypt at the time of the Prophet Abraham (a.s) as well. The king called Pharaoh used to arrest any beautiful woman who came to his country, and murder her husband (in case she was married), and then ask her brother (in case she had one) to release her to him.

When the Prophet Abraham (a.s) with his wife Sarah left the city of Urfa for Egypt after Nimrod perished, upon crossing the border the Pharaoh's men asked Abraham (a.s) about the woman accompanying him. Abraham (a.s) told them that she was his sister in religion, hoping to take them in by falling back upon a legal device for getting around the law. Upon his answer they let Abraham (a.s) free, but they took Sarah away to the palace.

It is narrated in Bukhari:

"When Sarah came to the palace, she immediately made ablution and offered two units of prayer. She sought refuge in Allah. And Allah took care of her."

And the Pharaoh who attempted to approach Sarah was out of breath because Allah was protecting her.

And eventually the Pharaoh was paralyzed and alarmed. He finally let Sarah free. Moreover, he gave her his slave Hajar as a gift. The Pharaoh told the high officials of the palace who were bewilderedly watching him:

"– This woman is a jinn. If she were to stay with me a bit longer, I would have perished. I gave her my slave Hajar as a gift not to be harmed by her!"

So, this was a result of the two units of prayer offered by Sarah.

Therefore, the Prophet (ﷺ) used to direct his household to perform a prayer when faced with any difficulty or calamity, and also read the following verse from the Qur'an:

"Enjoin prayer on your people, and be constant therein. We ask

you not to provide sustenance: we provide it for you. But the (fruit of) the Hereafter is for righteousness." (Taha 20:132).

The Prophet (ﷺ) also let us know that the prophets before him also held fast to prayer when faced with any difficulty:

"The former prophets also used to hold on to prayer when faced with any tribulation or misfortune." (Fadail al-Amal, 249).

The Prophet (ﷺ) also said.

"Allah lends help to my people due to the prayers and the sincerity of the underprivileged." (Nasai, Jihad, 43).

Allama Sharani says:

"A country where people do not offer prayers is afflicted with problems and calamities. And a country where people offer prayers is kept away from them. Let nobody say 'I offer prayers, and it is not my business if others do not offer prayers'; for when a society is exposed to trouble or calamity it includes all members of it.

The Prophet (ﷺ) was once asked about this point as follows:

' – Are we to perish even though we have righteous people among us?'

The Prophet (ﷺ) answered:

' – Yes, when wickedness prevails...' (Muslim, Fitan, 1).

Therefore, every believer who has been given the inherent power is responsible to enjoin the good and prohibit evil."

On the other hand, the only way of being saved from the weight upon our shoulders through careless acts that draw Divine warning or calamity is to hold fast to prayer. Namely, salvation from sins is possible only by repentance and prayer. The Prophet (ﷺ) told a sinful person who came to him and prayed together with him in repentance:

"– Allah has forgiven your sins." (Muslim, Abu Dawud, Bukhari).

REGULAR PRAYER

The orders of Allah in the Qur'an are not said with the word "Pray!" but they are said with the words "Establish prayer!"

169

A prayer that is offered properly restrains the believer from sensual inclinations; it gives the believer ecstasy. It is said in the Qur'an:

".. **And establish regular prayer: for prayer restrains from shameful and unjust deeds; and the remembrance of Allah is the greatest (thing in life) without doubt...**" (Ankabut, 29:45).

Prayer restrains the believer from misdeeds either before prayer or after it, and of course, during prayer. If prayer does not restrain one from misdeeds that means s/he does not pray regularly. The Prophet (صلى) says about the prayers of these kinds of people:

"Whoever is not restrained from clear and ambiguous misdeeds by the prayer he does, he moves away from Allah." (Jam' al-Fawaid, I. 339)

Therefore, the most important point to be observed during prayer is pious reverence.

PRAYERS DONE UNWARILY

A prayer that is done improperly and a prayer in which Satan steps in, is equivalent to a blow being struck on the person who prays it. It is said in the Qur'an:

"**So woe to the worshippers who are neglectful of their prayers, those who (want but) to be seen (of men), but refuse (to supply) (even) neighborly needs.**" (Maun, 107:4-7).

Exegetes of the Qur'an identify three forms of heedlessness in prayer:

1. Being careless when the time of prayer is due and delay it to do at another time.

2. Not sensing prayer spiritually though being physically at prayer.

3. Not taking heed of the precepts of prayer.

Mawlana Jalal al-Din Rumi says:

"**I asked my intellect about 'what is faith?' And my intellect leaned over the ear of my heart and whispered: 'Faith consists of manners.'**"

The greatest of manners is reverence towards the Lord. And it is best displayed with worship, particularly with prayer.

Being unaware about the requirements, precepts, and contents of the prayer is a compromise that Satan uses to strip off blessings. The inclination of the praying person towards unwariness allows Satan recourse to act. And, of course, a prayer that Satan weakens is not accepted.

Some people display themselves as strong defenders of Islam, but they do not duly perceive the importance of prayer, and they are heedless about it. They underestimate the Qur'anic and Prophetic orders and advice, and they remain indifferent to prayer. They neglect both pious reverence and the precepts of prayer. They perform prayers as if they wished to be free from it as soon as possible. May Allah save us from this kind of indifference.

Those careless people are like those who go bankrupt. They have nothing left but weariness. The Prophet (ﷺ) says:

"There are many of those who pray, but they only get weariness and exertion." (Nasai).

"Allah does not appreciate the other good qualities of those who do not pray regularly." (Tabarani).

Then again, the Prophet (ﷺ) describes one's negligence of proper prayer as "theft." He says:

"The most wicked thief of humans is the one who steals from his prayer." (Ahmad and Hakim).

And as this kind of theft is done on behalf of Satan the thief gets nothing but weariness. And the thief should remember the words of Allah in this regard:

"So woe to the worshippers who are neglectful of their prayers..." (Maun 107:4-5).

As this verse propounds, those who are lazy cannot approach prayer, and those who are not able to overwhelm their unsubmissive self cannot penetrate into the spirit of prayer, and thus they cannot benefit from it. Whoever prays without observing the precepts of prayer, and offer his prayer not realizing that he is in Allah's presence, and holds worldly concerns in remembrance during prayer, that means he is not really praying. And his prayer remains in this world.

So, the prayer that is supposed to mature one's faith in the heart ends up causing deprivation in the hands of such unwary people. And prayers of such individuals bring them nothing, but eternal torment. The Qur'an says:

"The hypocrites – they think they are over-reaching Allah, but He will over-reach them: when they stand up for prayer, they stand without earnest-ness, to be seen of men, but little do they hold Allah in remembrance." (Nisaa 4:142).

THOSE WHO KEEP THEMSELVES AWAY FROM PRAYER

A saint of Allah warns those who are not among those who pray:

"Those who refrain from prayer because of worldly possessions will be resurrected and assembled with Qarun for judgment. Those who do not pray because of being possessed by their power of ruling and administration will be resurrected with *Pharaoh*. Those who do not pray because of being a high and influential official will be resurrected with *Haman* (the minister of Pharaoh) and those who keep away from prayer because of inordinate love of gaining profit in business will be resurrected with Ubay bin Khalaf , an enemy of the Prophet."

Those who neglect prayer live an unproductive life. They do not have the light of Divine beauty in their faces. None of their deeds are rewarded. Their supplications to Allah are not accepted. They are also deprived of the love of saintly people. Their entire experience is in pain in accordance with the maxim *"you die as you live."* Their graves turn into a pit of hell where they find the rage of Allah against them. They are questioned strongly and finally thrown into hell .

As narrated in a hadith of Bukhari, the Prophet (ﷺ) used to ask the companions after morning prayers if they had any dreams. Those who did used to tell their dreams and the Prophet (ﷺ) used to interpret them. One day he again asked and then said:

"I had a dream. Two persons came and took me away."

Then he told them the rest of the dream describing to them the fea-tures of paradise and hell, particularly the suffering there. The story of a man in hell was related as follows: One of the men was being struck on the head with a stone. The stone hit so strongly that it was bouncing off. This happened over and over again.

The Prophet (ﷺ) asked the two persons who took him away:

"– Who is this person?"

They answered:

"– This man preferred sleeping to offering the obligatory prayers and he gave up reading the Qur'an though he earlier had learned how to read it."

Satan particularly tries to keep the servant away from prayer. Satan wants to make sure that the servant is kept away from Divine Mercy, as he knows the fact that "he who has no prayer has also no religion." (Taberani)

Therefore, foresighted believers protect themselves from the traps of Satan in this regard and they care about prayer and do their best to make up the prayers they had been unable to offer in their proper time.

The Prophet (ﷺ) says:

"Whoever forgets his prayer, let him immediately offer it whenever he remembers; there is no other way to atone for it." (Muslim, Masajid, 314). If the message of this saying to make up what is owed is not observed, the servant will be afflicted with a wretched state in the Hereafter.

PRAYER AS A MEANS OF DIFFERENTIATION

The Prophet (ﷺ) advised anyone who became Muslim:

"The symbol of Islam is prayer. Whoever prays in time, paying attention to the details, and whole-heartedly, this person is a believer." (Fadail al-Amal, 255-256).

He used to teach those who embraced Islam how to pray and he let them know that prayer is the pillar of religion, and it distinguishes the believer from the disbeliever.

The Companions of the Prophet (ﷺ) regarded the avoidance of

prayer as equal to disbelief. Abu Bakr used to tell the people who were around when it was time for prayer:

"O people! Arise! Extinguish the fire you are in with prayer!"

Prayer is not only a means of distinction between the believer and the disbeliever, but it also distinguishes between believers with regard to their having different degrees. Abu Hurayra narrates this hadith:

"Two persons from the tribe of Udaa came to the Prophet (ﷺ) to embrace Islam. Later, one of them was martyred on the battlefield. The other died a natural death one year after him. I dreamed that the one who died one year after entered paradise before the one who was martyred. I was amazed and said:

'Is not the degree of the martyr higher? Should not he have entered paradise first?'

When I told the Prophet (ﷺ) about this he said:

'Do not you see how much reward the latter has? He fasted in the month Ramadan during the extra year after the first was martyred. He also offered more than six thousand units of prayer.'" (Ahmad, ibn Maja).

Regarding another occasion of this kind the Prophet (ﷺ) commented to the companions:

"Has not the person who died a year after worshipped more?"

"Certainly", they replied.

Then the Prophet said:

"Has not he prostrated more than the one who died a year earlier?"

"Certainly", they answered.

And the Prophet (ﷺ) said:

"There is as great a difference between them as between the sky and the earth."

The privilege of prayer is stated in the following sayings of the Prophet (ﷺ):

"Allah did not enjoin anything superior than belief and prayer. If He were to enjoin anything superior, He would enjoin it on the angels. Whereas some of the angels bow down and some of them prostrate night and day."

"Prayer is the most valuable striving (Jihâd)."

"When the individual stands up for prayer Allah turns towards him. When he completes the prayer, Allah turns away." (Fadail al-Amal, 256).

"If there comes a disaster or calamity from the sky the people in mosques are saved from it.." (Fadail al-Amal, 256).

"The key to paradise is prayer." (Tirmizi, Taharat, 3).

"Prayer is the sacrifice of every pious believer." (Kuzai, Musnad, I, 181).

"The person who neglects a prayer is like the person who has lost all his wealth and family." (Nasai, Ahmad).

As prayer is so superior and important, Islam demands training in the early years of life for it. The Prophet (ﷺ) advises us to be very serious in this regard:

" Order your children to pray at the age of seven. At the age of ten (if they do not) beat them lightly. Let them also sleep by themselves (at this age)." (Abu Dawud).

SUMMING UP

It is noteworthy that prayer often begins due to a distress of the heart when passing through a test or affliction and progresses into experiencing joy on the occasion of celebration of the Eids. If we establish a symbolic connection here, we may say that those who regularly pray in this world will be rewarded with a festival in the Hereafter for prayer includes the meaning to lead the servant to perfection and Divine reward. In short, prayer provides the following physical benefits:

Prayer requires physical acts that are healthy for the body. It also organizes one's time during the day and regularizes one's entire life.

Prayer provides spiritual benefits as follows:

It provides, when performed properly, the joy of being in Allah's presence, meditation, comfort in the time of fear, pleasure in the time of joy, sustaining the spiritual character of the soul, maintenance of faith, and a good relationship with the Divine Being.

Prayer provides the following sociological benefits:

The sense of coming together, knowing one another, friendship, and reinforcement of the bonds of brotherhood.

It must be stated here that no excuse is acceptable for not attempting to offer prayer. Even those who are on the battlefield are supposed to pray by turns. And there can be no excuse for women as well, apart from those related to female health.

The Prophet (ﷺ) was so serious about prayer that he warned us even when he was in his last moments of life:

"Be careful about prayer!"

We should forever be awake about prayer taking heed of the above warning.

Those souls who pay attention to this warning and perceive the importance of prayer, let it become the dearest joy of their life. They pull away from this transitory world, and reach annihilation in Allah when they stand up for prayer.

A sincere worshipper needs to embody the following qualities for the acceptance of his/her prayers.

"1. Those who remain steadfast to their prayer;

2. And those in whose wealth is a recognized right for the (needy) who ask and him who is prevented (for some reason from asking);

3. And those who hold to the truth of the Day of Judgment;

4. And those who fear the displeasure of their Lord;

5. And those who guard their chastity;

6. And those who respect their trusts and covenants;

7. And those who stand firm in their testimonies;

8. And those who guard (the sacredness) of their worship;

Such will be the honored ones in the Gardens (of Bliss)." (Maarij, 70:23-35).

O my Lord! Please, let our prayers have the honor of being offered in their true meaning and wisdom , and let them be regarded as an ascension (mi'raj) to You! Let our prayers be our joy, and the delight of our souls both in this world and the Hereafter!

Amen!..

*

MINOR ABLUTION, MAJOR ABLUTION OF THE BODY, ABLUTION WITH SAND OR EARTH IN THE ABSENCE OF WATER (DRY ABLUTION)

1. Minor Ablution (Wudu)

Obligatory Requirements (Fardh) of Minor Ablution

1. Washing the face.

2. Washing both hands and arms thoroughly up to the elbows.

3. Moving the palm of the wet hand over one-fourth of the head, starting from the front of the forehead to the back of the head.

4. Washing the feet up to the ankles.

The Voluntary Acts (Sunnah) performed by the Prophet (ﷺ) in the Minor Ablution:

1. Declaring the intention that the act is for the purpose of worship and purity.

2. Saying at the start, بِسْمِ اللهِ الرَّحْمنِ الرهِيم "In the name of Allah, the most Merciful, the most Compassionate."

3. Beginning by washing both hands up to the wrists.

4. Cleansing the teeth with a toothbrush (miswak) whenever possible, if not, then rubbing with the fingers.

5. Doing the washing from the beginning to the end without any break.

6. Rubbing the areas of ablution.

7. Rinsing out the mouth with water three times.

8. Gargling (not to be done when fasting).

9. Cleansing the nostrils by sniffing water three times.

177

10. Washing three times.

11. Beginning to wash from the right side.

12. Beginning to wash the hands and the feet from the fingertips and toes.

13. Wiping the beard with wet hands.

14. Moving the ring on the finger so that no part remains dry.

15. Rubbing wet fingers into the grooves of both ears and cavities.

16. Passing both hands over the back of the head to the neck.

17. Moving the palm of the wet hand over the whole head.

18. Making sure that water has reached between the fingers and the toes.

2. Major Ablution of the Body *(Ghusl,* bath)

Obligatory Acts (Fardh) of the Major Ablution:

1. Gargling to the throat.

2. Washing the nostrils.

3. Washing the whole body.

The Voluntary Acts (Sunnah) performed by the Prophet (ﷺ) in the Major Ablution.

1. Clear intention that it is for the purpose of purity and worship.

2. Saying at the start, بِسِمِ اللهِ الرَّحمنِ الرَّهِيم "In the name of Allah, the most Merciful, the most Compassionate."

3. Washing any dirt from the body.

4. Washing the private parts.

5. Making a Minor ablution before the Major ablution.

6. Washing the whole body three times and making sure it covers every part of the body.

7. Washing the head first, then over the right and then the left shoulders, and then rubbing the body.

8. Washing the feet last.

3. Dry Ablution with Sand or Earth in the Absence of Water (*Tayyammum*)

Obligatory Acts (Fardh) of Dry Ablution:

1. Declaring the intention that the act is for the purpose of worship and purity.

2. Wiping the hands on clean sand or earth twice and anointing the face and arms respectively.

The Voluntary Acts (Sunnah) performed by the Prophet (ﷺ) in Dry Ablution:

1. Saying first, بِسمِ الله الرَّ همن الرهيم "In the name of Allah, the most Merciful, the most Compassionate."

2. Doing all acts in proper order.

3. Doing the acts without stopping.

4. Moving hands forward first and then back while wiping on the earth.

5. Keeping the fingers separated.

6. Shaking the hands off when lifting from the earth.

4. Prayer

There are twelve requirements for prayer. Some of them are external prerequisites. These are called "conditions of prayer." And some of them are internal prerequisites. These are called "pillars of prayer."

The Conditions of Prayer:

1. Purification from invisible impurities: This requires purity from invisible dirt or dust. It is done by performing Minor ablution, Major ablution, or dry ablution.

2. from visible dirt: This requires that the entire body, the clothes worn, and the ground used for prayer be free from all kinds of dirt or impurity.

3. Proper dress: Dressing properly in such a way so as to meet the moral regulations aimed at covering the private parts. For the male, the body should be covered at least from the navel to the knees. For the female, the whole body should be covered except the face, the hands and the feet. If one-fourth of the part of the body becomes open then the prayer is void.

4. Facing the Ka'bah: Facing the right direction, the Qiblah, the direction of the Ka'bah at Mecca. If one's direction is turned during prayer his prayer is nullified.

5. Time: Obligatory prayers are to be done at fixed times. They cannot be advanced or postponed.

6. Intention: Declaring the intention of prayer with the heart. In the case of prayer in congregation the leader of the prayer should declare that he is the leader, and the congregation should declare that they are subject to the leader.

The Pillars of Prayer:

1. Reciting "آللَه اَكبَر Allahu Akbar is the Greatest" at the start: This is done by raising the hands up to the ears while saying "Allah is Greatest."

2. Standing: Those who have sufficient strength are required to stand to begin prayer and if unable, they may sit or recline.

3. Recitation: It means reciting at least three verses from the Qur'an while standing.

4. Bowing Down: After standing we bow down with our hands placed on our knee.

5. Prostration: It means prostrating on the floor with the forehead, nose, palms of both hands, and knees touching the floor.

6. Sitting Upright: This is done by sitting at the end of the prayer so as to read the blessing called *"at-Tahiyyat."*

Necessary Conditions of Prayer:

1. Commencing the prayer by saying "Allah is the آللَه اَكبَر Greatest."

2. Recitation of the opening chapter of the Qur'an (*al-Fatiha*) in all units of prayers both obligatory and voluntary.

3. Recitation of the al-Fatiha before verses from the Qur'an.

4. One should recite a minimum of three short verses from the Qur'an after and in addition to al-Fatiha. This should be done in the first two units of any obligatory prayer and in all units of voluntary prayers.

5. Placing the nose together with the forehead on the floor while prostrating.

6. Doing two prostrations one after another in each unit of prayer.

7. Doing all acts properly.

8. Sitting upright after two units of three or four unit prayers.

9. Reading the blessing called *"at-Tahiyyat"* while sitting upright.

10. Standing up after sitting upright to continue the three or four unit prayers.

11. Reading out loud by the Imam of the opening chapter (*al-Fatiha*) and a passage from the Qur'an in the first two units of the morning, evening, and late evening prayers if offered in congregation, and also in the Friday congregational and Eid prayers.

12. Reading in a low voice in all units of the noon and late-noon prayers, and also in the third and fourth units of the evening and late-evening prayers.

13. Reading out loud the opening chapter (*al-Fatiha*) and the passages from the Qur'an in the *Tarawih* prayer, and in the *Witr* prayer offered during the month of Ramadan.

14. If prayer is offered in congregation, the individuals apart from the leader of the prayer are not required to read the opening chapter (*al-Fatiha*) and the passages from the Qur'an.

15. Reciting the *Qunut* (devotion) supplication in the last unit of the three unit *Witr* prayer (performed at the end of the late evening prayers.)

16. Saying the special prayers related to the Eid prayers.

17. Ending the prayer with greetings directed to the angels on the right and the left shoulders.

18. Making the prostration of forgetfulness (*sajda-us -sahw*) in case of any minor mistake made during prayer.

19. Prostration when a verse of prostration is recited in prayer.

The Voluntary Features of Prayer Performed by the Prophet (ﷺ):

1. Raising the hands up to the ears when beginning the prayer, and also at the beginning of *the qunut* prayer of the *witr* prayer and then placing the right hand on the left hand just below the navel or on the chest (females put their hands on the chest).

2. Before reading *al-Fatiha*, reciting the *"subhanaka"* in the first unit of each prayer and then saying, "I seek shelter in Allah from the rejected satan"

3. Saying "Ameen!" silently (according to Hanefi fiqh) after *al-Fatiha* in all prayers whether done in congregation or separately.

4. Saying "Allah is Greatest" before and after every act between different sections of the prayer.

5. Saying سَمِعَ اللهُ لِمَنْ حَمَدَهُ "Allah hears those who praise Him. Our Lord, praise be to You!" while rising after bowing down.

6. سُبْحَانَ رَبِّيَ الْعَظِيم Saying "Glory to my Lord, the Greatest" three times while bowing down, and سُبْحَانَ رَبِّيَ الْأَعْلَى "Glory to my Lord, the Highest" three times while prostrating.

7. Placing the palms on the knees while bowing down, and holding the elbows straight, and the head level with one's back.

8. Placing the knees, hands, and face on the floor respectively while prostrating; and removing them in reverse order; and placing the face in between the hands in prostration.

9. Placing the hands on the knees while sitting upright; reading "at-Tahiyyat" during the first sitting; and reading "at-Tahiyyat" and *as-Salah alan nabiyy* (the blessing on the Prophet) in the final sitting.

10. Turning the face to the right and to the left respectively at the end of the prayer with the words أَسَّلَامُ عَلَيْكُمْ وَرَ حْمَةُ الله "Peace and the Mercy of Allah be upon You!"

Good Manners in Prayer

Focusing our eyes on the place of prostration while standing; on the feet while bowing down; on the hands placed on knees while sitting upright; and on the shoulders while turning our face to the right and to the left at the end of the prayer.

Prostration of Forgetfulness (*sajdatus sahw*)

The prostration of forgetfulness is performed when some requirements are forgotten or done incorrectly in order to make up for the error by making two extra prostrations and then reciting *"at-Tahiyyat"* and *as-Salah alan nabiyy* (the blessing on the Prophet) before ending the prayer.

Such acts as forgetting to read the *Qunut* supplication in the *Witr* prayer; bowing down before reading passages from the Qur'an after *al-Fatiha*; forgetting to sit upright after the first two units; and not doing prostration if a verse of prostration is recited in the prayer, require the prostration of forgetfulness.

However, if one forgets to perform the prostration of forgetfulness and ends the prayer without performing it, it is not necessary to perform the prayer over again.

ZAKAT AND INFAQ

وَيُطْعِمُونَ الطَّعَامَ عَلَىٰ حُبِّهِ مِسْكِينًا وَيَتِيمًا وَأَسِيرًا

"And they feed, for the love of Allah, the indigent, the orphan, and the captive,-" (Insan, 16:8)

$\mathcal{M}$an is the finest creation of Allah among the rest of creation. However, the natural or acquired differences between individuals such as race or nation or being strong or weak, healthy or sick, educated or illiterate, rich or poor do not change every essential human Allah-given value. They serve to establish an order and harmony in society. Through these differences people are able to benefit from each other in different ways.

In particular, the different financial states of poverty and richness, as two opposite realities, possess a significant place in the order of society. Allah has created a world where people, sometimes temporarily and sometimes permanently, become rich and poor in order to test them spiritually in different situations. Consequently, these two states possess a deep meaning and wisdom for those who would understand. Merely being rich is not a virtue as being poor is not a vice; they are only part of Allah's Divine pre-determination (Allah's distribution). They are the manifestations of Allah's Wisdom. Allah the Almighty states in the Qur'an:

"We distribute among them their livelihood in the life of this world, and We have exalted some of them above others in degrees, that some of them may take service from others; and the Mercy of your Lord is better than what they amass. And were it not that

mankind would have become one community (through love of riches), We might well have appointed, for those who disbelieve in the Beneficent, roofs of silver for their houses and stairs whereby to mount and for their houses doors and couches of silver whereon to recline. And ornaments of gold. Yet all that would have been but a provision of the life of the world- and the Hereafter with your Lord would have been for those who were Allah-fearing" (Zukhruf: 43:32-35)

"Allah grants abundant sustenance, or gives it in scant measure, to whichever He wills of His creatures: for behold, Allah has full Knowledge of everything." (Ankabut:, 29:62)

As these verses inform us, the distribution of wealth is not the same for everybody but does this mean that this is an injustice? Since the responsibility to use wealth is according to one's capacity, the answer is no. Those who have more wealth will have the burden of more responsibilities than those who have less and all will be judged accordingly. Thus, a certain dynamic equilibrium is made to function in society. Islam, in order to prevent human beings from slavishly working to amass wealth and a consequential tendency to become selfish, greedy and proud and to prevent the poor from developing negative feelings towards the rich such as jealousy or hatred, commanded the payment of Zakat. Through the payment from the total wealth one has had control for at least one year, a social balance combining justice, mutual respect and love between the poor and the rich is maintained. It should be borne in mind that neither the poor nor the rich have the knowledge of whether they are to permanently remain in the degree of poverty or richness they find themselves in at a particular time. The poor must not accept living off charity as a necessarily permanent condition of their life but must strive to acquire wealth while the rich must strive to spend it in a manner pleasing to Allah and not simply hoard it. It is also emphasized that whatever is spent for the sake of Allah will eventually be replaced either in this world or in the next.

The role of the government must not be overlooked in helping to facilitate conditions to help people remove themselves from everything which keeps them in chronic poverty and also in preventing the rich from exploitation of the poor, misuse of their power and influence or unfair or illegal business practices. Just as incentives are given to help businessmen so also there should be programs for education, training, and basic health and social services.

Therefore, Zakat is one of the most essential duties in Islam relating to the rights one owes to others who are the beloved of Allah and His servants.

Allah the Almighty, with His Divine Wisdom and Knowledge tests his servants according to their resources. Allah will hold the rich responsible concerning how they have earned their wealth, whether it was from legal or illegal means, whether they paid the poor-due and other voluntary charity. For the rich, this command is a serious challenge to test whether or not they will fulfill their obligations towards the less fortunate members of society who need help for their basic needs. If they successfully pass this test, they will be highly rewarded in paradise.

"And spend of that wherewith We have provided you before death cometh unto one of you and he says: O my Sustainer! If only thou wouldst reprieve me for a little while I would give alms and be among the righteous. But Allah reprieves no soul when its term cometh, and Allah is informed of what ye do." (Munafiqun, 63:10-11)

On the other hand, the poor are tested in a different way. Allah the Almighty, does not ask them to pay anything and drive them deeper into poverty. Their test is to be patient, not to complain without good reason or to revolt against society, taking from what others have rightfully earned, and to preserve their purity and uprightness. If they pass this test successfully they will be abundantly rewarded in the Hereafter and their suffering in the world will be replaced by eternal bliss and heavenly riches.

The commandment of paying the Zakat is mentioned in the Qur'an twenty seven times together with the establishment of the daily prayers (salât). This shows the significance of the commandment. Only in one place is the commandment of establishing prayers and paying alms mentioned separately but this time Allah the Almighty confirms that those who pray to Allah in true prayer, will naturally fulfill their obligations. In Islam, commandments are divided into two areas, huququllah, the rights we owe directly to Allah- like prayer and huququlibad, the rights we owe to others, like Zakat. We must spend out of the wealth we have been given and we must also spend of ourselves. They occupy the highest position in their categories. Although Islam separately evaluates the fulfillment of each commandment and the ignoring of one commandment does not affect the other ones, the case of alms-due is different. If a believer does not pay the alms due his prayers will not be accepted. The Prophet (ﷺ) says:

"If a person prays but does not pay the alms his prayers have no value." (Munavî, Kunûz al-haqâik, p.143)

Therefore, the first caliph of Islam, Abû Bakr considered those who rejected paying Zakat as apostates even though they accepted performing their prayers. He declared war against those who did not pay what is considered as the right of the poor over the rich. Allah the Almighty states in His Holy Qur'an:

"And in their wealth the beggar and the outcast had due share." (Dhâriyât, 51:19)

And the Prophet (ﷺ) said: If you pay your alms, you pay the rights of what you owe to the poor in your wealth. (Tirmidhi)

If the rich pay what is due to the poor, the rest of their wealth is made blessed for them. In other words, the wealth of the rich is purified from all sorts of harm. When passed to the poor and disadvantaged sections of the society, the rich can enjoy their wealth with peace of mind knowing that the poor have also been satisfied regarding their essential needs. The following verse confirms this reality:

"Take alms out of their property, you would cleanse them and purify them thereby, and pray for them; surely your prayer is a relief to them; and Allah is Hearing, Knowing." (Tawba, 9:103)

The distribution of alms pleases the poor but it also benefits the rich more than anything else because they are thus blessed in both worlds. Zakat means "cleaning and purifying" and it cleans man from the diseases of the heart. It cleanses wealth from the rights of others and purifies it. As a matter of fact, this is also the role of the Prophets i.e. they purify people from spiritual diseases.

In addition, alms given with a willing and generous heart helps to establish a bond of love and sincerity between the rich and the poor. From very ancient times there has been a continuous conflict between the poor and the rich. Generally, the rich looked upon the poor as worthless and ignorant people, they despised and judged the poor simply for their poverty. On the other hand, the poor maintained an anger and jealousy towards the rich. This kind of relationship is still the prevalent one in most societies of the world. However, all the Divinely revealed religions contain commandments to look after others and to show mercy and love towards the weak. If today, every rich person paid his obligatory alms, there would not be any needy person in society. We should bear in mind that this is the minimum requirement that a Muslims should pay, and that there is no limit to the amount of voluntary charity (sadaqat)a believer who possesses a perfect faith in Allah can give. At the time of Umar b. Abdulaziz, the Umayyad caliph, the governors could not find enough poor people to distribute the alms due to, since there were not enough poor people around. They asked the caliph what to do with the alms the state had collected from the rich. All the rich people had paid their rightful amount of alms. Consequently, this time period in the history of Islam has been accepted as the brightest period after the first four caliphs of Islam.

Hadrat Jalaladdin Rumi describes the significance of helping the poor in a very fascinating way:

Though it (the poor) is one filled with knowledge, it hath a house filled with smoke (poverty and need): open a window for it by listening (to his problems). (Masnawî, III. 485)

Hence, Islam treats the social wounds of society emanating from poverty and richness. On the other hand, non-Islamic systems have been unable to achieve any comprehensive or consistent success in handling this delicate problem. They either went to the extreme of denying or severely limiting the right of personal wealth and private ownership or they idolized acquiring personal wealth. They either denied the right of the poor to ask help from the rich or they completely left it to them to ask help from others, leading to a chronic life of begging. Islam handled this problem through admonishing the rich about the benefits of giving in charity, secretly and openly and through encouraging the poor to be patient and not to be a permanent burden on society but rather to do their best to earn their livelihood.

In reality, obligatory alms giving is one of the highest values that Islam has introduced to humanity. The difficulties and sufferings of the poor, the destitute, the orphans, and the widows are lessened through the institution of Zakat and other kinds of charity. It is also through Islam that slaves were enabled to become free. Slaves were able to buy back their freedom from the sources of charity. Freeing slaves without receiving any payment was also encouraged as a worthy act and for remission of sins.

In addition to alleviating poverty Zakat has another very important function. It prevents people from drowning in the swamp of unending payments of interest. If needy people are not helped they will be forced to borrow at high rates of interest. Borrowing seems easy at first but in reality it is nothing but a means of taking advantage of the poor. Through giving, the poor do not need to borrow for essentials. Those who charge interest on loans to those in desperate conditions take advantage of the situation whereas those who distribute alms to the poor in fact share their burden. They do not expect any worldly return from the poor; they only help them in order to attain the pleasure of Allah the Almighty. Without having any collateral to offer a bank, the poor are forced to turn to loan companies. When the loan cannot be fully paid in a short time the amount of the original loan doubles and triples until only the interest on it can be paid and the borrower becomes permanently indebted.

A greedy person never feels satisfied with the amount of wealth he gathers; the more he gets the more his greediness increases. On the other hand, those who give alms do not develop greed, they are contented with little from worldly things. The people who devour interest develop an immense greed for wealth and they do not mind destroying the lives of others to increase their wealth. It is possible to see examples of such people in the big trade centers of the world. The following verse on the other hand advises us not to use interest in business transactions:

"Allah will deprive usury of all blessing, but will give increase for deeds of charity: For He loveth not creatures ungrateful and wicked." (Baqarah, 2:276)

Those who are involved with interest in their businesses lose the blessing of Allah and as a result they become bankrupt in the Hereafter. This bankruptcy can happen in this world and those who made great fortunes out of interest and other illegal ways lose them in a short time. Either a calamity, a disease or wasteful or mistaken spending consumes their wealth in a short time. The harm of interest is not only personal, it also has a destructive effect on the social fabric of the society. Through interest gained without gainful work or productive investment, the rich become richer and the poor become even poorer. It destroys the unity of the society. Because of these destructive results such people lose the chance to acquire spiritual wealth as well as eternal bliss.

On the other hand, distribution of Zakat establishes social harmony and order and will bring blessings in this world as well as in the Hereafter. The following incident is a good example of such generosity and social solidarity:

One day a beggar asked Hadrat Ali for some money. Ali (may Allah be pleased with him) asked his sons Hadrat Hassan and Hadrat Hussein to bring some golden coins from home.

The boys obtained them from their mother and gave them to Hadrat Ali who gave them all to the beggar even though they needed this money to buy flour.

Hadrat Ali was just entering his house and at that moment someone who wanted to sell his camel approached Ali saying him: "Take this camel for 140 dirhams and pay later, leaving the camel with him." After a very short time, another person came, and bought the camel from Ali for 200 dirhams, paying in cash.

Hadrat Ali paid his 140 dirham debt to the person from whom he had bought the camel and gave the rest of the money to his wife, Hadhrat Fatimah, and told her that this is the reward that is promised by Allah through His Prophet (ﷺ); we gave six dirhams and Allah the Almighty paid us back ten fold and he recited the following verse:

"Whoso bringeth a good deed will receive tenfold the like thereof," (An'am, 6:160)

In addition to this good news, the following verse states that giving the poor-due and charity will open the doors of mercy and prevent calamities:

"Is there any Reward for Good - other than Good?" (Rahman, 55:60)

The following incident is a good example of the great benefits of giving charity:

Once, several thieves forced their way into a shop and the owner, an old man had no choice but to give up all the money from his safe. However, before he opened his safe, one of the robbers remembered the shopkeeper. He turned to his friends holding his gun and said: "You cannot rob this man unless you kill me first."

His friends were very surprised about this unexpected behavior and asked:

"We have robbed many shops so far and what is so different about this person that we should not rob him as well? Leave us and let us do the job once more"!

He answered:

"Do you know who this old man is? He is the one who helped my family when I was spending my time drinking, gambling and neglecting my family. He looked after my family like a merciful father and financed the education of my children. Please do not insist on this and let us leave this man alone."

As a result all the robbers apologized and left the shop without even taking a penny.

This is the example of how charity drives away evil.

The best example of helping the poor and solving their problems is witnessed in the life of the Prophet Muhammad (ﷺ). He wanted to make generosity an inseparable characteristic of every Muslim. Hence he stated: The giving hand is superior to the receiving hand (Bukhari, Zakat, 18).

He strongly praised the donators of charity in the following hadith: "There is no envy except in two cases: a person to whom Allah has given wealth and he spends it in the right way, and a person to whom Allah has given wisdom (i.e. religious knowledge) and he gives his acts accordingly and teaches it to the others." (Bukhari, *Volume 2, Book 24, Number 490*)

The following prayer is also a good example of how much he loved the poor and the weak members of society: "O my Lord! Enable me to live as the poor, sustain me as a poor person and resurrect me (on the Day of Judgment) among the poor." (Tirmidhi, Zudh, 37)

He made his house like a refuge for the poor, dedicating some part of his house to the poor emigrants known as Muhâjirs (the emigrants).

In his hadith he states that the poor will enter Paradise forty years before the rich since they have no wealth for which to give account. (Tirmidhi, Kitâb al-Zuhd)

"The rich are in fact the poor (being little rewarded) on the Day of Resurrection except him to whom Allah has given wealth which he gives (in charity) to his right, left, front and back, and does good deeds with it."

In this way Islam teaches that neither poverty nor richness is a virtue by their basic nature, the virtue lies in the way that a person behaves. A poor person can also contribute to the society very positively; hence he should be taken seriously. To this effect, the Prophet (ﷺ) states that if a poor person has no financial power to give charity, his good conduct and heartfelt sweet words will be considered as his charity. In this way Islam gives an equal chance of attaining rewards both for the rich and the poor. Money and wealth are not the highest values; the important thing is how one behaves in their absence and presence.

One should behave like a human being with full dignity both in poverty and in richness. Neither of them is bad if a believer behaves properly in these situations. Of course, we are not suggesting that poverty is something good, what we are saying here is that when poverty is an unavoidable reality of life, a Muslim should behave with dignity while trying to free himself from it.

There is another important wisdom behind the duty of the poor-due and voluntary charity. It aims to prevent a monopoly of vast amounts of capital in the hands of a few, individuals. If wealth is in the hand of a few it usually results in the abuse of the poor. If richness is made an instrument of abuse and pride, a terrible consequence for the rich is unavoidable. Everyone in the society, the poor and the rich need each other spiritually or materially as part of the wisdom and plan of Allah, the Almighty. It should be known that everything including our personal possessions belong to Allah. Man only possesses things metaphorically not in reality. Allah the Almighty states in the Qur'an:

"O ye men! It is ye that have need of Allah: but Allah is the One Free of all wants, worthy of all praise." (Fâtir, 35:15)

As this verse narrates, man possesses nothing, he is in need of Allah in all conditions even when he is rich. We are living in Allah's domain and surviving with the sustenance He grants us. However, due to Allah's wisdom, not known to us, man thinks he possesses things in a real sense. We forget that we are being tested through what we possess. Solomon(a.s.), who had a great wealth and a kingdom unequalled in human history, lost all his wealth all of a sudden. But Allah gave him back his kingdom, when he asked forgiveness from Allah. A friend of Allah therefore warns us saying that we should not run after sustenance but rather after the Sustainer.

Wealth is a trust given to man for a limited period in order to test him. He is not allowed to use it according to his inclination. Man should make use of his wealth as Almighty Allah, the Real Owner of wealth commands him. If it is used against the will of Allah, it causes man to become corrupt and commit injustice against his fellow human beings. Wealth has this enormous potential for harm, when it is loved without any restraint. Therefore, Allah the Almighty calls worldly wealth a affliction *(Fitna)* when it is idolized as an end in itself instead of a means. For such ill-favored people Allah states:

"They who hoard up gold and silver and spend it not in the way of Allah, unto them give tidings (O Muhammad) of a painful doom," (Tauba, 9:34)

"On the day when it will (all) be heated in the fire of hell, and their foreheads and their flanks and their backs will be branded therewith (and it will be said unto them): Here is that which ye hoarded for yourselves. Now taste of what ye used to hoard." (Tauba, 9:35)

The Prophet (ﷺ) also warns us against the potential dangers of miserliness and holding onto wealth selfishly, only for satisfying the ego.

"There is never a day wherein the servants (of Allah) get up at morn, but are not visited by two angels. One of them says: O Allah, give him more who spends (for the sake of Allah), and the other says: O Allah, bring destruction to one who withholds." (Muslim Zakat, *Book 005, Number 2205*)

On the other hand, he praises those who spend for the good of the community saying that charity drags man to Paradise whereas miserliness drags him to Hell.

"Generosity is a tree in Paradise whose branches extend to the world. Whoever catches a branch of it, it takes him to Paradise. Miserliness, on the other hand, is a tree in Hell whose branches are in the world. Whoever grabs it, it takes him to hell." (Bayhaki, Shuab al-Iman)

These are clear warnings from the Prophet (ﷺ) concerning the terrible end of the miserly people who do not fulfill their financial responsibilities towards society such as paying the alms due, and 'ushr (i.e, the commandment for farmers to pay one tenth of the harvest to the poor).

These verses and the hadiths confirm that when the love of wealth finds a place in the hearts of people they will steal the rights of the poor with their wealth. Faced with these clear Divine warnings, we should be very careful to fulfill our obligations towards the poor and to try to give more than two and half percent of our total wealth, which is the minimum requirement of Islam. The following verse gives us the guidance concerning the principles of charity:

"And they ask thee what they ought to spend. Say: that which is superfluous." (Baqara, 2:219)

The companions of the Prophet (ﷺ) understood very well the significance of charity and they competed with each other in donating their wealth. When the Prophet (ﷺ) asked the help of his companions at the battle of Tabuk, Umar brought half of his wealth, thinking that he exceeded all the rest. However, Abu Bakr donated his entire wealth for Islam. When the Prophet (ﷺ) asked: "What did you leave for the needs of your family?" He answered: "I left Allah and His messenger (for their needs)."

The following incident shows the Sufi concept of charity. One day a faqih (Islamic jurist) asked the famous Sufi Shibli, in order to test his knowledge of Islamic law, the amount of Zakat that a Muslim must pay since at that time some scholars thought that Sufis were ignorant of Islamic law.

Shibli asked the faqih: "Do you want the answer according to the school of the faqihs (the scholars) or the faqirs (the Sufis)?"

The faqih said: "According to both."

Shibli stated: "According to the faqihs a year in duration in total must pass over wealth before it is taxable. Thus, over 200 dirhams, you pay one fortieth which is 5 dirhams. However, according to the Sufis you give away the entire 200 dirhams and thank Allah that you have gotten rid of the responsibility (of the wealth)."

The faqih disliking his answer responded with sarcasm: "We have learned Islam from Muslim scholars (not from Sufis)."

Shibli on the other hand gave him an answer that shattered the prejudice of the faqih saying: "We have learned Islam from the close companion of the Prophet (ﷺ) (i.e. Abu Bakr) who put all his wealth at the disposal the Messenger of Allah and gave thanks to Allah (for ridding himself from the heavy responsibility) (Mektûb, 34, Üçüncü Yüzyyıl)"

The Prophet (ﷺ) led the way in giving charity, as he was the best example of the spirit of continuous giving. The following example from his life shows this very well. One day he had slaughtered a sheep for his family. They distributed most of the meat when the Prophet (ﷺ) asked his wife Aisha (may Allah be happy with her) how much was left from the sheep, she answered: "only the shoulder of the sheep remains" (the rest having been distributed). The Prophet (ﷺ) on the other hand understood this charitable act from a different perspective and said: "That means that except for the shoulder the rest of the sheep remains for us." By this he (ﷺ) wanted to say that by giving most of the sheep for the needy we made it our real possession in the Hereafter to benefit from the eternal rewards given by Allah. On the other hand, the part we kept for our own consumption will only satisfy our hunger for a short time and that its usefulness will not extend to the Hereafter. When compared to its use in the Hereafter, the short-lived satisfaction is like a waste.

If he had some money at home, he could not sleep without first giving it away as charity due to his high spiritual level. However, he did not command this level of charity to the general body of Muslims, and he directed them to be balanced and asked them to give according to their capacities. For example, although he accepted all the wealth of Abu Bakr he advised another companion of his to give some of his wealth and to keep the rest for his own use. (R.M. Sâmî, Tebük Seferi, p.66)

In other words, Islam does not require people to give up all their wealth; it only encourages them to give according to their spiritual and material capacities after fulfilling the obligatory ones. However, some of the companions like Abu Dhar deduced from the example of the Prophet (ﷺ) that it is illegal to save money for the future without using it for the good of the community.

Abdurrahman b. Awf was another good example that followed the high example of the Prophet (ﷺ). He would feed the poor when he himself was hungry. He would not mind the difficulties that he would face but on the other hand would strive to comfort others and remove their difficulties. The companions had adorned their hearts with the feeling that the wealth they possessed was only a trust given to them by Allah.

In short, those who desire to reach eternal bliss should know that they are not the real owners of their worldly possessions but rather their keeper on behalf of Allah, the real Owner, and one day they will give account for their management of His possessions. The following verse clearly reminds us of this fact:

Then on that day you shall most certainly be questioned about the gifts. (Takathur, 102:8)

Fully understanding the terrible consequences of this warning the Sufi mystics never forget that using halâl (religiously legal) things will be accounted for and harâm (religiously illegal) things are punishable.

Hence, the rich people who spend their money in order to please their ego and base desires are in fact carrying wood for their own fire. It is a great virtue to work hard and to acquire the necessities of life. However, the right action is to do that without putting the love of wealth in the heart by being able to give it in charity. Otherwise, richness is nothing but the work of a porter who carries things for others and cannot personally own them. Similarly, wealth that is not spent in the way of Allah will be passed to the heirs but the full responsibility will belong to the one who gathered it in the first place.

The intention behind earning wealth should be to attain the following level that the Prophet(ﷺ) directs us: "The best of mankind is the one who benefits them most" (tabarânî, Majmûat'u-Awsât, VI, 58) Money should be kept in the pocket not in the heart.

It should be known that the prayers of the poor and the helpless for the well being of the rich are a source of peace for them. This is a spiritual help from the poor to the rich. It should be emphasized once more that poverty is not a shame as it may be the manifestation of Allah's mercy in the Hereafter.

The generous rich and the honorable poor who patiently face difficulties are equal in attaining Allah's pleasure and attaining a high state of human perfection. On the other hand, Islam denounces the rich who behave with pride and vanity. In addition, the people who act like being poor in order to easily attain their needs without any trouble are also scorned by Islam. Therefore, the Prophet (ﷺ) took refuge in Allah from the mischief of richness and poverty: "O Allah, I seek refuge in Thee from the trial of Hell-Fire; and from the torment of Hell-Fire; and from the trial of the grave and torment of the grave; and from the evil of the trial of affluence and from the evil of the trial of poverty." (Bukhari, *Book 035, Number 6534*)

Hence, whoever has the quality of contentment with what he has in trust and submission to the will of Allah, they are the real rich. If one wants to be really rich he should make others benefit from the worldly possessions and advantages he has. The intention of a good Muslim is to be a person who benefits society with his tongue and hands, i.e. to use all his limbs for the good of society.

Giving the poor-due and other acts of charity are in fact the expression of one's thankfulness to Allah. In return Allah promises more favors to those who give thanks for His generosity.

Allah the Almighty states in the Qur'an: And when your Lord proclaimed:

"If ye give thanks, I will give you more; but if ye are thankless, lo! My punishment is terrible." (Ibrâhîm, 14:7)

The Prophet (ﷺ) also confirmed this promise in the following Hadith:

"O son of Adam! Give to others as you too will be given to." (Bukhari and Muslim)

Woe to those who say," I have earned this wealth by my personal endeavor and look down upon the poor. They are preparing a terrible end for themselves like Qarun as narrated in the Qur'an":

Qarun was a person who lived in the time of Moses (a.s.). In the beginning he was a good person. However, after he became very rich he could not protect the purity of his heart and lost his good characteristics. His wealth made him proud and arrogant. The Qur'an narrates the amount of his richness:

"Now Qarun was of Moses' folk, but he oppressed them; and We gave him so much treasure that the stores thereof would verily have been a burden for a troop of mighty men. When his own folk said unto him: Exult not; lo! Allah loves not the exultant;" (Qasas: 28:76)

Qarun did not listen to his folk and closed his ears to their advice as well as to the advice of Moses (a.s.). When Moses (a.s.) asked him to pay the alms due of his wealth, he forgot that he owed his success to Moses (a.s.) and said:

- Do you covet my wealth? I have earned it myself.

The Qur'an narrates the story as follows:

"But seek the abode of the Hereafter in that which Allah hath given thee and neglect not thy portion of the world, and be thou kind even as Allah hath been kind to thee, and seek not corruption in the earth; lo! Allah loveth not corrupters, He said: 'I have been given it only on account of knowledge I possess.' Knew he not that Allah had destroyed already of the generations before him men who were mightier than him in strength and greater in respect of following? The guilty are not questioned of their sins.

Then went he forth before his people in his pomp. Those who were desirous of the life of the world said: Ah, would that we had the like of what hath been given unto Qarun! Lo! He is the lord of rare good fortune.

But those who had been given knowledge said: Woe unto you! The reward of Allah for him who believeth and doeth right is better, and only the steadfast will obtain it. So We caused the earth to swallow him and his dwelling-place. Then he had no host to help him against Allah, nor was he of those who can save themselves.

And those who had envied his position the day before began to say on the morrow: "Ah! it is indeed Allah Who enlarges the provision or restricts it, to any of His servants He pleases! Had it not been that Allah was gracious to us, He could have caused the earth to swallow us up! Ah! Those who reject Allah will assuredly never prosper."
(Al-Qasas, 28:77-82)

This is a terrible end for those who lose themselves in the love of wealth and forget the Hereafter. It is a tragic scene of how one lost the eternal bliss and richness due to ambition.

A poet descries the end of Qarun in the following lines:

What kind of richness is this O Qarun!

It caused you to be a beggar who is not shown mercy

Now in the Hereafter he lost all he possessed and became a beggar since the Hereafter is for those who served Allah piously, with sincerity, fearing His wrath. The following verse clearly explains the causes of why one loses the rewards in the Hereafter:

"That Home of the Hereafter We shall give to those who intend not high-handedness or mischief on earth: and the end is (best) for the righteous." (Qasas, 28:83)

Jalaladdin Rumi (may Allah bless his secret) wonders at the terrible end of the covetous people who go to the Hereafter bankrupt.

For Rumi the worldly wealth should be spent for the sake of Allah and man should not be its slave. Otherwise, man who is the slave of wealth will be the cause of man's going to the Hereafter empty-handed.

According to Rumi, most people become slaves to worldly possessions. Like snakes they wait at the feet of wealth abasing themselves to a very low situation returning to the heavens empty-handed. If wealth is not spent in the way of Allah it has no value at all in the eyes of Rumi.

There is one example that is similar to the example of Qarun among the companions of the Prophet (ﷺ). There was a poor man named Thalabah among the companions who had a greed for wealth.

Hence, he came to the Prophet (ﷺ) to ask for his prayer that he become rich. The Prophet (ﷺ) politely refused this request by saying:

"Little amount of wealth for which you can give thanks to Allah is better than much wealth for which you cannot give enough thanks to Allah."

Thalabah gave up his desire for sometime but later he felt an even greater urge to be rich and came back to the Prophet (ﷺ) repeating the same request: O Messenger of Allah! Please pray to Allah so that I become rich!

This time the Prophet (ﷺ) gave him the following answer:

"Am I not a good example for you? I swear by Allah that if I wished those mountains would turn into gold and silver, and they would follow me wherever I go, but I did not want it."

Thalabah tried hard to give up this desire but could not get rid of the idea that if he was rich he would help the poor and receive great rewards from Allah." The call of the ego had overpowered him hence he came back to the Prophet (ﷺ) and said:

"I swear by Allah who sent you as a prophet, if he makes me rich I will protect the poor and fulfill my obligations."

Upon this insistence the Prophet (ﷺ) prayed: "O my Lord! Please give the amount of wealth that Thalabah desires from You."

Upon this prayer, Allah the Almighty gave great wealth to Thalabah. After a short while, he became very rich, his flocks of animals covered the hills of Madinah. However, Thalabah, who was called as the bird of the mosque thus far, started to neglect the mosque and came to the congregational prayers less than before. This continued until he was able to come to the mosque only on Fridays for the general congregational prayer, (which is the basic minimum for congregational prayer for a Muslim). This continued for a while but later he even forgot to come to the Friday prayers.

Having learned of this situation the Prophet (ﷺ) commented about him:

"What a pity for Thalabah, he destroyed himself (his pious life before becoming rich)."

The ignorance and heedlessness of Thalabah did not even stop here and continued until one day he said to the officials of the Prophet (ﷺ) who came to him in order to collect the alms-due from his wealth: (At that time the officials of the state used to collect the alms due in order to efficiently distribute it to the poor.)

"What you are doing is daytime robbery."

In that way he did not even give the minimum amount of charity that was prescribed by the Qur'an. He had forgotten all the promises he made that he would spend much of his wealth for the poor and the needy. Hence he became a hypocrite, one whose words and deeds contradict each other.

The Qur'an describes the psychology of such people in the following verses:

"And there are those of them who made a covenant with Allah: If He gives us out of His grace, we will certainly give alms and we will certainly be of the good. Yet when He gave them of His bounty, they hoarded it and turned away, averse." (Tawba, 9:75-76)

Thalabah, having ignored the advice of the Prophet (ﷺ) lost the Divine bliss and became a miserable person in the Hereafter since he was deceived by the glamour of transient wealth. Hence he deserved to be poor eternally. When he died in great pity the advice of the Prophet (ﷺ) was ringing clearly in his ears:

"Little amount of wealth for which you can give thanks to Allah is better than much wealth for which you cannot give enough thanks to Allah."

He did not heed the warnings of the Prophet (ﷺ) concerning the dangers of the wealth and died in a terrible situation in endless pain. He stupidly destroyed his eternal bliss in return for a short-lived happiness, of which he had thought of as an endless pleasure. (Ahmed Shahin, Tarihin Şeref Levhaları, p.27)

As understood from many life examples, man by his nature selfishly loves the riches of the world. The ego finds great satisfaction in gathering unlimited wealth. However, once one has been deceived by this satanic thought one will never be satisfied with what he attains. The following hadith succinctly explains the greedy nature of man:

If the son of Adam possessed two valleys of gold, he would covet the third Only earth can satisfy the hunger of the son of Adam...(Bukhari, Muslim)

With the increase in wealth there usually is a corresponding increase in greed to accumulate even more. Once a person is immersed in the love of worldly possessions then he/she loses all the humanistic values such as mercy, love and sacrifice. Giving charity becomes a very difficult thing with the ego saying: "Do not give now, wait until you become richer and then you can give even more in charity."

Such people lose their spiritual balance as well as the order of their bodies. Since they do not use the chance given to them in this world they become the object of the following hadith:

"Those who said "I will do it tomorrow" have utterly lost."

The above story of Thalabah is not only an example of man's greedy nature, it is also a good example for the terrible consequences of not respecting the good way of supplication and prayer. When the nature of one's destiny is forced, then these kinds of terrible results are inevitable. The Prophet (ﷺ) although knowing the fate of this man, still prayed for Thalabah in order to show his community a living example of the dangers of greediness. Therefore, when we ask something from Allah the Almighty we should not trust our mind very much and should add to our supplication, "If it is acceptable in the Divine sphere of things and if it is for our good, please accept our supplication." Otherwise, we can be damaged by not seeing the harm which is hidden in the seeming favor we desire. Supplication, like giving charity can change the conditional destiny (Qader-i Mukayyad) of man. However, we should not solely trust our rationality when we ask from Allah for the change of our destiny since it is not always good for us. Supplication is a favor from Allah and a commandment. However, when we fill our supplications with the desires of the ego and the rational mind, we should not insist that the contents of our supplications are correct and for our good. Hence we should add the phrase at the end of every supplication:

"O My Lord! Please fulfill my desire if it is for my good."

Using wealth in accordance with the Divine commandments can eliminate the dangers of greed. This is an obligation for the well being of societies and individuals both in this life and in the Hereafter.

IMPORTANT RULES OF PAYING ZAKAT

The Poor-due is paid at 2.5 % out of our wealth once in a lunar year.

The commandments of the Qur'an mostly involve a lunar year, which is 355 days. Most countries today use the solar calendar, which is 365 days hence this ten-day span should be added to the rate of Zakat. This will be approximately %2.6. In addition, in countries where high inflation exists the value of the alms due should be counted according to a stable value. In some countries there is almost a 100 %inflation rate. Hence, if we pay it according to our initial assessment of wealth but at the end of the year, the poor will receive only half of what we must pay.

Another important rule is that the alms due is paid to the individual only. Beneficiaries of donations such as mosques, schools, hospitals, are not entitled to receive this. We can help them with other kinds of charity. It must be known that the food we serve to the poor also cannot be accepted, since the poor cannot possess it.

The Qur'an clearly defines who can receive Zakat. In this way these people will be able to live like human beings without being degraded by having others look down on them. Islam also aims to prevent people from resorting to begging by providing for their essential needs.

One day a villager came to the Prophet (☼) and asked for financial help. The Prophet (☼) seeing that he was fit and strong asked him:

What do you have in your possession?

The man answered: I have a cotton bag and a bowl.

The Prophet advised him: Sell these two and buy an axe, cut wood from the forest and in this way you can earn your livelihood. (Abu Dawud, Kitâb al-zakât)

This Muslim followed the advice of the Prophet (☼) and in a short while he escaped his poverty.

Islam is a religion of balance. It does not forbid the needy from asking for help for their needs but it encourages them to be self-sufficient. For those who make asking and begging a habit the Qur'an says:

"And of them is he who defameth thee in the matter of alms. If they are given thereof they are content, and if they are not given thereof, behold! they are enraged." (Tauba: 9:58)

Such people lose their dignity and wish for an easy life. The

Prophet(ﷺ) did not like such people and advised them to work. One day a person came to the Prophet(ﷺ) asking to receive alms. In reply, the Prophet (ﷺ) stated:

Allah the Almighty, did not leave the beneficiaries of Zakat to the will of the people, not even to the will of the prophets. He named eight classes of people and said," if you fall into one of these groups you can take your share from the alms." (Bayhaki, Sunanu'l-Kubrâ, VII, 6)

The Prophet (ﷺ) showed great meticulousness when he distributed Zakat. At that time the Prophet (ﷺ) personally collected it from the rich and distributed it to those groups specified in the Qur'an. Of course, this does not mean that we cannot help people in any way we like but this is not counted as the obligatory alms due. One can spend money for other good purposes as a supererogatory act of charity. The Prophet (ﷺ) rejected giving alms to those who did not deserve it, but for the distribution of supererogatory charity he did not reject anyone. Since the Qur'an commands:

"Therefore the beggar drive not away," (Dhuha, 93:10)

The Prophet (ﷺ) states that it is the result of good moral characteristics that a Muslim should not leave those who open their hands (i.e. ask help) empty handed even if we only give one date. (Bukhari, Kitâb al-zakât)

Inspired by this hadith, my father Mûsâ Efendi, used to give charity even to those who made begging a trade and would say: "We should keep giving in order not to get too accustomed to not giving and becoming miserly."

Islam is a very balanced religion; on the one hand it advises the rich to donate generously for the poor and other good purposes, on the other hand it advises the poor person to work hard for his sustenance and not to resort to begging. Some people might think that so much encouragement for giving might create a class of parasites who live off the charity of the rich. In order to curb such an abuse of the mercy of others, Islam allows asking the help of others only in extremely difficult conditions. Asking from others degrades one's social status as well as dignity. Therefore the Prophet (ﷺ) conditioned many of his companions not to ask anything from anybody when he accepted their pledges.

However, it is the duty of good Muslims to search for the genuine needy people who do not like to ask people openly and are too shy to mention their financial difficulties. In the following hadith the Prophet (ﷺ) defines the poor as those who do not possess the financial capacity to meet their daily needs:

Narrated by Abu Huraira:

Allah's Apostle said, "The poor person is not the one who goes around to people and ask them for a mouthful or two (of food) or a date or two but the poor is that one who has not enough (money) to satisfy his needs and whose condition is not known to others, so that others may give him something in charity, and who does not beg of people." (*Bukhari, Volume 2, Book 24, Number 557*)

In this hadith the Prophet (ﷺ) warns us that those who go around asking people can get their essential needs hence we should concentrate on those who do not ask and patiently bear poverty. The Holy Qur'an emphasizes the significance of giving charity to those people in the following verse:

"(Charity is) for those in need, who, in Allah's cause are restricted (from travel), and cannot move about in the land, seeking (trade or work): the ignorant man thinks, because of their modesty, that they are free from want. Thou shalt know them by their (unfailing) mark: They beg not persistently from all and sundry. And whatever of good ye give, be assured Allah knoweth it well." (Baqara, 2:273)

As understood well from this verse those who pay alms should investigate those to whom they wish to give Zakat. If the giver of alms due does not do this and finds out later that the receiver of the charity was not really eligible for it, then he should pay the same amount again since the first was invalid. However, if he makes a mistake after making careful research, then he is excused and does not need to repay the alms due.

Secondly, we should give the ownership of the alms to the poor; the recipient should really possess it.

When paying the alms, the following principle is important. Firstly, our own body has a right over us, then our family members and then relatives come according to their closeness in blood ties. Islamic inheritance laws regard these ties as essential rules. The ones with rights also have different priorities: the first are those with closeness in blood ties and with urgency of need.

When we choose the recipients of alms we take into consideration the urgency of their need as well as their closeness to us. If a stranger and a relative have the same degree of urgency we prefer the relative but if the stranger has a more urgent need then he is to be preferred. Preferring one's relatives should not be taken to imply neglecting people who are really suffering in miserable conditions.

These principles show that Islam is a religion of mercy as well as a force which promotes a balanced life. The most beautiful fruit of faith in Allah is to show mercy to others. A heart that has no mercy for others, is in fact not a living heart, it is actually dead. The Basmalah (recitation of Bismillahir- Rahmanir-Raheem), the phrase that all Muslims recite when they start a new action, gives preference to the names of Allah that are related to His mercy: **"In the name of Allah, Most Gracious, Most Merciful."** (Fatiha, 1:1)

The first chapter of the Holy Qur'an also brings forth the attributes of Allah's mercy.

"Praise be to Allah, the Cherisher and Sustainer of the worlds; Most Gracious, Most Merciful" (Fatiha, 1:2-3)

In addition, the life stories of Sufis are full of merciful acts towards the creation of Allah.

The Prophet (ﷺ) in many of his sayings emphasized the significance of showing mercy in order to attain Allah's mercy. He said in one of his hadith that our mercy should engulf all of the creation:

"Show mercy to those on earth so those who are in Heaven will show mercy to you. (Abu Dâvud, Adab, 58)

Fulfillment of the financial commandments of Islam, such as zakat, optional charity and 'ushr are some of the most important keys in receiving this mercy.

'USHR

Ushr is the tax that Islam obliges farmers to pay on their harvest. This is one of the commandments of Islam that is almost forgotten by most Muslim farmers. Ushr means in Arabic one tenth, that is one tenth of the harvest should be given to the poor if the harvest is realized without irrigation. If the farmer spent extra resources such as on irrigation then he only needs to distribute 5% of the harvest to the poor.

Those who do not distribute ushr are as guilty as those who do not pay their Zakat. Giving some of the harvest means giving thanks to Allah for his providence. Those who do not give the rights of the poor, the traveler and other beneficiaries of the ushr, are in fact usurping the rights of the poor regarding wealth, which is in fact, the grace of Allah.

According to a narration there was a generous man in Yemen near Sana. He had date palm gardens and other fields yielding a good harvest. Every harvest season he would abundantly distribute the ushr to the poor. When he passed away his children became greedy and said to each other:

"- Our family is very large and we do not have much harvest. This year let us collect the harvest before the poor hear about it and we will keep all of it for ourselves."

Having decided this, they went to their garden the next morning. When they reached the garden, they could not recognize it and they asked each other: Did we come to the right place? Alas, their garden had been destroyed and blackened by lightening

When their father had distributed the ushr tax generously, Allah had blessed the garden and had given an abundant harvest.

The following true story from the Qur'an clearly shows us the grave consequences of being miserly and not fulfilling the commandment of ushr.

Lo! We have tried them as We tried the owners of the garden when they vowed that they would pluck its fruit the next morning, And made no exception (for the Will of Allah); Then there came on the (garden) a visitation from thy Lord, (which swept away) all

around, while they were asleep: So the (garden) became, by the morning, like a dark and desolate spot, (whose fruit had been gathered). And they cried out one unto another in the morning. So they went off, saying one unto another in low tones: No needy man shall enter it today against you. And in the morning they went, having the power to prevent. But when they saw the (garden), they said: "We have surely lost our way: (Qalam, 68:17-26)

Allah the Almighty teaches us a lesson that the ungrateful people who do not share with others what has been given to them by Allah will have a terrible end even in this world. Since Allah knows the secrets of the hearts, nothing is hidden from His knowledge.

Hadrat Rumi in the following verse very nicely clarifies the futility of love of wealth that causes mercilessness and greed:

"He dreams that he has wealth and is afraid of the thief who may carry off his sack of (gold).

When Death pulls his ear and makes him start up from slumber, then he falls mocking at his fears." (Mas. III, 2640-41)

The following verse is also an indication of the guilt and pity that the miserly people will feel when they are resurrected in the Hereafter as they wake up from a deep sleep:

"And spend something (in charity) out of the substance which We have bestowed on you, before Death should come to any of you and he should say, "O my Lord! Why didst Thou not give me respite for a little while? I should then have given (largely) in charity, and I should have been one of the doers of good." (Munâfiqûn, 63:10)

However, at that time it will be too late to fulfill the opportunity that has been given to us in this world. While this verse informs us of the terrible end for those who have not fulfilled their financial duties towards society, it also implies that we must use the chance given to us and give generously in charity.

Spending (for the sake of Allah - infâq), is mentioned in the Qur'an more than 200 times and this emphasis shows that a good believer is the one who dedicates his wealth and his life to Allah. The Prophet (ﷺ)

used to meet people from Madinah secretly when he started preaching Islam. Twice he met the groups coming from Madinah and took pledges from them. In the second Aqaba pledge meeting, when Abdullah b. Rawaha asked the Prophet (ﷺ):

"- O Prophet what do you lay down as conditions in Allah's name and for yourself in order to accept our pledge."

"- My condition, in the name of Allah, is that you should worship Him, and not associate partners with Him. My conditions are that you will protect me as you protect your own lives and properties."

The people of Madinah asked again:

"If we do that what are our rewards?"

The Prophet (ﷺ) answered: "Paradise!"

Being very happy with the reward, the people of Madinah said: "What a good and profitable bargain. We will never break our promise and we never wish that others break their promises to you (on these conditions)." (Ibn Kathir, Tafsir, II, 406)

Upon this conversation, Allah the Almighty, sent down the following verse:

" Lo! Allah hath bought from the believers their lives and their wealth because the Garden will be theirs: they shall fight in the way of Allah and shall slay and be slain. It is a promise binding on Him in the Torah and the Gospel and the Qur'an. Who fulfilleth His covenant better than Allah? Rejoice then in your bargain that ye have made, for that is the supreme triumph." (Tawba, 9:111)

How does Allah buy our lives and properties? Martyrdom; giving our life for the sake of Allah is, as a matter of fact, selling it to Allah. Sumayya, the first person who was killed for her belief in Islam gave her life freely in the path of Allah. Thus, she bought her share in paradise and she occupied the throne in the hearts of believers, waiting for Judgment Day in order to receive her great reward. Following her example, we should turn to charity with our full heart.

In the battle of the Dardanelles (Gallipoli), the Turkish army even did not have enough bullets but by freely sacrificing their lives, they defeated the enemy. There are many other examples in history, that those who sacrifice their lives and wealth in the way of Allah will eventually become victorious.

The selling of wealth to Allah is achieved through giving charity. Allah the Almighty, counting the attributes of Allah-fearing people says: "This is the Book; in it is guidance sure, without doubt, to those who fear Allah; Who believe in the Unseen, are steadfast in prayer, and spend out of what We have provided for them." (Baqara, 2:2-3)

Charity is of many kinds. Charity begins with giving out of what is at hand. Giving even half of a date is considered as an act of charity and even this small amount of charity protects the believer from hell-fire. The Prophet (ﷺ) considers all Muslims as rich in the sense that there is something that all Muslims can give in one way or another. The Prophet (ﷺ) informs us that glorifying Allah, commanding what is good, helping those who suffer from injustice, counselling the believers, giving happiness to the hearts of Muslims, to remove things from the road that are harmful to any passers-by and so on, are all considered as acts of charity. The real richness according to Islam lies in the heart of the Muslim. People are only as rich as they feel. The smile of those who are rich in their hearts is also considered as a charitable act. Those who are rich in their hearts are happy and distribute happiness to their friends. What charity can be better than giving happiness to those who are around us? On the other hand, there is no cure for those who are poor in their hearts. In other words, real richness does not lie in possessing much wealth; it is the richness in the heart. Since the real Muslims are rich in their hearts, they give charity from what they possess. Charity is the perfect manifestation of a believer's sensitivity to his feelings of mercy and self-sacrifice.

The lives of the companions of the Prophet (ﷺ) are full of such examples. One of the most striking examples of self-sacrifice is manifested in Hadrat Omar's life. When his army opened Jerusalem to Islam, he set off together with his slave to receive the keys of the city. They were riding the camel by taking turns. When they approached the city it was the slave's turn to get on the camel. The slave did not want to enter Jerusalem riding while his master was walking. However, Omar who was rich in heart insisted that the slave should use his turn, so Omar entered the town on foot.

Another example can be seen in the life of Hadrat Ali, the fourth caliph and son-in-law of the Prophet (ﷺ). All in the family were fasting but they had very little food to break their fast. However, a poor person came to them in the evening and asked for some food. They gave all their food to this poor person and all went to sleep hungry. The next day near sunset when the time to break fast approached an orphan arrived asking for some food. Again they gave their food. The following day they finally had some food to eat but a slave came asking for food. Performing the same charity again they showed the highest example of self-sacrifice and charity.

This generosity of heart was shown by the companions even with their last breath. At the battle of Yarmuk, a man was offering water to three companions who were injured in the fight. Each one of them refused to drink and offered the water to his wounded compatriot hence the water circulated among them but none of them drank since they all passed away before the water came back.

These are the highest examples of giving charity and called îthâr in Arabic. Îsâr is more than giving charity, it is the preference of others over your rights; it is to give what you need to others. This kind of charity is almost non-existent in modern societies today. People simply do not understand the significance of this much generosity. However, if we contemplate what the world would be like if every individual considered the well being of others more than his own, we would see that we would be able to live the life of paradise in this world. Therefore, we should encourage ordinary Muslims to give their obligatory alms due and to increase this amount even more as voluntary charity. In addition, we should carry out the distribution of charity through institutions and organizations that work professionally. This can be achieved through training sincere people who are hard working and self-sacrificing. It is also a duty incumbent upon the Ummah (Muslim nation) to establish

215

hospitals, dormitories for those who have no accommodation and soup kitchens.

In short, giving charity generously should be an essential characteristic of a believer. The following verse clearly considers giving charity as an inseparable feature of a Muslim:

"Those who spend (freely), whether in prosperity or in adversity; who restrain (their) anger, and pardon (all) men; - for Allah loves those who do good."(Al-i Imran 3:134)

Jafar as-Sâdik, who is an important figure from the offspring of the Prophet's grandsons, manifested all the qualities of a believer that are mentioned in the above verse. He had a slave that looked after the housework. One day he brought soup to Jafar (may Allah be pleased with him) but spilled it on him. As his entire garment was spoiled by the soup, Jafar looked directly at him. The slave realizing his displeasure said:

"O my Master! Allah the Almighty describes the believers in the Qur'an as those who restrain their anger, and recited the verse above."

Upon hearing it, Jafar said: "I have restrained my anger."

This time the slave read the second part of the verse saying: "Allah the Almighty, states that good believers pardon people's mistakes".

Jafar said: "I have forgiven your mistake".

Upon this the slave stated: "Allah states in the Qur'an that He loves those who give with benevolence".

Upon hearing this nice answer, Jafar said: "You can go now as a free man, I have freed you".

In that way he applied all the commandments of the verse in his life and set a good example for the rest of the Ummah.

As the Prophet (ﷺ) stated, a sinful woman was forgiven due to her mercy for a thirsty dog by giving it water. She attained paradise due to this simple of act of mercy while on the other hand, another woman was destined for hell for her unmerciful act to a cat, by walling it up and allowing it to starve. These are important examples and indications as to how a believer should behave towards others. A believer should be very merciful, self-sacrificing, and generous to others.

The real generosity, which will be acceptable in the sight of Allah, is the one that one gives from one's valuable and beloved possessions. If one gives charity from valueless things, this will not be regarded as worthy.

In the Time of Happiness, (the age of the Prophet (ﷺ)) people accommodated the poor companions in the Mosque. They were called the People of the Bench and their sole duty was to study Islam, hence they could not earn their livelihood. The Prophet (ﷺ) and his rich companions would supply their needs including food. Some of the companions sent them spoiled dates as food. The People of the Bench were obliged to eat these spoiled dates due to excessive hunger. Upon this sad incident the following divine warning arrived from Allah the Almighty:

"O ye who believe! Give of the good things which ye have (honorably) earned, and of the fruits of the earth which We have produced for you, and do not even aim at getting anything which is bad, in order that out of it ye may give away something, when ye yourselves would not receive it except with closed eyes. And know that Allah is Free of all wants, and worthy of all praise. (Baqara: 2, 267)

In another verse, Allah the Almighty informs us that in order to be close to Allah we should give charity from our beloved possessions.

"By no means shall you attain to righteousness until you spend (benevolently) out of what you love; and whatever thing you spend, Allah surely knows it." (Al-i Imrân, 3:92)

When this verse was revealed the companions of the Prophet (ﷺ) started racing with each other to give their favorite and most loved possessions. The companions who were listening to the Prophet (ﷺ) felt this verse in the depths of their inner worlds. They were reckoning themselves about being able to give what they liked the most. Suddenly a companion stood up. This companion whose face was bright with the light of faith was Abu Talha (may Allah be pleased with him). He owned a big garden with six hundred date trees in it that was very close to the Prophet's Masjid and he loved that garden very much. He used to invite the Prophet (ﷺ) to his garden often and get his blessing.

217

Abu Talha said: "O Messenger of Allah! The most beloved to me in my property is this garden in the city that you also know. Right at this moment, I give it to the Messenger of Allah for the sake of Allah. You can dispose it the way you like and give it to the poor." After he finished his words he went to the garden to carry out this beautiful decision. When Abu Talha reached the garden he found his wife sitting under the shade of a tree. Abu Talha did not enter the garden.

His wife asked: "O Abu Talha! Why are you waiting outside? Come on in!" Abu Talha said: "I can not enter inside, you should also take your belongings and leave." Upon this unexpected answer his wife asked in surprise: "Why, O Abu Talha? Isn't this garden ours? "No, from now on this garden belongs to the poor people of Madina," he said and gave the news of the good tidings in the verse and told excitedly about the charity he made.

His wife asked: "Did you give it on behalf of the two of us or just yourself?"

He answered: "On behalf of us." He heard the following words from his wife in peace: "May Allah be pleased with you, O Abu Talha! I used to think about the same thing when I saw the poor people around us, but I could not find the courage to tell you. May Allah accept our charity. I am leaving the garden and coming with you, too!" It is not difficult to predict the climate of happiness that would surround the world if this moral quality was rooted in the souls of people.

The commentators of the Qur'an explain the Arabic word al-Birr, meaning righteousness, the highest point of charity, as paradise, the mercy of Allah and His pleasure with us. The same word is explained in another verse in the Qur'an:

"It is not righteousness that ye turn your faces towards the east or west; but it is righteousness- to believe in Allah and the Last Day, and the Angels, and the Book, and the Messengers; to spend of your substance, out of love for Him, for your kin, for orphans, for the needy, for the wayfarer, for those who ask, and for the ransom of slaves; to be steadfast in prayer, and practice regular charity; to fulfill the contracts which ye have made; and to be firm and patient, in suffering

and adversity, and throughout all periods of panic. Such are the people of truth, the Allah-fearing. (Baqara, 2:177)

Hence, those who attained to the level of al-Birr in giving charity in reality attained all other good qualities as well. Emphasizing this fact the Prophet (ﷺ) stated:

"Whoever applies this verse in his life Allah will be granted perfection in his faith." (Nasafi, Madârik al-Tanzîl, I, 249)

In these days, brotherhood and solidarity have been lost, on the contrary hatred and enmity has increased in the society due to ignoring the problems of the poor. In order to fight these negative feelings we need to declare a campaign of charity and donation. We must imagine that we could be in the shoes of the needy. Hence, giving charity to the poor is in fact to give thanks for the favors of Allah upon us. The great Sufi Aziz Mahmud Hudayi invited even the kings to the campaign of giving charity. In his letter to Sultan Selim the Third he wrote:

"Like your grandfather Suleiman the Magnificient who brought the water to the people of Istanbul from faraway springs (called Istirancalar) you must supply wood to the poor this winter."

Fighting against poverty and the campaign to raise charity is not only important for us but it is also very important for our family. As we train our youngsters to perform their prayers at an early age, in the same vein, we must train our children in order for them to give charity and to share the sorrows of others. This is an obligation that we should fulfill when our children are young, otherwise they will not be able to give charity as an adult. They should grow up keeping in mind that wealth in reality belongs to Allah.

Those who want to be upright in Islam should never stop giving charity in the path of Allah even if their means are restricted. We should shoulder those who are in a miserable condition or at least we should pray for their well-being. Even sharing their sorrows emotionally is considered as an act of worship in the sight of Allah the Almighty. We should also keep in mind that in these times the greatest act of charity is to train people who will work in the institutions of charity and spend for these kinds of institutions. As a great thinker once said:

"The difference between the developed and undeveloped countries is a bunch of well educated people"

The world is really thirsty for these kinds of educated people. If Islam is in a horrible condition and Muslims are suffering from injustices the reason is that we do not have this high quality of people. We must shake laziness off from ourselves as we start to struggle to exemplify what it is to be a true Muslim. Doing this is possible only if we sacrifice for the good of the people.

Establishing charitable foundations institutionalizes this sacrificing and giving in charity. Establishing foundations means to dedicate wealth for the service of Allah and making it eternal. The perfection of Islam can be reached through showing mercy and love towards His creation with a smiling face. To sacrifice both our wealth and lives in the way of Allah is, as a matter of fact, to buy paradise.

One's wealth and children possess the highest capacity to prevent one from the path of Allah. In order to warn from these dangers Allah the Almighty states in the Qur'an:

"Your possessions and your children are only a trial, and Allah it is with Whom is a great reward." (Taghabun, 64:15)

"O you who believe! let not your wealth, or your children, divert you from the remembrance of Allah; and whoever does that, these are the losers. (Munafiqûn, 63:9)

"Therefore be careful of (your duty to) Allah as much as you can, and hear and obey and spend, it is better for your souls; and whoever is saved from the greediness of his soul, these it is that are the successful." (Taghabun, 64:16)

"If ye lend unto Allah a goodly loan, He will double it for you and will forgive you, for Allah is Responsive, Clement," (Taghabun, 64:17)

As may be understood from the above verses, according to Islam the poor and the weak are a trial for the rich in terms of whether they will fulfill their duties or not. The doors of Paradise will be open for the rich through the prayers of the poor. Through charity, wealth is not allowed to be a cancerous cell in the body. Hence, the foundations of charity are monuments of mercy and the best places where charity is distributed. They are a bridge between the rich and the poor. Through the existence and abundance of these kinds of institutions the feelings of resentment and hatred between the rich and the poor will not find a fertile soil for growth.

It is worth noting that our ancestors, the Ottomans, established hundreds of thousands of charitable foundations. Although many of them have been plundered in recent history, nevertheless 26,798 still are standing on their own. The Ottomans, who practiced Islam sincerely, demonstrated to the world the endless mercy of Islam. This mercy was so limitless that it not only included their fellow human beings but also reached to the animal kingdom. Some of these foundations are dedicated to animals that are injured or could not migrate to their habitats in winter months. The network of foundations surrounded the society and treated all kinds of social problems.

In other words, charitable foundations are manifestations of the responsibility that Muslims feel towards the society. They are an outcome of the belief that we should love creation for the sake of Creator. Allah the Almighty, named all the facilities of life as a trust given to man for a limited period. Wealth, offspring, and health are all given to man as a trust and they should be used in the way of Allah. If they are used in His way they will bring blessings and good rewards in the Hereafter.

When the companions of the Prophet (ﷺ) heard the commandment of Allah with regards to giving charity they brought whatever they had to the Prophet (ﷺ). The verse **"Do they not know that Allah accepts repentance from His servants and takes the alms, "** (Tawba, 9:104) gave them the greatest motivation for giving charity wholeheartedlly.

We should also realize that charity may not only be given materially. Whatever Allah has given us should be used in the way of Allah. The companions of the Prophet (ﷺ) donated their lives and their wealth to invite people to Islam. They reached the far ends of the world in their time in order to spread the religion of Allah. Qusam son of Abbâs (the prophet's uncle) and Muhammad son of Uthman (Caliph and son-in-law of the Prophet) gave the best examples of personal charity in spending their lives in order to spread Islam. They traveled as far as Samarqand to spread the light of Islam. As a result of their sacrifice, this area has produced some of the greatest scholars of Islam such as Bukhari, Imâm Qâsânî, Imâm Tirmidhi, Shâh Naqshbend, and many others.

Similarly, today the greatest charity is to practice Islam fully and wholeheartedly to present it as a way of life.

THE ETIQUETTE OF SPENDING

When one gives Zakat and sadaqat (compulsory and voluntary charity)it is very important to act correctly. The one who gives should thank the one who receives the charity since through him the giver is receiving great rewards from Allah by fulfilling his duty. The donor is also protected from calamities and harm due to his charitable acts and it constitutes a shield against all sorts of distress.

The Qur'an teaches us the following good manners when one gives charity:

"O you who believe! Do not make your charity worthless by reproach and injury, like him who spends his property to be seen of men and does not believe in Allah and the last day; so his parable is as the parable of a smooth rock with earth upon it, then a heavy rain falls upon it, so it leaves it bare; they shall not be able to gain anything of what they have earned; and Allah does not guide the unbelieving people." (Baqara, 2:264)

Alongside advocating giving charity this verse very clearly teaches us how to be careful in the act of giving it. In other words, if the donators belittle the poor or break their hearts with harsh words or acts, Allah will not place value on their charitable acts. When one helps someone there should be no expectations and it should be done for the sake of Allah only.

It is narrated on the authority of Abu Dharr that the Messenger of Allah (may peace be upon him) observed: There are three persons with whom Allah would neither speak on the Day of Resurrection, nor would look at them nor would absolve them and there is a painful chastisement for them. The Messenger of Allah (may peace be upon him) repeated it three times. Abu Dharr remarked: They failed and they lost; who are these persons, O Messenger of Allah? Upon this, he (the Holy) Prophet) observed: They are: the dragger of his lower garment (out of pride), the one who reminds about being obligated to, the seller of goods by false oath. (Muslim, Imân, 1,192)

All these show that those who lay obligation on the receivers of charity and those who hurt the feelings of the poor will be punished by Allah. Hence, these bad qualities are grave sins in giving charity. Allah looks at people's hearts and values them and as Rumi has stated: "Give your existence and wealth in charitable acts so as to buy people's hearts. The supplications of their hearts on your behalf will enlighten your dark grave."

According to Rumi the poor are an opportunity for the rich to express their gratitude to Allah. As Allah bestowed upon them favor they can similarly reflect on Allah's bounty to the poor. Hence their hearts should not be broken:

"Inasmuch as the beggar is the mirror of bounty, take care! Breath is hurtful to the face of the mirror." (Mesa. 2748)

The poor are mirrors of Allah's bounty, (Mesa. 2748) since the poor turn their faces to charity loving people and by supplying them with an opportunity to donate for the sake of Allah, the poor in fact prepare the path of salvation for them. In addition, the poor develop love and respect for the rich due to their generosity. In that way, the mercy and love residing both in the rich as well as in the poor flourish.

In other words, Allah made the poor function as mirrors for the rich so that they can see their generosity. Rumi describes the terrible end of the heartless rich in the following way: "Those good-hearted rich people who lost their existence in Allah became the manifestation of Allah's generosity. Having a share in the Divine generosity they have eradicated their existence in pure generosity. Except for those of them who do not attach their hearts to worldly possessions, the rich will be the poor in spirituality. Their external riches are but the lifeless paintings of their

223

unfortunate states. These are people who are heedless of reality and with no souls. Do not approach them to become friends with them; do not throw bones to pictures of dogs"!

"Such people are slaves to their interests. They are ignorant of the Divine thirst."

Rumi warns us not to befriend such people: "Do not put the plate of food in front of the dead. Such people will be miserable beggars in the Hereafter.

The dervish that wants bread is fish on land. He has the form of a fish but he is fleeing from the sea. He loves Allah for the sake of gain: His soul is not in love with Allah's Excellence and Beauty." (Mesa. I, 2750-55)

In sum, we should not be cheated away from Divine sustenance in the Hereafter by the glamour of worldly pleasures such as having nice food and drink. If we do not want to lose in the Hereafter, we should be surrounding the needy with our generosity.

Another important principle is to give charity in secrecy, that is, not to reveal those who receive charity. When charity is given in openness to the poor, they will lose their feelings of shyness and in time they will be accustomed to asking help from others and become lazy. They will lose their desire to work. Secondly, giving it openly causes the donor to feel pride and conceit. Hence, giving charity in secret is good both for the one who receives as well as for the one who donates.

However, at times, in order to urge others to give charity, one can donate in open so as to be a good example to others. In this way, ordinary people are urged to follow suit. Therefore, the Qur'an states:

"If you give alms openly, it is well, and if you hide it and give it to the poor, it is better for you; and this will do away with some of your evil deeds; and Allah is Aware of what you do. (Baqara, 2:271)

The commentators on the Qur'an infer from this verse that the obligatory alms due should be given openly, but the supererogatory acts of donation should be fulfilled secretly.

The best way of giving charity is to give with the right hand so that even the left hand does not have any knowledge of this giving. As has been made clear in the hadith, such charity loving people will be under the shade of the Divine Throne on the Day of Judgment. Our ancestors also acted in this as far as giving charity is concerned. The Ottoman Sultan, Fatih the Conqueror put forward the following conditions in his charter of foundation:

"I am Sultan Fatih Mohammed, the conqueror of Istanbul. I have handed over my 136 shops, that I have earned with the work of my hands, as a charitable foundation with the following conditions:

In the soup kitchen that I built in the complex near to the mosque, the widows of the martyrs and their children, the poor of Istanbul will be fed. However, those who cannot come to the soup kitchen to have food for some reason, their food should be taken to their homes in closed containers after it is dark so as they will not be humiliated for receiving charity."

As may be clearly seen in this charter, Sultan Fatih acted in a most sensitive way to protect the feelings and honor of the poor, and made rules that served this purpose. The subjects of such a king did not behave but like him. They would put the charity money in envelopes into the stones of charity (these are stones with holes on their top so as the charitable people put their financial donations inside and the poor would take them whenever they needed, these stones are placed in the mosques and the poor would take the money without having to be ashamed of anyone.

This is the highest mode of good behaviour since the rich do not know who has received it and the poor do not know who has donated the money. In that way the rich are protected from being proud over the poor and the poor are protected from the feeling of indebtedness to the donor.

The main purpose of religion after faith in Allah is to produce good charactered people with deep understanding and to produce a peaceful society. Such a perfect society can be realized when the individuals' hearts are merciful and caring, leading them to give voluntary charity as well as the obligatory alms.

We are living in the kingdom of Allah with the sustenance bestowed on us by His grace. Those who neglect the acts of worship that demand financial sacrifice, do not they know that everything belongs to Allah and from whom they are withholding His wealth.

Love grows through sacrifice in the path of the beloved. According to the level of his love, the lover sacrifices for the beloved. Sometimes the lover even gives his life in order to please his beloved. Since charity is given for the sake of Allah, He states in the Qur'an that it is He who takes the charity through the hands of the poor:

"Know they not that Allah doth accept repentance from His votaries and receives their gifts of charity, and that Allah is verily He, the Oft-Returning, Most Merciful?" (Tawba, (9:104)

In order to emphasize the same truth the Prophet (ﷺ) states:

"Undoubtedly, when a donator gives charity, Allah is the first to receive it even before the needy, and then He gives it to the poor. "(Munawî, Kanz al-Hakâik)

Therefore, the most important characteristic of charity is that it should be given sincerely for the sake of Allah. Those who give charity should never feel proud or superior over those who benefit from their donations; they should not expect them to feel grateful. Such negative feelings will erase the good rewards of donations. On the contrary, those who give should thank those who receive their charity. Only in this way will Allah accept our worship of giving charity. The following verse describing the noble ways of charitable acts by Ali and Fatimah teach us the code of behavior that we should follow:

"And they feed, for the love of Allah, the indigent, the orphan, and the captive,- (Saying),"We feed you for the sake of Allah alone: no reward do we desire from you, nor thanks. "We only fear a Day of distressful Wrath from the side of our Lord." But Allah will deliver them from the evil of that Day, and will shed over them a Light of Beauty and (blissful) Joy." (Insân, 76:8-11)

If the donors have such sublime feelings, those who receive their charity also benefit from their feelings. Their good intentions and sincerity is reflected in the hearts of the poor. If they do not really deserve the charity after receiving it, they change their bad ways. The following incident narrated by the Prophet (&) exemplifies this positive transformation:

Allah's Apostle (&) said, "A man said that he would give something in charity. He went out with his offering of charity and unknowingly gave it to a thief. The next morning the people said that he had given his charity to a thief. (On hearing that) he said, "O Allah! All the praises are for you. I will give alms again." And so he again went out with his alms and (unknowingly) gave it to an adulteress. The next morning the people said that he had given his alms last night to an adulteress. The man said, "O Allah! All the praises are for you. I gave my alms to an adulteress. I will give alms again." So he went out with his alms again and (unknowingly) gave it to a rich person. (The people) next morning said that he had given his alms to a wealthy person. He said, "O Allah! All the praises are for you. (I have given alms) to a thief, to an adulteress and to a wealthy man." Then someone came and said to him, "The alms which you gave to the thief might make him abstain from stealing, and that given to the adulteress might make her abstain from illegal sexual intercourse (adultery), and that given to the wealthy man might make him take a lesson from it and spend his wealth which Allah has given him, in Allah's cause." (Bukhari, zakat, *Volume 2, Book 24, Number 502)*

It is interesting that the manifestation of the meaning of this hadith is seen in the life of a friend of Allah, namely Sâmî Efendi, narrated by Mûsâ Efendi:

One day someone signaled for us to stop the car and when we stopped he asked:

"O hadji, father give me money to buy cigarettes for the sake of Allah." His friends did not want to give him money. However, our sheikh said: "Since he asked our help it is better to give." The poor man, when he saw this kind behavior, told them he had changed his mind, and would buy bread with this money and not cigarettes. And he left us with great pleasure.

Out of curiosity, one of the companions of the Sheikh in order to see how this man spent the money, followed him. To his surprise, the man, as he promised bought bread with the money.

This is a living example of how charity which is only given for the sake of Allah changes the hearts of those who receive it. Therefore, when we give charity we should scrutinize our feelings more than the one who benefits from our donation.

O my Lord! Please make your limitless mercy the never-ending treasure of our hearts.

Amen!

THE REQUIREMENTS OF ZAKAT

Zakat on wealth has five conditions:

1- To be Muslim, to be sane, to be free and to reach the age of maturity,

2- To have excess wealth called nisâb, more than necessary for the basic necessities of life, (house, food, car and so on) for a year,

3- The possession should be increasing in value,

4- The passing of a lunar year over the wealth and,

5- Valid ownership of the property or wealth.

The kind of property for which alms due has been required:

The basic limit of giving alms due changes according to the property one has and this limit in sheep and goat is forty, in cattle it is thirty and camels five. In order to pay alms due on gold, it should weigh at least 81 grams and for silver the amount is 561 grams. When the amount of wealth and property reaches this level one needs to pay alms due as described in the law books of Islam.

The recipients of Alms due:

Allah the Almighty clearly explains those who are eligible to receive the alms due.

"Alms are only for the poor and the needy, and the officials (appointed) over them, and those whose hearts are made to incline (to

truth) and the (ransoming of) captives and those in debts and in the way of Allah and the wayfarer; an ordinance from Allah; and Allah is knowing, Wise. (Tawba, 9:60)

1- Poor: According to Islam anyone who has insufficient wealth to require payment of the alms due is poor. So anyone who cannot give alms due can receive it. Even if such people are employed they can still benefit from it due to their needs.

2- Indigent: According to Islam those who do not have sufficient food for one day are called indigent (miskîn). Such needy ones are living in deep poverty like homeless people.

3- The collectors of the alms due who are employed by the state

4- And those whose hearts are inclined (to truth)

5-Slaves: Alms due may be paid to slaves so that they may gain freedom from their masters. But today there are no legally acquired slaves.

6- Those in debt are people whose debts exceed their possessions.

7- Those in the way of Allah include the fighter in the path of Islam, the students and those who were left without money on their way to pilgrimage.

8- The wayfarer: Those who lost their money during their travel and have been left helpless. Such people can benefit from alms even if they are rich in their hometown.

On the other hand, there are also some people that are not qualified to benefit from the alms due. One cannot give to ones father, mother, grandparents, son, and daughter. The close relatives should be taken care of from other kinds of charity. Also, those who are rich and those who are non-Muslims cannot receive the alms due.

'Ushr: The alms of crops:

Farmers should pay alms on their crops. According to the Hanafi School of Islamic Law one needs to give one-tenth of the crops each time they are harvested. If a body of land yields a crop more than once, then each time the alms should be given. The guardians of an insane person or the executors of the will of a recently dead person should pay 'ushr out of their crops. However, 'ushr is paid on long-lasting storable products such as wheat and barley and is not paid on quickly perishable items such as fruits and vegetables.

If the land is irrigated through natural ways such as from rivers or rainwater the amount of 'ushr is one tenth. However, if the farmer has to pay money for irrigation, then he only gives one twentieth of the crop. 'Ushr is paid out of the whole crop and the farming costs are not extracted from the value of the crops.

If 'ushr is paid on the crops there is no need to pay it again on their products after they have been processed. Examples here would be olives and seeds that are made into oils.

'Ushr is given when the crops are completely harvested. Before they are collected one is not required to pay its alms. However, one can pay close to the harvesting time when the crops are quite ripe.

If one collects some of the crops before the harvest time, it should be made up afterwards. Such as if one collected ten kilos of grapes, one should pay a kilo of more alms after the full harvest.

All these kinds of alms show that Islam does not leave the poor and needy to the mercy of the law. One needs to pay these financial obligations as a part of worshipping Allah. In this way Islam wants to create a balanced and just society.

PILGRIMAGE TO MECCA

A personal as well as a social act of worship
that gives life to the hearts

"In it are clear signs, the standing plase of Ibrahim, and whoever enters it shall be secure, and pilgrimage to the House is incumbent upon men for the sake of Allah, (upon) every one who is able to undertake the journey to it; and whoever disbelieves, then surely Allah is Self-sufficient, above any need of the worlds." (Âl-i İmrân, 3:97)

$\mathcal{P}$ilgrimage is the fifth pillar of Islam and it is a duty that has been continuing to resurrect the hearts of the believers from the first prophet Adam (a.s.) to the last Prophet Muhammad (ﷺ). It is a sublime way of worship making us realize the secret of the words" die before you die."

Pilgrimage is not a new invention of Islam, prior to Islam pilgrimage was established in Mecca. However, the Arabs had changed it into a kind of immoral ceremony. The tribe of Quraish who had an eminent place among other Arab tribes used to worship at the Ka'aba dressed in a normal way. However, the other Arabic tribes both men and women, used to visit the Ka'aba and circumambulate around it naked. It was up to the Quraish tribe to cover them and dress them, and if they do not give clothing to the visitors, they would continue to worship in a naked state. Also, these people used to sacrifice animals to spread their blood on the walls of the Ka'aba. Instead of using the meat of the sacrifices in a beneficial way, they used to burn their flesh. Islam erased all these evil pilgrimage rites that were made up by the Arabs and many other superstitious acts. According to Islam, the main purpose behind the acts of all worship is to remember Allah, to ask His forgiveness and to glorify His words. Islam, by removing the superstitions that were added by the Arabs purified the Hajj returning it to its original pure form.

Pilgrimage possesses many benefits for the believers both in this world and in the next. Allah's limitless mercy manifests itself in the times of pilgrimage in these sacred lands. Those Muslims, who are engulfed in the mercy and forgiveness of Allah, meet each other in an atmosphere of love and respect and establish bonds of brotherhood among themselves.

Through Hajj we take lessons from the submission of the prophets Abraham (a.s.) and Ishmael (a.s.) and can appreciate their strong trust in Allah. As related in the Qur'an, when Abraham (a.s.) received the commandment to sacrifice his son for the sake of Allah, he submitted to the Divine Will. In the same vein, Ishmael (a.s.) stoned Satan who wanted to urge him to revolt against his father and escape from being slaughtered. As Ishmael (a.s.) slaughtered the Satan, we should stone our low desires and ego. The Hajj is also an enormous gathering of different nations and different colors that reminds us of the Day of Judgment, where people will be gathered before the Divine court without discrimination of color and nationality. This shocking scene will break the barriers of race and nationality, making all of humanity brothers and sisters, hence making the bond of faith as the strongest one among all other bonds.

In Hajj, all the Muslims wear white seamless garments, replacing their normal garments. This symbolizes the soul's separation from the dress of the ego and its elevation over the human weaknesses, the low desires of the flesh.

The place in which the Hajj is performed has also a special place in the lives of Muslims. These are holy places in terms of the Divine blessings and spirituality, possessing Divine signs. In these places, one is always reminded of the limitless mercy of Allah and His endless blessings. The Qur'an describes the holiness of these Divine climates as the signs of Allah and alternatively as the sacred places of Allah.

Another purpose behind the pilgrimage is that the pilgrim experiences the same things that the companions and the Prophet (ﷺ) lived through in these holy lands. These holy lands that were watered by the tears of the lovers of Allah, from Adam (a.s.) to Muhammad (ﷺ), engulf so many recollections of the Holy Prophet (ﷺ) and his companions. Those who attentively fulfill the rites of the Hajj, as a matter of fact, follow in the footsteps of these holy persons.

In the holy lands, we remember the prayers of the previous prophets of Allah, such as Abraham (a.s.) who said: **"Our Lord! Make of us Muslims, bowing to Thy (Will), and of our progeny a people Muslim, bowing to Thy (will); and show us our place for the celebration of (due) rites; and turn unto us (in Mercy); for Thou art the Oft-Returning, Most Merciful.** (Baqara, 2:128)

In this way, we repeat the same prayers as they have made and receive the blessings of Allah when we are blessed by the acceptance of our supplications.

The Muslims are always burning with desire to visit these holy lands. The poets wrote their best poetry about these lands. One of them addressing the morning breeze sings:

O the morning breeze! If one day you pass through the holy lands, take my greetings to the Prophet (ﷺ) of man and jinn.

Those who could not afford to visit these places would send their greetings through the winds. They would see off those who were going on pilgrimage with their best prayers.

In particular, the friends of Allah who could not control their love for these lands, would often go and pray in these holy lands through the miracle of tayy al-makan, meaning that the long distances were folded up for them and they would reach these lands in a few seconds.

Some of the lovers of Allah even carried those who had no means to go for Hajj in their miraculous ways. The following story is a well-known one among the Sufis, through which the great Sufi master Azîz Mahmûd Hudâî turned to Sufism.

At that time Hudâî was the judge of Bursa, an important Ottoman town. One day an interesting court case was presented to him. A woman came to him complaining:

"O Honorable Judge! My husband intends to go to Hajj every year but due to poverty he could never set out for the journey. He was very insistent to go to Hajj this year as well, but he could not. However, a few days before pilgrimage time he disappeared and came back five or six days later claiming that he visited the holy lands and became a pilgrim. How is it possible to be a pilgrim in such a short time? I want to get a divorce from such a great liar."

In order to check this story out, Hudayî summoned the husband to the court and asked him whether his wife's reports about him were correct or not. The husband answered:

" Honorable Judge! Whatever my wife reported about me is correct. I have really gone for pilgrimage. I have even met some other pilgrims from Bursa and I entrusted with them some of my possessions so they could bring them back home."

The judge was shocked, and asked the husband:

"How is it possible that you went on pilgrimage and came back in less then a week?" Since at that time, with even the fastest means of transportation, it was a long trip, taking many months.

The man answered: "Sir! I was very sad at being unable to go on pilgrimage. I had gone to visit a friend of Allah, Mehmed Efendi and told him of my plight. He told me to close my eyes and when I opened them again I was there at the Ka'aba".

The judge, who had never witnessed such a strange case in his life before, denied the truthfulness of these words and did not accept the man's testimony.

However, the man still under the influence of this extraordinary trip and sacred visit, asked the judge the following question:

"O Respected Judge! Satan the enemy of Allah can also go around the world in a second why then cannot a friend of Allah in one moment go on pilgrimage."

The Judge, Mahmud Hudâyî, finding this answer very reasonable postponed his verdict until all the pilgrims returned from the holy lands in order to check whether he was there or not. After many weeks the pilgrims returned, and Hudâyî asked them whether this man was with them at the Ka'aba fulfilling the duty of pilgrimage. To his surprise, they confirmed that he was there. The Judge had to reject the case against him since the man was not a liar.

After this interesting incident, Hudâyî found Mehmet Efendi, a well known Sufi of the times and through him Hudâyî reached the well known Sufi master Uftâda. He became a follower of him for spiritual training. After his spiritual training under the guidance of Uftâda, Hudâyî reached a very high station in the Sufi path and himself became a great Sufi master. His tomb, in the Uskudar district of Istanbul, is frequented by visitors throughout the day.

In short, one does not intend to see the sands of the deserts but to visit Abraham (a.s.)'s habitat and his son Ishmael (a.s.)'s offspring. One goes there to see the places in which the Prophet (ﷺ) was born, lived and spread Islam, in order to inhale the same air that was breathed by the Prophet (ﷺ). It is to follow in the footsteps of the Prophet (ﷺ) and to see his signs in these lands as stated in the Qur'an: **"Lo! the first Sanctuary appointed for mankind was that at Becca, a blessed place, a guidance to the peoples."**(Al-i-Imrân, 3:96)

Therefore, those who can look at these places with the eyes of their hearts can see the blessings of Allah and as a result their love for Him circulates in their veins. Wherever they look they see the signs, hence they experience spiritual ecstasy, losing themselves. As a result, they continuously remember Allah, chanting His names and praising His glory. They spend their time in these holy lands with utmost respect and care towards the Divine signs as stated in the verse:

"That (shall be so); and whoever respects the signs of Allah, this surely is (the outcome) of the piety of hearts. (Hajj, 22:32)

Hence, Hajj is not only a physical act of worship, it is above all a spiritual act of worship. Al-*"Hajj al-Mabrûr,"* a good Hajj, as described by the Prophet (ﷺ) consists from beginning to end of goodness and beautiful acts and includes repentance from sins, supplications to Allah and asking forgiveness, which are the highest form of worship. Therefore, the hearts attain the blessings and mercy of Allah. A pilgrim, as a matter of fact, promises Allah to keep the highest standards of morality and acts of worship after he returns to his home as well. The following supplication of Abraham (a.s.) while he was building the Ka'aba guide us in how to pray in these holy lands:

"Our Lord! and make us both submissive to Thee and (raise) from our offspring a nation submitting to Thee, and show us our ways of devotion and turn to us (mercifully), surely Thou art the Oft-returning (to mercy), the Merciful." (Baqara, 2:128)

The loving hearts of Muslims who go on pilgrimage realize that they are walking on the same path that the Prophet (ﷺ) once walked on and feel great excitement. As an example, when they walk over the hill of Safâ, they visualize the Prophet's sermon to the unbelievers inviting them to Islam. The master of the worlds, addressed the Meccans from this hill saying:

"If I tell you that enemy is approaching behind these hills to attack you so take your precautions, would you believe me?"

The Meccans answered: "We believe in you even though we do not see behind the mountain. Since you are Muhammad the trustworthy, (Muhammad al-Amîn), we never doubt your words."

Upon this the Prophet (ﷺ) said:

"As you would trust me in this news, you should also believe me that there is only one Allah who has created this world. The idols you worship are but pieces of stone, earth or wood. Leave these idols and believe in one Allah. Know that Allah has sent me as a prophet to you."

Hearing this invitation to this Divine message, his uncle Abû Lahab and other non-believers retorted: "Have you called us for this?" Then they departed from the Prophet (ﷺ) without accepting his invitation although they accepted the truthfulness of his call, they submitted to their base desires and followed their ancestors' crooked ways.

However, the Prophet (ﷺ) never gave in to their hostile attitude and tried his best to serve the Divine truths to the hearts of humanity like serving the water of life to the thirsty. In pilgrimage we have a chance to contemplate all these brave acts of the Prophet (ﷺ).

In Mecca, we can hear the reflections of the teaching of the Qur'an by the Prophet(ﷺ) in *Dâr al-Arqam*. (This is the house of Arqam, a companion of the Prophet(ﷺ) where he could teach Islam secretly to the early Muslims). We can extend our cups to fill from the blessings of the lives led by the companions after the emigration to Madinah. When we visit the cave of Thawr, we have our share from the three spiritual nights that the Prophet spent with Abu Bakr and we join their talks. Through this spiritual association between the Prophet (ﷺ) and Abu Bakr, the roots of the golden chain of (Naqshbandiyya) was established. We can taste the sweetness of faith experienced in love and ecstasy in this cave. In Madinah, we experience the memories of the Prophet (ﷺ) and his companions, and then we return back to Mecca, this time imagining the conquest of the Mecca by the Prophet (ﷺ). When we look at the mountains around Mecca, we can visualize the fires that were burned by the companions to scare the Meccans before the conquest. We can hear as if the call of the adhan were raised by Bilâl again, as he, for the first time, did after the conquest of Mecca, lifted the azan over the Holy Ka'aba. We can hear the Prophet (ﷺ) reciting the verse: **"And say: Truth hath come and falsehood hath vanished away. Lo! falsehood is ever bound to vanish."** (Isra, 17:81)

After visualizing all these events, we can internalize these outward signs in our hearts, thinking that the Ka'aba of our heart has been polluted by the idols of base desires, hence by the spiritual power we attain through the Hajj we try to knock over these idols and keep our heart clean for Allah only. In that way, we make our heart the location of Divine manifestations. From the weakest to the strongest believer the duty of Hajj contains a vast treasure of Divine manifestations according to their perception capacities. Therefore Hajj is a comprehensive act of worship presenting a vast amount of spiritual benefits to the Muslims. Through Hajj, a believer exposes himself to the rain of Divine blessings and gets rid of the shackles of the nafs (tempting soul).

At Arafât, the Muslims gather in the hundreds of thousands in order to supplicate to their Lord. This vast meeting also reminds us of the Day of Resurrection, when all human beings will be gathered in the Presence of their Creator. Today all of them, dressed in the same garments, are equal. They are all helpless and in need of Divine Mercy. It is

239

the practicing of the Hereafter in this world and preparing for that day from today. Muslims present their most sincere prayers for Allah and repent of their sins. The believers open a new and clean page for the rest of their lives, promising Allah to lead a life of obedience and submission to Allah.

Arafât is the microcosm of Resurrection Day, heads and feet are uncovered, there are only for men, two pieces of cloth, one covering the top another the bottom. No one has the power to look around, thinking only of his or her own destiny.

Arafât is a place of forgiveness and taking refuge.

At Arafât, arising in the morning and in groups getting together is a reminder containing very old memories for Muslims as old as the history of humanity in the world. The first human being, our father Adam (a.s.) and mother Eve had eaten the forbidden fruit and were removed from paradise to different corners of the world. Adam (a.s.) asked the forgiveness of Allah for the sake of Prophet Muhammad (ﷺ) knowing that he had a high place in the sight of Allah. Allah accepted his supplication and they were forgiven. Allah sent an angel who guided him to Mecca. Meanwhile, Eve who had fallen in the area of Jeddah was also guided to Mecca by an angel. They met once again on the plain of Arafât, on the day of "arafe" (day before the standing in Arafat) in the afternoon. They cried for their sins and together asked for the forgiveness of Allah.

Out of His endless mercy and love for humanity Allah accepted their prayers and permitted their offspring to make the same supplications at the same time every year until Judgment Day. Allah promised a comprehensive forgiveness and salvation for those who followed the footsteps of Adam (a.s.) in asking His forgiveness in the same place. Therefore on the day of Arefe, the pilgrims go up to the plain Arafât to ask the forgiveness of Allah.

After this re-union, Allah the Almighty ordered Adam (a.s.) and Eve to take Mecca as their home. In remembrance of this, Mecca is called Ummu'l-Qurâ, the Mother of Cities. Hence, we can see the universal aspects of Islam in the pilgrimage. In Mecca, all human beings regardless of color, nationality, and financial status become brothers and sisters, remembering that they all come from the same father and mother, namely Adam (a.s.) and Eve. Over there, the rich, the poor, the ruler, the ruled, the lettered and the unlettered, all stand in the same square, dressed in the same seamless garments. Although there are many political and social problems in Islamic countries, the atmosphere of peace and brotherhood in these holy lands is really fascinating. People experience peaks of sacrifice and mutual love that would set an example to the rest of the nations all over the world. Many international institutions and organizations could only dream of that amount of love. We can even claim that no other religion achieved so much in harmonizing so many different colors and nations in such a successful manner. The reason is that Islam places spirituality and religion as the basis of brotherhood, not any material benefits. Any other brotherhood or solidarity based on material benefits is bound to collapse due to people's hunger for power and wealth. Only when the souls are educated in self-sacrifice and love can there then be real brotherhood.

Muzdalifah, referred to in the Qur'an as *"al-Mash'ar'ul-Haram"*, the sacred gathering, is a place replete with the manifestations of Divine Love and Mercy. This is a place where the hearts should forget all else except the Power and Kingdom of Allah and expose themselves to the manifestations of Divine blessings.

After the days of Adaq (votive offerings) are completed, the pilgrims sacrifice animals (*"Kurban"*) to glorify the name of Allah in memory of the spiritual sacrifice of Abraham (a.s.), and through the sacrificing of animals in the imitation of Abraham (a.s.), we receive the spiritual state he possessed. Those who received this blessing and felt the Abrahamic (a.s) breezes from their sacrifice, automatically recite the following verse of the Qur'an, which is in fact the declaration of Abraham (a.s.): **"For me, I have set my face, firmly and truly, towards Him Who created the heavens and the earth, and never shall I give partners to Allah."** (An'am, 6:79)

"Say: "Truly, my prayer and my service of sacrifice, my life and my death, are (all) for Allah, the Cherisher of the Worlds: He hath no

241

partner. This am I commanded, and I am first of those who surrender (unto Him)." (An'am, 6:162-163)

The great prophet Abraham (a.s.) recited the following words on his way to Damascus from Bâbil (Babylonia) as witnessed by Allah.

He said: "I will go to my Lord! He will surely guide me! "O my Lord! Grant me a righteous (son)!" (Saffat, 37:99-100)

This verse indicates that there is a trip that should be taken from one's heart to Allah, Who is the best of the friends. Through this trip a believer can reach Allah.

The Qur'an continues to narrate the story of how Abraham's (a.s.) supplications were answered:

"So We gave him the good news of a boy, possessing forbearance." (Saffat, 37:101)

And when he attained to working with him, he said: O my son! surely I have seen in a dream that I should sacrifice you; consider then what you see. He said:

O my father! do what you are commanded; if Allah please, you will find me of the patient ones. (Saffat, 37:102)

So when they had both submitted their wills (to Allah), and he had laid him prostrate on his forehead (for sacrifice), We called out to him.

"O Abraham! Thou hast already fulfilled the vision. Lo! thus do We reward the good. For this was obviously a trial- (Saffat, 37:103-106)

"And We ransomed him with a momentous sacrifice: And We left (this blessing) for him among generations (to come) in later times: "Peace and salutation to Abraham!" Thus indeed do We reward those who do right. Surely he was one of Our believing servants." (Saffat, 37:107-111)

Hadrat Abraham (a.s.), due to a Divine sign, from Allah took Hagar and their son Ishmael (a.s.) to Mecca. Then he returned to his other wife Sarah. He would sometimes visit his family and son. On one of these visits, Prophet Abraham (a.s.) had seen Mecca in his dreams. In this dream he was sacrificing his son Ishmael (a.s.). Abraham (a.s.) doubted the origin of this vision, whether it was divinely inspired or a temptation of Satan. However, having seen the same dream three times he was certain that the dream had a Divine origin. Two of these dreams were seen in the last two days before the current time of Eid-ul-Adha (Festival of Sacrifice) and the third dream was seen on what is now the first day of Eid.

According to sources, Allah the Almighty, asked Abraham (a.s.) to slaughter his son since he had promised Allah that if he had a son he would sacrifice him for Allah. Allah tested him whether he would keep his promise or not. However, Abraham (a.s.) did not break his promise and told his mother Hagar to wash him and to spread musk over him. Abraham (a.s.) told Hagar that he was going to take him to a friend. He also told Ishmael (a.s.) to take with him a knife and rope, telling:

"O my son! I will make a sacrifice to Allah."

Together they set out to the place named Arafât where the pilgrims gather on the day of Arafeh. Satan was waiting for an appropriate time, and disguised like a man, he approached our mother Hagar and asked her: Do you know where Abraham (a.s.) is taking your son?

She replied: To his friend.

Satan retorted: No he is taking your son to slaughter.

Hagar replied: No he likes his son very much.

Satan explained: Abraham (a.s.) will slaughter him because Allah commanded so.

Hagar showed great trust in Allah and replied: If Allah has commanded, then this is a good thing, we trust in Him.

Satan having failed to tempt our mother Hagar, this time hurried to Ishmael (a.s.) in order to tempt him. He asked the same questions to Ishmael (a.s.):

"Do you know to where does your father take you?"

Ishmael (a.s.) replied: "To fulfill the commandment of Allah."

Satan provoked: "You know that your father will slaughter you."

Upon hearing this Ishmael (a.s.) insulted the Satan: "Go home the cursed one! We follow the commandments of our Lord lovingly." Then he threw stones to him.

243

This time he rushed to tempt Abraham (a.s.) saying:

"O old man! Where do you take your son? Satan has cheated you in your dream, your dreams are not divinely but satanic temptations."

Abraham (a.s.) said: "O Satan! Go away from me immediately!"

He collected seven pebbles and stoned Satan three times in different places. Hence the habit of stoning Satan has been taken from Father Abraham's (a.s.) memory, this practise is repeated by all the pilgrims. This unequalled sacrifice has been eternalised by Islam by making the stoning an essential part of the rituals of pilgrimage.

When they were going to Arafât from Mina, there was great excitement among the angels. They were telling each other:

"We glorify Allah! (How strange is it that) a prophet is taking another prophet in order to present him as a sacrifice."

Abraham (a.s.) explained the nature of their trip and the commandment of Allah concerning his son Ishmael (a.s.) saying:

"O my son! In a vision, I have been ordered to slaughter you as a sacrifice to Allah"

Ishmael (a.s.) asked: "O my father! Is it Allah who commanded you to offer me as a sacrifice?"

Abraham (a.s.) answered in the affirmative. Upon hearing this answer Ishmael (a.s.) gave the following reply:

"Father! Do as you are commanded. Allah willing you will see that I will be a forbearing person." In that way he showed that he would gladly sacrifice his life in order to fulfill the commandment of Allah.

According to the narration, when Abraham (a.s.) put the knife to the neck of Ishmael (a.s.), having seen the seriousness of the situation Gabriel, the archangel became more excited and troubled than ever before. At that moment, the first thing Gabriel did was to remove the sharpness of the knife. The Mercy and Help of Allah the Almighty came at that point since Abraham (a.s.) proved that he would sacrifice even his most valuable son for the sake of Allah. As a replacement Allah sent a ram from paradise. They together sacrificed the ram and glorified Allah for this favor.

Hence, when Muslims sacrifice animals to Allah, these incidents should be kept in mind. The main purpose is to show that we take lessons from the complete submission of Prophet Abraham (a.s.) and to practice these characteristics in our lives. Otherwise, slaughtering an animal possesses no value in the eyes of Allah if the spiritual meaning is lost. The Qur'an, in order to emphasize this reality, warns us:

"It is not their meat nor their blood, that reaches Allah: it is your piety that reaches Him" (Hajj, 22:37)

After offering their sacrifices to Allah, the pilgrims shave their heads in order to show that they are Allah's slaves. Before the advent of Islam, when a master freed his slave he would first shave his head, as a symbol that this person was a slave. Therefore, the Muslims repeated this tradition in order to show that they are only the slaves of Allah and will follow His orders. In other words, this shaving of the head is symbolically the dedication of our lives to Allah's will.

Mina, where Hadrat Abraham (a.s.) and Ishmael (a.s.) stoned Satan, is a holy place that bears witness to their submission and trust.

Stoning Satan also symbolizes the stoning of one's internal Satan i.e. his nafs. It is also remembering how Hadrat Abraham (a.s.), Ishmael (a.s.) and Hagar successfully stoned the Satan, not yielding to His temptations.

Stoning in the old times meant cursing since people would curse their enemy through stoning. The attribute of Satan, in Arabic, "rajîm", as a matter of fact, means "the stoned" signifying that he is "cursed."

There is another significance in stoning which reminds us of the event in the history of Islam when Abraha, a Christian general from Yemen, wanted to destroy the Ka'aba. As narrated in the Qur'an, Abraha jealous of the Ka'aba, attacked Mecca with his big army including some elephants. However, Allah the Almighty, destroyed this army by sending an army of birds that dropped tiny stones onto the army. Through these stones the mighty army of Abraha was destroyed. Hence, stoning is done in the memory of this incident.

In short, stoning Satan means to curse Satan and to clean the heart from Satanic influences in order to be able to turn to Allah with full dedication. The Prophet (ﷺ) states in a tradition that the aim of stoning is nothing else but to establish the remembrance of Allah. (Mishkat, Tirmidhi)

In another hadith, the Prophet (ﷺ) describes Hajj as stoning Satan, running between the hills of Safâ and Marwa, and circumambulating the Ka'aba. The main purpose behind all these acts is the remembrance of Allah. (Tirmidhi, Nasâî).

Safâ and Marwa are the two hills between which Hagar was running in desperation in order to find water for her and her thirsty son Ishmael (a.s.). Then, Allah the Almighty gave them the well of Zamzam, which is till today giving water to the pilgrims. In order to remind us of this incident, the running (sa'y) between these two hills has been made among the rituals of the pilgrimage.

In order to show the significance of these two hills, Allah, Most High, states n the Qur'an: **"Behold! Safa and Marwa are among the Symbols of Allah.** (Baqara, 2:158)

The Ka'aba is a very important center that all Muslims face during their ritual worship. It is the place where the hearts of Muslims beat. As the heart is the location of the manifestations in the human sphere, the Ka'aba is the location of Divine manifestations in the worldly sphere. In other words, the Ka'aba possesses the same place as the heart possesses in the human body. In the Ka'aba we have the place of Abraham (a.s.) who is called by Muslims as Khalilullah (the friend of Allah). Allah, the Almighty, commanded the pilgrims to perform the prayer of circumambulation behind the place dedicated as his position. In that way they will follow his steps in submission to the will of Allah.

There is also the Black Stone, which is respected by all Muslims. Muslims kiss and greet this stone symbolizing their acceptance of their servanthood to Allah. This is also an indication of giving up the animal desires of the ego and the temptations of Satan.

This blessed stone also marks the beginning and end of the pilgrimage rituals. Although all the stones of the Ka'aba have been replaced in restorations, the Black Stone preserved its place, set in a corner. It has been kissed by millions of lips, and touched by millions of blessed hands. Hence, though it is an ordinary stone, it became a symbol of showing our love for the Ka'aba. Hadrat Omar states this reality when he kissed the Black Stone as

Abdullah b. Sarjis reported: I saw 'Umar b. Khattab (Allah be pleased with him) kissing the Stone and saying: "By Allah. I am kissing with full consciousness of the fact that you are a stone and that you can neither do any harm nor good; and if I had not seen Allah's Messenger (may peace be upon him) kissing you, I would not have kissed you." (Muslim, *Book 007, Number 2914*)

In short with all these characteristics, the Ka'aba is a shadow of the Divine Kingdom and a source of Allah's Mercy and Blessings. Allah's attributes of Mercy and Forgiveness manifest themselves here more than anywhere else in this Holy Land. It is the source of Divine Illumination and the sun that illuminates our hearts.

THE CONSTRUCTION OF THE KA'ABA:

According to a narration in religious books, Adam (a.s.) and Eve were separated from each other after the fall but later met at Arafât and walked together towards the west. Adam (a.s.) prayed to Allah that he would give him back the pillar of light that he was worshipping Allah around in paradise. Upon this prayer, the pillar of light appeared and Adam (a.s.) worshiped Allah by circumambulating around it.

This pillar of light disappeared in the time of the Prophet Seth (a.s), leaving only a black stone behind. However, he built the Ka'aba in the form of a pillar of light and placed this Black Stone next to it. Today what we call the Hajar al-Aswad is this stone. After the flood of Noah (a.s.), this building was left under the sands for a long time.

Later, Prophet Abraham (a.s.) by the command of Allah traveled to the surroundings of the Ka'aba and left his wife Hagar and son Ishmael (a.s.) to settle there. With his son, he located the foundations of the Ka'aba that had been built by Seth (Sheed) (a.s.) and rebuilt it. When he completed the construction of Ka'aba he prayed to Allah:

"And when Abraham prayed: My Lord! Make this a region of security and bestow upon its people fruits, such of them as believe in Allah and the Last Day" (Baqara, 2:126)

As a result of this prayer, we can say that in Mecca, most people enjoy the sweetness of faith as well as the good taste of the foods and fruits.

The Ka'aba has been rebuilt 11 times. The first time it was built by the Angels. The second time it was built by Adam (a.s.), the third by Seth (a.s.), the fourth by Abraham (a.s.), the fifth by the tribe of Amâlika, the sixth by Jurhumî tribe, the seventh by the Qusai, the leader of the Meccans, the eighth by the tribe of Quraish, the ninth by Abdullah b. Zubair who lived in the first generation named as (tâbiûn), after the death of the Prophet (ﷺ). It was rebuilt the tenth time by Hajjâj the tyrant and the eleventh time by the Ottoman Sultan, Murat IV.

The Ottomans showed great respect for the Holy Lands. The refined good manners which were a manifestation of this respect were beautifully exemplified during the reign of Murad IV. The Ka'aba was flooded and the walls were damaged. For repair, the chief architect, Ridvan Agha, was sent to Mecca. Having done the necessary research on the structure of the Ka'aba, he reported his findings. Due to his full respect for the Ka'aba, the House of Allah, he could not say that some of the walls were destroyed, saying instead, "Some of the walls of the Ka'aba have gone to prostration."

They also took precaution in order to prevent the beasts of labor from passing water over these sacred places. All these reveal the great respect that the Ottomans showed to these places. This high esteem started from the capital itself. At that time, when they crossed the Bosphorous, that first spot Muslims landed at was called Haram, since this land would connect them to the Ka'aba. Hence, they started to behave, as they are required to behave in the Haram. They did not approve of any disrespectful behavior on their way to Ka'aba. The memory of Nâbi the Poet is a very striking example of the Ottoman attitude towards these holy lands:

In the year 1678, he set out for pilgrimage accompanied by many statesmen. When they had a rest break, he saw that one of the high-ranking soldiers in the group had extended his legs towards the city of the Prophet (ﷺ), Madinah al-Munawwara. (In Ottoman culture extending the legs towards a person is considered rude). Nâbi felt very sorry for this heedless behavior of the general and composed the following poem:

Beware of the heedlessness, this is the place where the Beloved of Allah (lived)

This place is the loci of Divine glances, the post of Mustafa (Prophet Muhamad).

O Nâbi! Enter this place with full respect

This place is circumambulated by the angels and kissed by the prophets.

When the caravan approached to Madinah just before the sunrise prayer, Nâbi heard his poem recited by the muezzins of the Madinah. Nâbi was very exited to hear this and he rushed to learn how this happened, since he wrote the poem the night before and no one had learned it.

Nâbi found the Muezzin and asked him: "How did you learn this na'at."

The muezzin answered: "Last night in my sleep the Prophet (ﷺ) told me in a vision:

'From my community, a poet called Nâbi is coming to visit me and he is full of my love to the extreme. For his love for me, meet him with his own poem when he enters the city. Hence we learned the poem from him, and obeyed his command'."

Nâbi was sobbing and shedding tears like rain saying: "It means that the Messenger of Allah (ﷺ) included me among his nation, the sun of the two worlds accepted me as a member of his community."

As we have seen in the example of Nâbi, the important thing in the pilgrimage rites is to behave with the highest esteem towards the Prophet(ﷺ) and the House of Allah.

The Ka'aba, which is also called the House of Allah, has been a sacred place from the time of the first human being Adam (a.s.). The Qur'an commands visiting these places with special rituals:

"Lo! the first Sanctuary appointed for mankind was that at Becca, a blessed place, a guidance to the peoples; : Wherein are plain memorials (of Allah's guidance); the place where Abraham stood up to pray; and whosoever entereth it is safe. And pilgrimage to the House is a duty unto Allah for mankind, for him who can find a way thither. As for him who disbelieveth, (let him know that) lo! Allah is Independent of (all) creatures. (Âl-i Imrân, 3:96-97)

As a manifestation of the Islamic spirit, everyone is equal in the lines of congregational prayers. If the head of government comes late to the mosque he prays at the back. If a poor Muslim comes early he prays in the first line. People are required to pray wherever there is an empty place. Uniforms and epaulets are useless in the mosque. This concept of equality was manifested in the pilgrimage on even a fuller scale. As everyone is buried with a white shroud, all the pilgrims wear the same clothes and the difference of qualities in garments completely disappears. Pilgrimage represents a level of equality that is only repeated after death. As a head of state is buried in a white shroud, even the poorest is buried with the very same shroud. Pilgrims covering their chests with a large towel and their waists with a large towel reflect the state of the dead in their graves.

We should know that death is the inescapable law that Allah has enforced for all transient beings. The length of life is counted with complete precision so that even the number of breaths is counted and recorded. There is an appointed time of death (ajal) for every person and this may never change. We have never heard of anyone who escaped death. Since the time of our death is unknown to us we should not neglect to perform the duty of pilgrimage. Otherwise, the following bad news from the Prophet (☐) will be valid for us:

"If someone dies without going for pilgrimage even though he had the requirements of food, drink and transportation, there is no nothing that will prevent this person to die as a Jew or Christian." (Tirmidhi, Hajj, 3)

This clear warning of the Prophet (☐) reminds those heedless Muslims who do not perform this commandment even though they have the necessary means that they will be punished in the Hereafter.

The negligence of this commandment means to despise the commandment itself.

Pilgrimage is commanded to be performed at least once in a lifetime; therefore it is a great mistake for able Muslims to delay it. The Prophet (ﷺ) states that those who are required to perform pilgrimage should rush to do it. (Jâmu'l-fawâid, II, 77)

The House of Allah is full of the reminders of Abraham (a.s.) and his family's trust and submission to Allah. When we mention the words trust, submission and pilgrimage immediately the names Abraham (a.s.) and Ishmael (a.s.) come to our minds. Due to their sincerity, pilgrimage was made an obligatory act of worship that will continue until the last day of the world.

Trust in Allah means to depend on, to have full confidence in, and to appoint someone as a representative. In Sufism, it signifies one whose heart is filled with Allah, only trusting in Him and seeking refuge only in Him. When Allah the Almighty asked Moses (a.s.) about his rod he answered: " It is my rod, I lean on it..." Allah the Almighty said: "throw it down", since this dependence on the rod shadowed his full dependence on Allah.

Concerning to whom we should trust, Allah the Almighty, states in the Qur'an:

"In Allah let believers put their trust!" (Tawba, 9:51, Ibrahim, 14:11)

"So put your trust (in Allah) if ye are indeed believers." (Mâidah, 5:23)

"And whoever trusts in Allah, He is sufficient for him." (Talaq, 65:3)

The Prophet (ﷺ) states that if we trust in Allah fully, He will sustain us as he sustains the birds that leave their nests hungry in the morning and return to them with a full stomach in the evening.

Trust in Allah does not signify giving up all kinds of necessary steps, and to ignore the laws of nature. It means to put full trust in Allah after fulfilling the necessary conditions to reach a result and not to trust in the means itself, ignoring Allah's will. Rather the slave should seek refuge in the power of Allah.

Allah the Almighty states:

"And take counsel with them in the affair; so when you have decided, then place your trust in Allah; surely Allah loves those who trust." (Al-i Imrân, 3:159)

Allah is the helper of the believer in both worlds. Whoever puts full trust in Him, He suffices for the needs of the slave. Real happiness and bliss lie in returning to Him both on the personal and social level by asking his help and putting our trust in Him.

In Arabic, the word salima signifying submission and connotes the meaning of yielding (the will), and accepting the acts of Allah with pleasure.

The Prophet Abraham (a.s.) had filled his heart with the love of Allah. When the angels asked Allah: How can Abraham (a.s.) be your friend who has his life, possessions and family (that will keep him engaged from You). Then, Allah the Almighty showed the angels his submission to the Divine will in three different tests.

The first test was about his life, that when he was about to be catapulted into the fire the angels rushed to help him, but he refused their offer and said:

"I do not need your help. Who gave the power of burning to the fire? Allah is the best of helpers." In that way he took refuge only in Allah. As a reward of this sincere submission to Allah's power Allah the Almighty commanded the fire:

"We said: O fire, be coolness and peace for Abraham (a.s.)" (Anbiyâ, 21:69)

In the second test, he was tested about his wealth. Gabriel had gone to Abraham (a.s.) and begged for some of his flock. When he praised Allah he said: Take this flock and they are yours."

In that way, he also successfully achieved the test of sacrificing wealth for the love of Allah.

The real servanthood to Allah is nothing but submission to Him. However, submission is based on love and obedience. We have seen the best example of this submission based on love in Abraham (a.s.). His own life, family and wealth did not prevent him from fulfilling the Divine commands due to his full devotion and submission to Allah. In order to reward his sincerity, the rites of pilgrimage will be performed up until Judgment Day to symbolize his submission and trust in Allah.

His tongue reflecting the situation in his heart continuously would say:

"I submit myself to the Lord of the worlds." (Baqara, 2:131)

In addition to the examples of Abraham (a.s.) and Ishmael (a.s.) who showed unequalled levels of sacrifice and submission to Allah, the Prophet Muhammad (ﷺ) showed the rituals and essentials of pilgrimage in his farewell pilgrimage. In particular, his farewell speech that was made on this occasion is the best guidance for pilgrims until Judgment Day. In this speech he designated the basic rights and responsibilities of Muslims and strengthened the lines of Muslims with love and mercy.

Those who intend to go on pilgrimage should prepare themselves both spiritually and materially. Trust in Allah does not mean to ignore making provisions for the journey of pilgrimage. Some of the Yemenites would go to pilgrimage without taking any essentials such as food and drink saying: "We trust in Allah!" When they reached Mecca they would beg due to hunger. In order to warn about this kind of wrong conception of trust in Allah, the Qur'an states:

"And make provision, for surely the provision is the guarding of oneself, and be careful (of your duty) to Me, O men of understanding." (Baqara, 2:197)

As understood from the verse, a Muslim needs both kinds of provisions in the Holy Lands. He needs material provisions like enough food, and spiritual food like submission, patience and so on. Only the Muslim who has purified his heart from spiritual diseases can achieve this. Only through possessing such a heart can we understand the reality of the acts of worship, in particular the pilgrimage, as indicated by Rumi in the following story:

"Bâyazîd, the Shaykh of the community, was hurrying to Mecca for the Hajj (the greater pilgrimage) and Umra (the lesser one). In every city to which he went he would first search out the venerable (saints). He would roam about, asking, 'Who is there in this city that is relying on (spiritual insight)'? He did this since he believed that wherever he went in his travels he should search for a holy person.

Allah the Almighty, said in the Qur'an: **'Ask the followers of the Remembrance (zikr) if ye know not?'** (Anbiyâ, 21:7)

Therefore Moses (a.s.) was commanded to visit Khidr who had spiritual knowledge. Bâyezîd was looking for the Khidr of the time and he suddenly saw an old man with a stature resembling the new moon. He saw in him the majesty and the speech of holy men. His eyes were sightless and his heart was as illumined as the sun. Bâyezîd sat down before him and asked him about his condition. He found him to be a dervish and also a family man. The old man asked: 'Whither art thou bound, O Bâyezîd? To what place wouldst thou bear the baggage of travel in a strange land'? Bâyezîd answered: 'I start for the Ka'aba and have two hundred silver dirhams as provision for the road'. The old man told him: 'Place some of those dirhams before me and the other needy. First enter their hearts in order to open the eyes of your soul. Get an endless life. First fulfill the pilgrimage with your soul, and then continue the trip with a refined heart. Although the Ka'aba is the House of His religious service, my form is the house of His innermost secrets. The Ka'aba is the house built by Abraham the son of Âzar, my heart is the loci of Allah's majesty'.

If you have spiritual insight, circumambulate the Ka'aba of the heart. The heart is the Ka'aba of the body, made out of earth. Allah commanded us to visit the visible Ka'aba in order that we might attain to a Ka'aba of the heart that has been purified from impurities.

Know that if you hurt a heart which is the loci of Divine glances, even if you go to pilgrimage on foot the rewards you attain will not cover the sin of breaking someone's heart. A perfect man is a treasure that contains Divine secrets. If you want to see the manifestations of Divine light do not escape from the trials and difficulties." (see Mesa. II, 2218-2251)

Bâyezîd gave heed to these mystical sayings, and put them in his ear as a golden ring. Through the conversation of this sheikh, his heart received a share of mercy. He then continued his trip with a peaceful mind and heart.

Through these kind of beautiful examples, Rumi guides the hearts to the truth of the pilgrimage and advises the believers who intend to go on pilgrimage:

"When the time of pilgrimage arrives, go there with the intention of visiting and circumambulating the Ka'ba. If you go with this intention you will see the reality of Mecca".

The reason why Rumi gives the example of pilgrimage is that it is a very delicate act of worship. Many legal things that are allowed in other times of the year are forbidden in this time. Therefore, the pilgrim first should prepare his heart to be able to perform this difficult duty. From the first moment the pilgrim intends to go on pilgrimage, Satan tries his best to corrupt its quality. The pilgrimage journey seems very easy and enjoyable but it is full of difficulties. This is also true for the rites of pilgrimage hence the pilgrim needs to adorn himself with Patience and forbearance. Hence the pilgrim should pray: O my Allah! Please make it easy for me!

We should not forget when we chant at the pilgrimage time: *"Labbayk Allahumma Labbayk Lâ Sharîka laka Labbayk, Innal Hamda wanni'mata laka wal mulk lâ Sharîka laka"*.

"Here I am at your service O Allah, Here I am at your service (I respond to Your call, and I am obedient to Your orders) You have no partner, Here I am. Surely, all the praise and blessing and sovereignty are for You.You have no partner."

That, as a matter of fact, we confirm that we are answering His invitation. We are admitting that in the kingdom of heavens and earth there is no partner with Allah. Hence, we are promising to Him that we shall not obey the temptations of Satan and the ego.

Otherwise, if we perform the pilgrimage heedlessly, without obeying the principles we have recounted so far, it will not benefit us. In particular, those who go to the holy lands with illegal earnings and savings that are in conflict with the most essential principle of Islam, that is, no act of worship can be performed with religiously illegal earnings. Hence, their words "we are at your service" will signify that "we are not at your service" since we broke the most significant rule of the pilgrimage.

Hence we can say that the most important rule of the pilgrimage is halâl (religiously legal) earnings, then secondly a sincere heart. Every time the pilgrim says "labbayk" these words should light a fire in his heart. Only in that way can a believer approach Allah. Otherwise mere words without really meaning it have no benefit. Hadrat Husain's face, the grandson of the Prophet (⁂), would turn pale whenever he said "Labbayk" fearing that the answer from Allah would be "lâ labbayk." May Allah enable us to perform the pilgrimage with both our bodies and souls.

The principles of pilgrimage guide man to mercy and a more spiritual life. When he wears the special white seamless garment (called ihram) he leaves all sorts of rough and unkind behavior. It makes man kinder and nicer since hunting animals, plucking the plants, breaking the green branches of trees and hurting creatures are forbidden during the days of pilgrimage.

Allah the Almighty, states in the Qur'an:

"So whoever determines the performance of the pilgrimage therein, there shall be no intercourse nor fornication nor quarrelling amongst one another; and whatever good you do, Allah knows it; and make provision, for surely the best provision is the guarding of oneself, and be careful (of your duty) to Me, O men of understanding. (Baqara, 2:197)

The pilgrims will not fight and hurt others, they will behave nicely and kindly to others for the sake of their Creator. In particular, hurting the hearts of the believers is considered a big sin. Therefore Hadrat Omar would not kiss the Black Stone in order not to hurt other pilgrims due to the crowding.

In Islam, every kind of worship begins with an intention. The intention for pilgrimage begins with wearing ihrâm. Having put on this special garment, the pilgrim is transformed into a spiritual state, leaving his ordinary conduct. The white garment reminds him of death and the shroud. Hence he spends his time in contemplating death and how to make preparations for it. With all its eloquent principles, pilgrimage makes man attain the highest state as informed by the Qur'an:

"Surely We created man of the best stature." (Tîn, 95:4)

The Prophet (ﷺ) gives the following good news for the pilgrims: "The greater pilgrimage and the lesser pilgrimage cleanse the pilgrim's sins as the nitric acid of the goldsmith cleans gold and silver." (Nesâî, Tirmizî)

The following hadith also gives good news for the pilgrims: The Prophet (ﷺ) said, "Whoever performs Hajj for Allah's pleasure and does not have sexual relations with his wife and does not do evil or sins, then he will return as if he were born anew (without any sins remaining)." (Bukhari, Volume 2, Book 26, Number 596)

This good news is valid for those who have performed the Hajj in an acceptable way, which is called al-Hajj al-Mabrûr. Those who have achieved this level of pilgrimage also attain the following virtues:

1- Sense of responsibility,

2-Pardoning nature,

3-Keeping the body and actions pure,

4-Islamic brotherhood,

5-Concsciousness that superiority is only on the basis of taqwâ i.e. awe of Allah,

6-Legal earning

7-Sincerity

Hence, pilgrimage is not just an act of worship performed for Allah. It also develops man's capabilities. It develops the social, moral and political condition of the Ummah. It teaches the universal aspects of Islam more than any other act of worship.

On the personal level, pilgrimage gives man a chance to evaluate his actions and behaviors and to correct his mistakes for the future life.

Pilgrimage is obligatory once in a lifetime. However, as in the daily prayers and fasting, a believer can perform supererogatory pilgrimages as well. Some Muslims consider going on pilgrimage more than once as a waste of money. This kind of heedless remark borders on disbelief and only those who do not understand the purpose and the transformative power of Hajj can utter such a remark.

From the Age of Happiness (the time of the Prophet), Muslims have always practiced the supererogatory acts of worship with devotion and love. These willingly performed acts of worship bring the servant closer to Allah as stated in the well-known hadith. They give depth and insight to the soul. They render the Muslim more generous and merciful. Allah becomes their eyes by which they see, the ears by which to hear. In short, their acts such as hearing, thinking become guided by the Divine Light.

This spiritual development can be realized through supererogatory acts of worship and showing mercy to the creation. The great Imam Abu Hanifah, went on pilgrimage 55 times. I think this shows the significance of the pilgrimage and there is no need for extra words.

THE LESSER PILGRIMAGE (UMRAH)

In addition to the Hajj, (the greater pilgrimage) which is performed only on fixed days of the year, one can also perform the lesser pilgrimage called Umrah at any time of the year. Due to its performance at any time, it is also called the lesser pilgrimage.

In Umrah, the pilgrim is not required to visit Arafât. The pilgrim only circumambulates the Ka'aba and runs between the hills of Safâ and Marwâ. If it is performed in the month of Ramadan , the Prophet(ﷺ) said that its reward will be as high as the reward of the greater pilgrimage.

When we visit the tomb of the Prophet(ﷺ) in Madinah, we should realize that this is a place where we should be able to increase our love and respect for the Prophet (ﷺ). Only he was addressed as "My beloved" by Allah. Allah the Almighty, also commanded us to love His messenger in the following verse:

"Say: If your fathers and your sons and your brethren and your

mates and your kinsfolk and property which you have acquired, and the loss of trade which you fear and dwellings which you like, are dearer to you than Allah and His Messenger and striving in His way, then wait till Allah brings about His command: and Allah does not guide the transgressing people. (Tawba, 9:24)

Qady Iyâd deduces from this verse that Allah obliged the Ummah to love Himself as well as His Messenger. Hence nothing should be dearer to us than the Prophet (ﷺ). Neither our house, nor our family, or our work!

Therefore, Imâm Mâlik considers the honorable grave of the Prophet as holier than the Ka'aba itself since all worlds and the creation were created for his sake. For this reason we should visit Madinah after completing the pilgrimage. Through visiting and smelling the earth of this land we should pay our humble respects to the Prophet (ﷺ). In that way we can benefit from his blessing.

The Prophet (ﷺ) informs us that visiting him after his death is the same as visiting him in his lifetime. (Dâraqutni, Sunan, II, 278)

However, one should show great respect while visiting the tomb of the Prophet (ﷺ). One day, while Imâm Mâlik was in the mosque of the Prophet(ﷺ), Abu Jâfar Mansûr, the Caliph of the time, came to the mosque in order to ask him a few questions. A scholarly debate started between them. However, with the fervor of the debate, the caliph started to raise his voice. Imam Mâlik warned him and said:

"O Caliph lower your voice here. Here, Allah warned more virtuous people than you not to raise their voices, referring to the verse:

"O you who believe! do not raise your voices above the voice of the Prophet, and do not speak loud to him as you speak loud to one another, lest your deeds become null while you do not perceive."" (Hujurât, 49:2)

The Caliph appreciated the Imâm's high manners in the presence of the Prophet (ﷺ) and asked him:

"- O Imâm! Shall I turn my face during supplication towards Rawdha (the tomb of the Prophet) or towards the Ka'aba"?

Imâm Mâlik answered: "When in Madinah turn your face towards Rawdha, for the creation and the Ka'aba were created for his sake. All humanity needs the intercession of Prophet Muhammad (ﷺ). (Qâdi Iyâz, Şifâ al-Sharif)

Some Muslims ignore this fact and prevent Muslims turning their faces towards the Rawdha. They say "Greet the Prophet (ﷺ) and leave him. Turn your faces towards the Ka'aba." They forget that the Prophet (ﷺ) is alive. The Qur'an informs us that martyrs are alive and similarly the prophets who occupy a higher place than them, are also alive. In particular, the Honored leader of the worlds, the Prophet Muhammad (ﷺ) possesses an extraordinary life.

*

In short, the greatest gift that pilgrims should take back to their countries is the good characteristics of the Holy Lands. They should carry back memories by continuing to practice the good virtues they cultivated during their visit. They will thus functions as windows for the spiritual beauties of the Holy Lands to reach those who have not yet gone.

The spiritual architect of Pakistan, Muhammad Iqbal asked the following questions to the pilgrims who had just returned from pilgrimage:

"You have visited Madinah "the Enlightened." With what have you filled your hearts from the spiritual market of Madinah? The material gifts you have brought such as the head coverings, the prayer beads and prayer rugs will fade away after a short while. What have you brought as the spiritual gifts of Madinah that will not fade away?

Among your gifts have you brought the characteristics of submission and trustworthiness of Abu Bakr, the justice of Hadrat Omar, the generosity and modesty (hayâ) of Hadrat Uthman. Will you be able to give to the Ummah, which is suffering from a thousand different problems, a hope from the "Time of Happiness" (Asr-i saâdah)?"

May Allah make us among those who have benefited from the spiritual blessings of the Holy Lands and make us among those who have visited the Messenger of Allah with a sensitive, burning heart.

May Allah grant us a life of submission to Allah and trust in Him. Let our Refuge and Helper be only Him. May Allah make us fulfill the duty of pilgrimage with a heart that feels the blessings of the Holy Lands.

THE HOLY MONTH OF RAMADAN
AND FASTING

"The month of Ramadan in which was revealed the Qur'an, a guidance for mankind, and clear proofs of the guidance, and the
Criterion (of right and wrong). (Baqara, 2:185)

The holy month of Ramadan is a month of opportunity for reward granted to us from Allah, the Almighty. In this month we remember the value of the favors Allah has given to us, which we normally take for granted and for which we do not give sufficient thanks.

The aim of fasting is to achieve taqwa (awe) and curb the selfish soul (nafs), to discipline it and bring it under control. Fasting must be performed in an attitude of worship if we really wish to benefit from its blessings. Because of fasting we can attain high qualities such as patience, a strong will, distancing ourselves from the base desires of the nafs. Like a shield, fasting also protects the honor of the believer by freeing him from the endless preoccupation for eating and drinking like the beasts.

One of the benefits of fasting is that it gives courage and resistance in times of famine and calamities. It also teaches us to be thankful and happy with the bounties of Allah, the Almighty. When we fast we understand the difficulties of the poor who suffer from lack of food, and as a result, our mercy for them is strengthened. This kind of understanding prevents social disturbances and class divisions. We can safely say that the nature of Islamic worship does not permit the class divisions we witness in other nations. Fasting(saum) and prayer (salât / namaz) make everyone equal in front of Allah. No one is exempted from these forms of worship except those who have a valid excuse.

Because of these positive effects of fasting, it was prescribed not only for Muslims but also for the previous nations. Allah, the Almighty, says:

"O you who believe! Fasting is prescribed for you, as it was pre-scribed for those before you, so that you may guard (against evil). For a certain number of days" (Baqara, 2:183-184)

Islam prescribes a variety of styles of worship for the believers. Different kinds of worship in Islam are meant to cure different kinds of spiritual diseases. These diseases increase especially in the easy times of prosperity and health. In the Meccan period, Muslims did not have a chance to develop such spiritual diseases, because the struggle to sur-vive under such difficult conditions occupied them. However, after the emigration to Madinah the financial situation of the Muslims improved. They were also safe from the persecution of the Meccan non-believers. In order to prevent Muslims from the harm that can come with the abuse of wealth and the enjoyment of bounties there was a need for a kind of abstention or restriction for using worldly posses-sions. It was time for fasting to be ordained in order to preserve the spiritual health of the believers.

As a matter of fact, fasting is like a medicine against the diseases, whether physical or spiritual. Hence, fasting is prescribed for a limited number of days, not for the entire year. If certain medicines for acute conditions are used all year the immune system of the body can get accustomed to it and it may not sufficiently benefit the user. Similarly, fasting should be carried out in determined times. If we fast continu-ously it does not help much to cure the illnesses and may weaken the body to the point of making it difficult to fulfill the normal responsibil-ities that Islam requires. Due to this reason, the Prophet (ﷺ) did not allow his companions to fast every day.

All Muslims are obliged to fast in the same month of the year, that is Ramadhan. This strengthens the bonds of unity in the Ummah as well as making fasting easier. This sense of unity gives our spiritual life extra richness and vividness. Another aspect of fasting is that the month of fasting is a lunar month. Hence it moves from one season to another throughout the solar calendar, and we fast on hot summer days as well as on short and cold winter days. Because each day of the year pays respect to Ramadan in a certain period, they are all blessed by it. This variety in the times of fasting also gives a variety of spiritual pleasure and tastes. This makes fasting easy and a different experience each time a believer fasts. We can see this richness also in the verse, which commands fasting. The verse first informs us:

"O you who believe! Fasting is prescribed for you", then in order to comfort us the verse states that it is also prescribed for other nations: **"as it was prescribed for those before you"** Finally the verse states that fasting is not meant for all the days of the year: **"For a certain number of days;"**(Baqara, 2:183-184)

After that, Allah, the Almighty, states the benefits of fasting, and its conditions:

"The month of Ramadhan in which was revealed the Qur'an, (is) a guidance for mankind, and a clear proof of the guidance, and the Criterion (of right and wrong). And whosoever of you is present, let him fast the month, and whosoever of you is sick or on a journey, (let him fast the same) number of other days. Allah desireth for you ease; He desireth not hardship for you; and (He desireth) that ye should complete the period, and that ye should magnify Allah for having guided you, and that you may give thanks.." (Baqara, 2:185)

This verse also shows us that the aim of fasting is to glorify Allah and to give him thanks. In this sense fasting has a positive influence on the rest of other kinds of worship. Shakik Balkhi says: "Worshipping Allah as he deserves is a difficult art. However, it can be achieved through solitude and fasting."

Reducing the intake of food is also a modern method of medical treatment. Dieting is the first condition of being healthy, even in the practice of modern medicine. By fasting the believers follow it in the best way, learning self-discipline.

Hunger is also a strong medicine, with which to control the nafs. It was narrated that when the nafs was created it had pride: It dared to say its Lord: "You are you and I am I." However, when Allah punished it with hunger it understood its mistake and professed its weakness and nothingness in front of its Creator. Hence for the health of the nafs there is no better cure than hunger.

Jalaladdin Rumi says: "The real nourishment of man is the light of Allah. Giving excessive material food is not good for him. The real food of man is Divine love and intelligence.

The discomfort of man is due to his forgetting his soul's nourishment and caring only for the nourishment of the body. This body is not satisfied. (It wants more and more) Because of this disease of greediness his face is pale and legs are shaky, his heart is beating with discomfort. Where is the worldly nourishment and where is the nourishment of infinity? (How great the difference between them)"

Allah said for the martyrs: "They are nurtured". There is no mouth and no body for this nourishment (they are taken by the soul).

Hadrat Lokman advises his son: When your stomach is full, your intelligence sleeps oblivious to wisdom and the limbs are lazy for worship.

A friend of Allah said: "I take refuge in Allah from the Sufi who fills his stomach with all sorts of food and corrupts it."

The Mother of believers, Aisha said: "Try to open the doors of the malakût (spiritual world)." They asked: "How?" She answered: "Through hunger and thirst."

The great friend of Allah Mahmud Sami Ramazanoghlu emphasizes the significance of eating and drinking little in his book Mukerrem Insan (The Perfect Man) and says: "They asked the doctors: What is the best cure, they answered: Eating little. The people of wisdom are asked how they found so much power and courage for worshipping Allah. They answered: Eating little. The ascetics are asked: What makes the tie between man and Allah stronger: They answered: Eating little. The scholars are asked: What is the best state for learning. They answered: being in a state of hunger (rather than satiety) and eating little."

There are so many benefits in eating little (never eating until the stomach is filled):

1. In moderate hunger there is clearness of mind and heart; the memory is stronger. In the state of being overly full, there is forgetfulness and foolishness.

2. In moderate hunger there is gentleness of the heart. The heart benefits and takes pleasure from worship and supplication. With a full stomach the heart is insensitive and takes no pleasure in worship.

3. In moderate hunger there is softness of heart and humility. Satiety produces insolence, conceit, pride and bragging.

4. In moderate hunger one thinks of the poor and hungry, whereas a man with a full stomach never remembers the poor and the needy.

5. In moderate hunger the appetite, needs and wishes of the animal soul are broken. When full the animal soul is strong and the desires find strength.

6. In moderate hunger the body is in an agile and aware condition. When full it feels sleepy and careless.

7. In moderate hunger one feels ready to worship and give service to Allah. When the stomach is full one feels lazy and lax.

8. In moderate hunger, the body is healthier. Sickness disappears. Overeating makes the body feel worn out and sick.

9. In moderate hunger the body feels light and spacious making, one cheerful.

10. In moderate hunger one feels more generous and ready to provide support for the poor with charity. On the other hand those who do not experience hunger at all, do not understand the sufferings of the poor. Also, for this, in the heat on the fearful Day of Judgment, the servant will come into a state of coolness and shade. Fullness produces a state that goes from stinginess to wasteful spending which leads to the destruction of the servant.

In other words, a full stomach urges the animal soul and ego to be active in order to satisfy its base desires. On the other hand, fasting when it is performed without going to the extreme opens up the faculties of meditation and makes the human heart more sensitive to the Divine realities. The following hadith summarizes what we have said so far: "Fast and find (both spiritual and physical) health." (Taberani)

269

The practices of the great Prophets of Allah also reveal to us the significance of fasting in order to reach spiritual perfection. Fasting was one of the most effective methods used by Allah the Almighty for perfecting the Prophets. Through fasting, the Prophets were prepared to receive revelation from Allah. As an example, Moses (a.s.) fasted 40 days and nights when he was waiting to receive revelation on the Mountain of Sinai. After this fasting period the Torah was revealed to him. Similarly, Jesus fasted the same number of days before he received the Injil (Evangel or Gospel).

Similarly, our Prophet Muhammad (ﷺ) spent a month in the cave of Hira near Mecca, worshipping Allah and contemplating His greatness. After this preparation period he received the Divine message from the archangel Gabriel, and his heart was filled with the light of the Divine Blessings.

All this shows that the real benefit of fasting is spiritual rather than physical. Hence when we fast we must only aim to worship Allah, the Almighty. If we aim for worldly goals such as cutting down on our spending for food or losing extra weight, we miss out on the real benefits. We can also say this for other acts of worship: For example, if one performs the daily salât for its value as exercise and to keep fit he is not considered as performing Allah's command. Rather, such a person is following the command of his ego under the guise of worship.

All acts of worship should be performed with only one aim in mind: to attain Allah's pleasure. To do this one needs to train and educate the heart, to clean it from such base thoughts. We also cannot attain Allah's pleasure through these sort of egoistic goals.

In order to benefit fully from the holy month of Ramadan, the following advice of the   Prophet (ﷺ) should be followed:

1-To repeat the Shahadah

2-To ask forgiveness from Allah and to chant his names

3-To perform all possible good deeds (a'mal al-sâliha) in order to attain Paradise

4-To refrain from what has been forbidden (harâm) so as to save ourselves from the flames of hell.

5-To give charity generously and to make those whose hearts are broken happy.

6-To give iftârî (food upon opening of the fast) to the believers.

Of course, there is no limit to what one can do as a good deed. Everybody should do his best in order to compete in doing any good that is for the good of the Muslim community. Ramadan is the season for perfecting the believers morally. As we are careful not to use our mouths for eating during Ramadan, we must similarly be careful not to use them for backbiting and useless talk. Otherwise, we miss the real target of fasting, which is to perfect the manners of the believer in accordance with Islamic morality.

Concerning this, the Prophet (ﷺ) said: "Fasting is a (protecting) shield as long as the fasting person does not harm his fast."

The companions asked the Prophet (ﷺ) how the fast is damaged. The Prophet (ﷺ) answered: "By lying and backbiting." (Nasâi, Mu'jam al-awsât)

The backbiters refrain from eating during the daytime but because of their backbiting they eat human flesh. Hence their physical fast becomes useless. For such people Sufian Sawri says:

"Backbiting breaks the fast."

Similarly, the famous scholar Mujahid says that backbiting and lying break one's fast. For those who contaminate their prayers (salât) and fasting (sawm) by backbiting, slandering and offending others in a heedless and cruel manner the Prophet (ﷺ) says: "Among many who fast their share is only hunger. There are many who perform night prayers and their share is only exhaustion." (Tabarâni)

In another similar hadith the Prophet (ﷺ) said, "Whoever does not give up forged speech and evil actions, Allah is not in need of his leaving his food and drink (i.e. Allah will not accept his fasting.)" (Bukhari, Vol. 3, Book 31, Number 127)

These hadiths clearly show us that it is very important to control our behavior in Ramadan. We must prepare our heart and mind for fasting. It should not be done heedlessly and carelessly. We must perform our salâts with extra care and attentiveness, strengthen our soul by the remembrance of Allah, recite the Qur'an with an attentive heart and mind, clean our wealth and our consciousness by giving charity and zakât. We should not forget that the Holy Qur'an was revealed in the month of Ramadan and we must show extra care in order to apply the injunctions of the Qur'an in our lives.

The real recitation of the Qur'an is performed by the heart. The external eyes function as glasses for the eye of the heart. There is a close connection between Ramadan and the Qur'an. Ramadan is the time to listen to the voice of the Qur'an; the voice which reminds us of our real destination, which we will arrive at after death. The Prophet (ﷺ) said: Fasting and the Qur'an will be intercessors on the Day Judgment." (Ahmad b. Hanbal, Musnad, II, 174)

"Fasting is half of patience." (Tirmidhi, Daawat, 86)

The reward of fasting will be determined in the Hereafter on the Day of Judgment: In a hadith al-Qudsi, as narrated by Abu Huraira:

Allah's Apostle said, "Allah said, 'All the deeds of Adam's sons (people) are for them, except fasting which is for Me, and I will give the reward for it.' Fasting is a shield or protection from the fire and from committing sins. If one of you is fasting, he should avoid sexual relations with his wife and quarrelling, and if somebody should fight or quarrel with him, he should say, 'I am fasting. By Him in Whose Hands my soul is ' The unpleasant smell coming out from the mouth of a fasting person is better in the sight of Allah than the smell of musk'. There are two pleasures for the fasting person, one at the time of breaking his fast, and the other at the time when he will meet his Lord; then he will be pleased because of his fasting." (Bukhari, Volume 3, Book 31, Number 128)

The Qur'an in the following verse enumerates the classes of those who will receive forgiveness and a mighty reward, mentioning those who fast:

"Surely the men who submit and the women who submit, and the believing men and the believing women, and the obeying men and the obeying women, and the truthful men and the truthful women, and the steadfast men and the steadfast women and the humble men and the humble women, and the almsgiving men and the almsgiving women, and the fasting men and the fasting women, and the men who guard their private parts and the women who guard, and the men who remember Allah much and the women who remember- Allah has prepared for them forgiveness and a mighty reward." (Ahzab, 33:35)

The Prophet (ﷺ) also informs us that the believer who fasts will be rewarded twice, once in this world and once in the next. In this world the reward is at sunset at the time of breaking the fast. The second is when he meets his Lord when he will granted a very high place. However, we are not informed of the reward in order to increase our love for fasting. In worldly contests sometimes rewards are kept hidden in order to increase the suspense for them.

Fasting is such a form of worship through which it one can learn how to value the favors of Allah, the Almighty. The fasting man gets a chance to understand the difficulties of poverty and hunger. Through fasting the believer saves himself from slavery to the material and attains the highest quality of self-control.

In addition to fasting, offering the tarawih salât in congregation after the late-night prayer of 'Isha, is also a sunnah in the month of Ramadan. In many places throughout the world the entire Qur'an is recited during this month and in this prayer. However, these salâts should be performed with devotion, slowly and not in a quick manner. Unfortunately, in some mosques people pray tarawih salât as if they are racing with each other. The Prophet (ﷺ) informs us that he made the tarawih prayers his sunnah so as to be followed by the Muslim community. He further statd that if a believer fasts in the month of Ramadan expecting reward only from Allah, and performs the tarawih salât, he becomes as sinless as on the day he was born from his mother. (Ahmad B. Hanbal; Nasâî)

Another important point in Ramadan is to have the meal at suhur. Suhur is taken before dawn begins, when the time of fasting starts. Normally people have their iftar (fast breaking meal) on time but most people neglect having suhur since it is taken very early. We must be strong-minded about having something, even if it is a glass of water. Concerning this subject as narrated by Anas bin Malik, the Prophet (ﷺ) says:

"Take Suhur as there is a blessing in it." (Bukhari, Volume 3, Book 31, Number 146)

As narrated by Sahl bin Sad: Allah's Apostle said, "The people will remain on the right path as long as they hasten the breaking of the fast." (Bukhari, Volume 3, Book 31, Number 12)

*

In order to realize the reality of the Holy Month of Ramadan one needs to open his heart to the rain of forgiveness and Divine Blessings. The rocks and the seas do not benefit from these rains, only fertile lands benefit from it. In other words, through awareness of Allah's presence and giving thanks to Him for his favors we should benefit from this month. The Prophet (ﷺ) informs us the following good news:

"When the month of Ramadan starts, the gates of the heaven are opened and the gates of Hell are closed and the devils are chained." (Bukhari, Volume 3, Book 31, Number 123)

This means that those who fast in the real sense of fasting do not commit sins. As shown by research conducted in Islamic countries, the crime rate falls to its lowest rate in the month of Ramadan. The evil of Satan is limited, however, the evil of the ego continues, hence Muslims should be vigilant against their base desires.

The Prophet (ﷺ) also informs us that in the month of Ramadan paradise adorns itself with all kind of charms and supplicates Allah saying: O my Lord! In this month, let people enter me. (Taberânî)

Fasting is described as physically refraining from food, drink and sexual intercourse but it also requires the protection of the soul from all animal-like desires and inclinations. The Sufis emphasize the spiritual dimension of fasting and consider it an essential part of fasting. As one refrains from eating and drinking similarly he should refrain from vices such as backbiting, lying, and other base desires. The Prophet (ﷺ) warns us in this regard and says: "Whoever does not give up false speech and evil actions, Allah is not in need of his abstaining from food and drink (i.e. Allah will not accept his fasting.)" (Bukhari, Kitâbu's-sawm, Volume 3, Book 31, Number 127: Tirmîdi, Bâvu's-sawm, Abû Dawud, sawm, 236, Ibn Maja, 122)

As required in this hadith we should refrain from all sorts of vices that will damage our fasting. In particular, the vice of anger and hostile behavior should be eliminated.

Allah's Apostle (ﷺ) said, "Fasting is a shield. The person observing fasting should avoid sexual relations with his wife and should not behave foolishly and impudently, and if somebody fights with him or abuses him, he should tell him twice, 'I am fasting." The Prophet (ﷺ) added, "By Him in Whose Hands my soul is, the smell coming out from the mouth of a fasting person is better in the sight of Allah than the smell of musk. (Allah says about the fasting person), 'He has left his food, drink and desires for My sake. The fast is for Me. So I will reward (the fasting person) for it and the reward of good deeds is multiplied ten times." (Bukhari, Volume 3, Book 31, Number 118)

Another name for the month of Ramadan is the month of patience and forbearance. Some commentators of the Qur'an explain the Arabic of fasting *sawm* with the words *sabr* meaning patience implying the similarity of these two words. With this respect, sawm is to be resilient against the base desires, and to be patient against the difficulties.

In Islam, patience occupies the central place among other good characteristics. Patience is half of faith and the key to salvation. Through it one attains paradise. Patience is to be resilient against unpleasant events without damaging our balance and to submit to the will of Allah. The prophets as well as the friends of Allah reached high states and the help of Allah through patience. Having to show patience in this world gives us a bitter taste but it will give sweet fruits in the Hereafter. In order to lessen the bitterness of patience we should contemplate the favors of Allah that are bestowed on us. We should think that there is wisdom behind the calamities and if patience is shown there will be great rewards in return. The most important principle in the concept of patience is that a Muslim should show it at the first strike of the calamity. When the pain of the disaster has lessened then patience will not be rewarded as such. The Divine name **"As-Sabûr"** is most beautifully reflected in the prophets and friends of Allah. As the most important legacy given to us, patience is the most important characteristic both in times of happiness as well as of calamities, in times of poverty as well as wealth.

*

In order to fast in the consciousness that Allah is with us we should carefully fulfill the components of fasting such as suhur, tarâwih, reciting the Qur'an, engaging in humble and earnest supplication and in the remembrance of the name (attributes) of Allah." The time of breaking the fast is a good time when Allah accepts the prayers and answers the supplications; it is the time of unity with Allah. To spend this time with others and to share the blessings is important since this is the source of mercy and spiritual contentment. Therefore the Prophet (ﷺ) advises us to share our food with the Muslims at iftar

"Whoever gives an iftârî (meal to break the fast) to a fasting person, he will be rewarded the same amount as the fasting person and the reward of the fasting person will not be lessened (due to extra reward given to the host). (Tirmidhi, Sawm, 90)

When the poor companions heard this tradition they came to the Prophet (ﷺ) and said that they did not have the means to give as much food as the rich. Upon this the Prophet(ﷺ) told them that even if they gave half a date or a little milk in order to open the fast they would be rewarded the same amount as the rich sahabis (Companions) who gave full iftaris.

*

In addition to obligatory fasting we should also perform voluntary fasting. The characteristic of the chosen slaves of Allah is trustworthiness. This can be reached through having good intention and purification of the ego. The Prophet (ﷺ) and his companions practiced voluntary fasting quite often under severe conditions in the heat of the Arabian Peninsula. Some of them even did not have garments to protect them from the fierce heat. They would fast even the very hot days. They would cover their bodies with their hands in order to protect them from the excessive heat. Under all these conditions they would continue voluntary fasting by feeling the taste of excessive spiritual contentment.

For those who fast voluntarily there are occasions where they might have to break their fast before sunset due to an invitation or some other reasons. Depending on the situation a believer may either prefer to complete the fast or can break it in order to please his friends and make up for it on a different day.

Abû Saîd (may Allah be pleased with him) narrated the following incident:

"One day I had prepared food for the Prophet (ﷺ) and his companions. When I served the food one of the companions said: "I am fasting." Upon this the Prophet (ﷺ) stated: "Your brother has invited you and made preparations for you and now you are saying that you are fasting. Break your fast now and make up for it on another day." (Tirmidhi, Abu Dawud)

"On another occasion the Prophet (ﷺ) and some of his companions ate food while Bilâl was fasting. The Prophet (ﷺ) commented upon the situation of Bilal and said: We are eating our sustenance, Bilal's sustenance is in paradise." (Ibn Majah)

These traditions give us the choice of completing a voluntary fast or breaking it, as the conditions require.

*

Allah will judge all our actions and life. The best of times are the ones that we spend with Him for His sake. When we enter the grave all our transient reminiscences, and memories will be buried as well. However only the good actions we have performed for the sake of Allah will benefit us. The Prophet (ﷺ) states that when a believer dies, his ritual prayers (salât) will rest above his head, his charity on the right and his fasting on the left. (Fadâil al-Amâl)

A lifetime spent that was not for the sake of Allah is a deception, like the vision in the desert heat. It has no reality but is only an illusion of the mind.

By the mercy of Allah, we follow the advice of the Prophet (ﷺ) and appreciate the great chance that the Holy months of many Ramadans offer to us so that way we can perform good actions and as we struggle to decrease our mistakes.

The Prophet (ﷺ) says: If people really knew the nature and blessings of Ramadan they would wish that Ramadan would continue all year. (Ibn Huzeyma, Sahih, III, 190)

The Holy Ramadan is a climate of forgiveness; in this month all the pillars of Islam can be performed except pilgrimage. However, Ramadan prepares the believers spiritually for the duty of pilgrimage by refining their morality. In pilgrimage, Muslims are trained to be nice and not aggressive, disobedient slaves.

Ramadan is a great opportunity for all the believers to attain Allah's pleasure. It is the season of blessing and salvation. As the Prophet (ﷺ) says: The beginning of Ramadan is mercy, its middle salvation and its end safety from Hell. (Ibn-i Huzeyme, Sahîh, III, p.191)

The month of Ramadan is like the season of spring where the trees bloom and the greenery is everywhere. Similarly the dry trees of faith find life in Ramadan through the water of good actions. However, those who do not know the value of Ramadan are in great loss as stated in the following hadith:

"One day the Prophet (ﷺ) asked us to sit closely around the minbar (the pulpit from where he gave his Friday sermon). Hence, we all gathered around. The Prophet (ﷺ) started to climb the stairs. On the first step he said: 'Amin', on the second step he again repeated the same phrase: 'Amin'. On the third step he again said: 'Amin'.

When he got down from the minbar we asked him:

"- O prophet we heard something that we have never heard from your before. Why did you say Amin three times?"

The Prophet (ﷺ) said:

- When I was climbing the first step, Gabriel came to me and said: the curse of Allah be on those who did not use the chance of Ramadan to attain Divine forgiveness. And I said: 'Amin'.

When I was on the second step Gabriel prayed: "Let be the curse be on those who did not say "peace be upon you" when your name was mentioned." And I said: "Amin!"

In the third step Gabriel again said: "Let upon the curse (of Allah) be on those who did not attain paradise although they survived to the old age of their parents or only one of them (i.e. those who did not serve either of their parents or both of them in their old age and attain the big reward as a consequence)."

I again said: "Amin!" (Hakim, Müstedrek, IV, 170)"

This hadith clearly indicates the miserable end of three groups of people. The first group are those who did not worship Allah in the month of forgiveness- Ramadan. The second group are those who did not say peace be upon him when his name was mentioned. And the last group are those who did not look after their parents in their old age. We should be very careful in these three important things if we want to enter Paradise.

*

In addition to fasting, the days of Ramadan should be valued and adorned with other good acts, in particular helping the disadvantaged. The orphans, the widows, the helpless, the sick, the poor and other needy groups should be supported financially and they should not be left alone to face their problems. They should be given a friendly hug, in that way the value of Ramadan will be realized. These kinds of charitable acts will cause Allah's forgiveness to burst endlessly. The good servants of Allah who fulfill these kinds of acts, will be covered with Divine Mercy and Blessings. Allah opens the doors of mercy and closes the doors of hell. The Prophet (ﷺ) states: "Charity prevents seventy kinds of calamities." (Suyûtî, al-Jâmiu's-Saghîr, v.II, p.52)

"Charity extinguishes the wrath of Allah" (Tirmidhi, Zakât, 28)

Luqman Hakim advised his son: "O my son! When you commit a sin knowingly or unknowingly, repent to Allah immediately and give charity."

In short, the charity given in the month of Ramadan is rewarded excessively and the prophet (ﷺ) states the exclusiveness of the month in the following words:

"O Messenger of Allah! Which charity is best in terms of reward."

The Prophet (ﷺ) answered: The charity given in the month of Ramadan. (Tirmidhi)

The friends of Allah divide the charity givers into different groups. The people of Sharîah (obedience to the law) give charity from their wealth. The people of haqîqah (reality) give from their souls in addition to their wealth.

The Gnostics (ârifûn) give from their hearts since their hearts are always in the presence of Allah. The lovers give from their souls since their souls are content with the manifestations of Divine destiny written for them. The charity of the rich is realized through the removal of money from their purse, the charity of the Sufis is to remove everything else other than Allah from their hearts.

The charity of the worshippers (abid) is from their nafs since they do not refrain from sacrificing their bodies in worship and service of Allah.

The generous people whose hearts are also rich do not resent donating their money to the poor. The poor and the weak become happy with the presence of the rich who give thanks to Allah for His favors (by donating their riches to the poor). As the April clouds water the dry lands with blessed rain, similarly the merciful, generous people manifest the mercy of Allah over His slaves.

The more sincerely and lovingly the rich donate, the more benefits and blessings are received by the one who receives. Such giving and taking become a source of felicity for both sides. The spiritual deepness of the donor is reflected from the one who receives. This is called a trade that without loss (tijâratan lan taburâ).

On the other hand Allah, the Almighty states in the Qur'an:

"O ye men! It is ye that have need of Allah: but Allah is the One Free of all wants, worthy of all praise." (Fâtir, 35:15)

Therefore the only real Rich One is Allah. All the slaves of Allah rich or poor should realize that they are always in need of Allah and feel the state of poverty to Allah at all times. The Sufis and great scholars in order to show the high status of poverty said: "Poverty is our pride!"

These words are a sign of wisdom. Since it is the preference of the richness of the heart over the richness of the worldly possessions. This feeling is the source of virtues both in the good-hearted rich and poor people. This phrase also implies to be content (kanaat) with what one has, even if it is a small amount.

If a rich person has the characteristic of feeling content with what he has he will protect himself from being miserly or prodigal. If a poor person has this characteristic he/she will lead a life of chastity and will only ask his needs from Allah. As Rumi states what befits to the generous is to donate to the poor and what befits to the lover is to sacrifice his life for the sake of the beloved.

The life of the Prophet (ﷺ) sets the highest example of giving charity, and the great scholar Ibn Qayyim describes the generosity of the Prophet (ﷺ) in the following way:

The Prophet (ﷺ) was not like anyone in giving charity. He never gathered worldly possessions in his house. If someone asked from him something he would not reply without giving neither too little nor too much. When he gave he would give without the fear of becoming poor. For him giving charity was the highest pleasure. His pleasure was much more than the one who received the donation for an urgent need. He was the most generous of people in giving in the way of Allah. His right hand was like a generous wind that scatters the bounties of Allah's mercy. If a needy person told about his suffering to him he would be very sad and would prefer the needy to his own needs and sometimes would give his own food and dress to the needy person. In the commentary of Hazîn it narrates that Hadrat Jabir said:

A little child came to the Prophet (ﷺ) and told him that his mother needed a shirt. At that time the Prophet (ﷺ) did not have any shirt except the one he was wearing. Therefore he told the child to come back later. The child left but after a while he came back again and told the Prophet (ﷺ) that his mother wanted the shirt the Prophet (ﷺ) was wearing.

Upon this, the Prophet (ﷺ) entered his room and took off the shirt and gave it to the child. After a short while the prayer time commenced and Bilâl started calling the believers to prayer by reciting azân. After making the azan the companions waited for the Prophet (ﷺ) to lead the congregation but he did not come to the mosque. When they went to his room in order to check what happened, they understood that the Prophet (ﷺ) would not come to the mosque since he had no shirt to wear. This led them to contemplate a long time about the generosity of the Prophet (ﷺ).

Umar b. Abdulaziz who was honored by being called the fifth rightly guided caliph of Islam due to his piety and justice stated: "The congregational prayers take you to half way to Allah. Fasting opens the gates of the King's palace and charity takes you to the presence of the King".

In conclusion, we should do our best to use this opportunity given to us in the current year. We never know if we shall be privileged again to reach the holy month next year. Apart from fasting and performing our prayers in the mosque we should recite the Holy Word of Allah. We must give charity generously to the poor. The Prophet (ﷺ) informed us that the best charity is the one which is given in the month of Ramadan. By combining all these good deeds we must turn to Allah in humbleness and sincerity. May Allah help us to perform fasting in the best way.

Ubayd b. Umeyr narrates: "Human beings will be resurrected in the Hereafter naked, excessively hungry and thirsty. Those who fed others for the sake of Allah will be fed, and those who gave water for the sake of Allah will be quenched, and those who gave clothes for His sake will be clothed."

The Prophet (ﷺ) says: "O human being! Give charity to others so as you will be donated to as well." (Bukhari, Muslim)

The reality of charity is explained in the best way by Rumi:

"Wealth does not decrease by giving charity, giving charity protects wealth from destruction.

The alms dues you pay become the guards of your purse, the salats you pray become your shepherd protecting you from the wolves and other troubles.

Those who sow grains at seedtime make their granary empty but at harvest time they receive back their seed many fold. In exchange for one empty granary they receive back many more full granaries.

On the other hand, if the wheat is not sown and is left in the granary, the fleas, worms and mice devour it."

Allah, the Almighty states in the Qur'an:

"And spend out of what We have given you before death comes to one of you" (Munâfiqûn, 63:10)

"Those who hoard up gold and silver and do not spend it in Allah's way, announce to them a painful chastisement," (Tawba, 9:34)

The alms due and voluntary charity are given for the sake of Allah. Therefore they should be given respectfully as if Allah is receiving them. The Prophet (ﷺ) emphasizing this point says:

"Without doubt, charity is received by Allah's Hands (of power) before it is taken by the hands of the poor. (Allah takes it first and then gives it to the poor). (Munawî, Kunuz al-Haqâiq)

The following hadith also clarifies this fact: Allah's Apostle said,

"If one gives in charity what equals one date-fruit of honestly-earned money -and Allah accepts only honestly earned money- Allah takes it in His right (Hand) and then enlarges its reward for that person (who has given it), as anyone of you brings up his baby horse, so much so that it becomes as big as a mountain." (Bukhari, *Vol. 2, Book 24, Number 491*)

The significance of charity is also stressed by the Qur'an since the verse confirms that it is Allah who receives the charity:

"Do they not know that Allah accepts repentance from His servants and takes alms, and that Allah is the Oft-returning (to Mercy), the Merciful?" (Tawba, 9:104)

Therefore a believer should be very careful when giving charity. The Qur'an describes the morality of giving charity in the following verse: **"O you who believe! Do not make your charity worthless by reproach and injury, like him who spends his property to be seen of men and does not believe in Allah and the last day;"** (Baqarah, 2:264)

In order not to cause injury and reproach, the friends of Allah stand up in front of the needy to give their charity as a token of modesty. The prophet Solomon (a.s.) did not give his heart to worldly riches, and removed all sorts of worldly love from his heart. He used to visit the poor and enjoyed sitting with them. He would say that the poor suit the poor. In that way he displayed great modesty in spite of great riches. He had really realized the meaning of the verse:

"O mankind! Ye are poor in your relation to Allah. And Allah! He is the Absolute, the Owner of Praise." (Fâtir, 35:15)

One day a heedless rich man asked him why he liked sitting with the poor:

"Why do you accompany the poor and eat with them?"

"Solomon (a.s.) answered: I only like those whose hearts are rich even though they are materially poor."

A water jug when its mouth is closed can travel in the sea for many miles without sinking. Similarly, a Muslim's heart, when it is filled with the love of Allah and is closed to egoistic desires, can survive in the storms of worldly oceans. It reaches high stations without sinking into the traps of worldly glamour.

A Muslim when his heart is tempered by generosity, mercy, modesty and love is not deceived with the glamour of the world and spiritually can attain high stations. Worldly adornments carry no value in the eyes of the soul. The only wish is that the heart be filled with the love and knowledge of Allah and in that way be able to fly in the heavens of Divine love.

*

In the holy month of Ramadan there is one particular night called Lailat-ul- Qadr (Night of Power) that should be spent in the worship of Allah. It is a special time when Allah spreads his mercy over the community of Muhammad (ﷺ). On this night, Allah bestows his spiritual treasures on Muslims. For its great value, Allah, the Almighty, revealed a chapter named the Chapter of Power. It is a remembrance left by Allah from the time of the Prophet (ﷺ) for those who aspire to spiritual realities and for those who would like to attain mercy and forgiveness.